PIMLICO

341

CONCEPTS AND CATEGORIES

Sir Isaiah Berlin, OM, who died in 1997, was born in Riga, capital of Latvia, in 1909. When he was six, his family moved to Russia: there in 1917, in Petrograd, he witnessed both the Social-Democratic and the Bolshevik Revolutions.

In 1921 his family came to England, and he was educated at St Paul's School and Corpus Christi College, Oxford. At Oxford he was a Fellow of All Souls, a Fellow of New College, Professor of Social and Political Theory, and founding President of Wolfson College. He also held the Presidency of the British Academy. His published work includes *Karl Marx*, *Four Essays on Liberty*, *Vico and Herder*, *Russian Thinkers*, *Against the Current*, *Personal Impressions*, *The Crooked Timber of Humanity*, *The Magus of the North*, *The Sense of Reality*, *The Proper Study of Mankind* and *The Roots of Romanticism*. As an exponent of the history of ideas he was awarded the Erasmus, Lippincott and Agnelli Prizes; he also received the Jerusalem Prize for his lifelong defence of civil liberties.

Dr Henry Hardy, a Supernumerary Fellow of Wolfson College, Oxford, is one of Isaiah Berlin's literary trustees. He has edited several other collections of Berlin's work, and is currently preparing his remaining unpublished writings and his letters for publication.

By the same author

KARL MARX
THE AGE OF ENLIGHTENMENT
FOUR ESSAYS ON LIBERTY
VICO AND HERDER

Edited by Henry Hardy and Aileen Kelly

RUSSIAN THINKERS ✓

Edited by Henry Hardy

AGAINST THE CURRENT ✓
PERSONAL IMPRESSIONS
THE CROOKED TIMBER OF HUMANITY ✓
THE MAGUS OF THE NORTH ✓
THE SENSE OF REALITY ✓
THE ROOTS OF ROMANTICISM

Edited by Henry Hardy and Roger Hausheer

THE PROPER STUDY OF MANKIND

CONCEPTS AND CATEGORIES

Philosophical Essays

___

ISAIAH BERLIN

Edited by Henry Hardy

With an introduction by
Bernard Williams

PIMLICO

Published by Pimlico 1999

2 4 6 8 10 9 7 5 3 1

Copyright Isaiah Berlin 1939, 1950, 1956
© Isaiah Berlin 1960, 1961, 1962, 1964, 1978

This selection and editorial matter © Henry Hardy 1978, 1999

Introduction © Bernard Williams 1978

The moral right of Isaiah Berlin and Henry Hardy to be identified as the author
and editor of this work respectively has been asserted in accordance with the
Copyright, Designs and Patents Act, 1988

This book is sold subject to the condition that it shall not,
by way of trade or otherwise, be lent, resold, hired out, or otherwise
circulated without the publisher's prior consent in any form of binding or
cover other than that in which it is published and without a
similar condition including this condition being imposed
on the subsequent purchaser

First published in Great Britain by
The Hogarth Press in 1978

Pimlico
Random House, 20 Vauxhall Bridge Road,
London SW1V 2SA

Random House Australia (Pty) Limited
20 Alfred Street, Milsons Point, Sydney,
New South Wales 2061, Australia

Random House New Zealand Limited
18 Poland Road, Glenfield,
Auckland 10, New Zealand

Random House South Africa (Pty) Limited
Endulini, 5A Jubilee Road, Parktown 2193, South Africa

Random House UK Limited Reg. No. 954009

A CIP catalogue record for this book
is available from the British Library

ISBN 0 7126 6552 8

Papers used by Random House UK Limited are natural,
recyclable products made from wood grown in sustainable forests;
the manufacturing processes conform to the environmental
regulations of the country of origin

Printed and bound in Great Britain by
Mackays of Chatham plc

Contents

Editor's Preface

This is one of five volumes published in Isaiah Berlin's lifetime in which I brought together, and prepared for reissue, most of his published essays that had not previously been made available in a collected form.[1] Until then his many writings had been scattered, often in obscure places; most were out of print; and only half a dozen essays had been collected and reissued.[2] These five volumes, together with the list of his publications that one of them (*Against the Current*) contains,[3] and two subsequent volumes in which I published much of his previously unpublished work,[4] made much more of his *oeuvre* readily accessible than before. Nevertheless, a good deal still remains unpublished, because Berlin felt that it needed revision, and he did not want it to appear in unrevised form in his lifetime. However, he placed no restrictions on posthumous publication, and I hope to make much of this material, which is of great interest and value, available in years to come. Indeed, the first instalment, Berlin's 1965 Mellon

[1] This volume was first published in London in 1978, and in New York in 1979. The other volumes are *Russian Thinkers* (London and New York, 1978), co-edited with Aileen Kelly; *Against the Current: Essays in the History of Ideas* (London, 1979; New York, 1980); *Personal Impressions* (London, 1980; New York, 1981; 2nd ed., London, 1998); and *The Crooked Timber of Humanity: Chapters in the History of Ideas* (London, 1990; New York, 1991). There is also a one-volume selection of essays drawn from these collections and their predecessors: *The Proper Study of Mankind: An Anthology of Essays*, ed. Henry Hardy and Roger Hausheer (London, 1997: New York, 1998).

[2] *Four Essays on Liberty* (London, 1969; New York, 1970) and *Vico and Herder: Two Studies in the History of Ideas* (London and New York, 1976). Other collections had appeared only in translation.

[3] Its currently most up-to-date version appears in the Pimlico paperback edition published in London in 1997.

[4] *The Magus of the North: J. G. Hamann and the Origins of Modern Irrationalism* (London, 1993; New York, 1994) and *The Sense of Reality: Studies in Ideas and their History* (London, 1996; New York, 1997).

Lectures on romanticism,[1] is published at the same time as this reissue of *Concepts and Categories*.

The essays in the present volume are Berlin's published contributions to philosophy, with the exception of 'Historical Inevitability' and 'Two Concepts of Liberty', which had already been reissued in revised form in *Four Essays on Liberty*, and 'Induction and Hypothesis',[2] which is the second contribution to a symposium, and, being in large part a reply to the first contribution, does not stand comfortably on its own, though it does not deserve to be neglected by students of Berlin's philosophical work.[3] 'The Purpose of Philosophy' first appeared in *Insight* (Nigeria) 1 No 1 (July 1962), and was reprinted in the *Sunday Times*, 4 November 1962, and as 'Philosophy's Goal' in Leonard Russell (ed.), *Encore*, 2nd Year (London, 1963: Michael Joseph); 'Verification', 'Logical Translation', 'Equality' and ' "From Hope and Fear Set Free" ' (the Presidential Address for the 1963–4 Session) all appeared in the *Proceedings of the Aristotelian Society*, vols 39 (1938–9), 50 (1949–50), 56 (1955–6) and 64 (1963–4) respectively; 'Empirical Propositions and Hypothetical Statements' was published in *Mind* 59 (1950); 'The Concept of Scientific History' appeared as 'History and Theory: The Concept of Scientific History' in *History and Theory* 1 (1960) and in Alexander V. Riasanovsky and Barnes Riznik (eds), *Generalizations in Historical Writing* (Philadelphia, 1963: University of Pennsylvania Press), and under its present title in William H. Dray (ed.), *Philosophical Analysis and History* (New York, 1966: Harper and Row); 'Does Political Theory Still Exist?' was published first in French as 'La théorie politique existe-t-elle?' in *Revue française de science politique* 11 (1961), and then in English

[1] *The Roots of Romanticism* (London and Princeton, 1999).

[2] *Proceedings of the Aristotelian Society*, supplementary vol. 16 (1937).

[3] Readers may like to have details of four other pieces in this area which do not appear here. There is a long review of Bertrand Russell's *A History of Western Philosophy* in *Mind* 56 (1947); 'Philosophy and Beliefs', *Twentieth Century* 157 (1955), is a conversation with Anthony Quinton, Stuart Hampshire and Iris Murdoch; 'An Introduction to Philosophy' is an interview with Bryan Magee in *Men of Ideas* (London, 1978); and 'Is a Philosophy of History Possible?' is a discussion with others in Yirmiahu Yovel (ed.), *Philosophy of History and Action* (Dordrecht/Boston/London and Jerusalem, 1978). For other reviews and smaller pieces, see the bibliography already cited.

in Peter Laslett and W. G. Runciman (eds), *Philosophy, Politics and Society*, 2nd Series (Oxford, 1962: Blackwell). Apart from necessary corrections and the addition of missing references, the essays appear here essentially in their original form.

I am greatly indebted to Bernard Williams, who not only wrote the introduction to this volume, but also played a crucial role in persuading Berlin that these philosophical essays were well worth reprinting. Without his support this volume would not have appeared. Berlin himself was unfailingly courteous, good-humoured and informative in response both to my persistent general advocacy of the whole project, which he continued to regard with considerable scepticism, especially in the case of the present volume, and to my often over-meticulous probings into points of detail. Pat Utechin, his secretary, was an indispensable source of help and encouragement at all stages, and Kate McKenzie kindly double-checked the proofs.

HENRY HARDY

May 1998

Author's Preface

Some of these articles were written more than a quarter of a century ago, when I was teaching philosophy in Oxford; when Dr Henry Hardy proposed to me that they should be included in a separate volume, I demurred. Although I do not think that there is anything in them that I should now wish to withdraw or change radically (I could not bring myself to re-read them), it seemed to me that they belonged too much to their time and place – they were not untypical of the kind of discussions and controversies, mainly about positivism, that went on in Oxford in the years immediately before and after the war, but I thought that they contained little or nothing worth resuscitating nearly thirty years later. I felt similar doubts about the articles written in the years that followed. Dr Hardy thought better of these pieces than I did, and when I continued to be obdurate, he proposed that we should go to arbitration and suggested that Professor Bernard Williams be appealed to. Bernard Williams is an original philosopher and a just and candid critic, and I therefore expected him to agree with me. When he said that he favoured republication, I could not, of course, help being pleased, and I accepted his verdict even though I wondered whether it was not more generous than just. Dr Hardy pressed his advantage and persuaded Professor Williams to back his judgement by writing an introduction to the volume. For this act of what I can only describe as heroic friendship I record my deep gratitude.

I have occasionally been asked what made me cease to teach philosophy as it is taught in most English-speaking universities, and as I believe it should be taught. The answer is best given by recording a conversation I had with the late Professor H. M. Sheffer of Harvard, whom I met there towards the end of the war when I was working at the British Embassy in Washington. Sheffer, one of the most eminent mathematical logicians of his day, said to me that in his opinion there were only two philosophical disciplines in which one could hope for an increase of permanent knowledge: one was logic, in which new discoveries and techniques superseded the old ones – this was a field of exact knowledge in which genuine progress occurred, as it did in the natural sciences or mathematics; the other was psychology, which he thought of as being in some respects still philosophical – this was an empirical study and obviously capable of steady development. And, of course, there was the history of philosophy: but this was not part of philosophy itself; as for logic and psychology, they differed from philosophy proper, to which – unlike history or classical learning – the notion of growth, of cumulative knowledge, did not seem to him to apply. 'To speak of a man learned in epistemology, or a scholar in ethics,' he said, 'does not make sense; it is not that kind of study.' He went on to say that philosophy was a marvellous province of thought, but it had not been helped, in his view, indeed had been gravely damaged, by what logical positivists, influenced by symbolic logicians like himself, were now doing; the kind of work that 'Carnap and Co.' (as he called them) were engaged upon repelled him – it would ruin real philosophy as he and his master Royce conceived it: 'If any work of mine has done anything to stimulate this development, I had rather not have been born.' Although I did not, and do not, agree with Sheffer's sweeping condemnation of the value and influence of logical positivism, or the rigid division he drew, repudiating his own earlier views, between logic and philosophy, his words made a profound impression upon me. In the months that followed, I asked myself whether I wished to devote the rest of my life to a study, however fascinating and important in itself, which, transforming as its achievements undoubtedly were, would not, any more than criticism or poetry, add to the store of positive human knowledge. I gradually came to the conclusion that I should prefer a field in which one could hope to know more at the end of one's life than when one had begun; and so I left philosophy for the field of the history of ideas, which had for many years been of absorbing interest to me.

My reason for telling this story is mainly historical, because of the light it throws on the conception of philosophy held towards the end of his life by one of the fathers of modern logic, about whose general views little or nothing, so far as I know, has been published; and also because somewhat inaccurate accounts of this conversation have been in circulation, one of which has recently found its way into print – and I thought it as well to set the record straight.

ISAIAH BERLIN

February 1978

Introduction

Bernard Williams

Isaiah Berlin is most widely known for his writings in political theory and the history of ideas, but he worked first in general philosophy, and contributed to the discussion of those issues in the theory of knowledge and the theory of meaning which preoccupied the more radical among the young philosophers at Oxford in the late 1930s. The medium was in good part personal discussion, particularly within a group including Stuart Hampshire, the late A. J. Ayer, the late J. L. Austin, and others.[1] In this selection from Berlin's more purely philosophical writings, the three papers which represent that earliest period of his concerns (only one of them written actually pre-war) involve the reader in a double displacement from what those philosophical conversations must have been like. The transition from dialectic to document is one thing – something that many philosophers of many schools have found problematical. Another thing is the transition from Berlin in person to Berlin in print.

It has been said that the kind of philosophical activity engaged in then by Berlin and his friends, like the 'linguistic philosophy' of the 40s and 50s which it helped to form, was essentially conversational and resisted publication. So far as the real point of the activity was concerned, as opposed to a certain manner, this has probably been exaggerated. Among 'analytical' or 'linguistic' philosophers, only Wittgenstein had an understanding of the nature of philosophy which (like that of Socrates) meant that something essential to the subject itself was lost in the transition to print. Nothing that Austin (for one) believed about the subject would have precluded him from writing a textbook, even, and Ayer has not declined to do so. The present

[1] See Berlin's own account, 'Austin and the Early Beginnings of Oxford Philosophy', in Sir Isaiah Berlin and others, *Essays on J. L. Austin* (Oxford, 1973), included in a later volume of the present selection, *Personal Impressions* (see p. vii above, note 1), and also Ayer's autobiography, *Part of my Life* (London, 1977), p. 160.

papers can, and surely do, preserve the point of those philosophical enquiries.

The second transition, however, from Berlin in discussion to Berlin in print, involves losses which are clear and determinate, even if they are hard to describe. The decorum of a journal article must attenuate that sense, which Berlin uniquely conveys, that no abstract or analytical point exists out of all connection with historical, personal, thought: that every thought belongs, not just somewhere, but to someone, and is at home in a context of other thoughts, a context which is not purely formally prescribed. Thoughts are present to Berlin not just, or primarily, as systematic possibilities, but as historically and psychologically actual, and as something to be known and understood in these concrete terms. This is one thing, besides a courteous nature, that makes Berlin a less than ruthless controversialist — a highly developed sensibility for what it is to be the other party, to see the world in that different way.

The agenda of philosophy for the group to which Berlin belonged before the war was set, in some part, by logical positivism. They were concerned with the conditions of sentences having a meaning, and with the connections between meaning and verification, where verification was construed in terms of sense-perception. Positivism both regarded natural science as the paradigm of knowledge, and took a strictly empiricist view of science, seeing scientific theory in operationalist terms as a mere compendium and generator of actual and possible observations. This set of ideas does not leave very much room for the historical imagination, nor for insight. It is hardly surprising that Berlin was never a positivist. But, seriously interested in philosophy at a time when philosophy's most pressing questions came from a positivist direction, he produced work which did not merely reject positivism programmatically, but argued its issues in its own kind of terms. Two essays in the present book are of this kind: 'Verification', and 'Empirical Propositions and Hypothetical Statements'. Both express a deep resistance to the operationalist ideas of positivism, which held that the meaning of our statements about reality is given directly by our procedures for finding out about it. Against this general conception, Berlin affirms that our understanding of reality already includes the conception of it as existing independently of us and our understanding; so that our reflection on what we mean when we characterise that reality cannot accommodate the positivist idea that truths about reality should be equivalent to truths about us.

This unacceptably idealist equivalence, as Berlin detects it to be, gets no better (as the positivists hoped) if categorical truths about reality are treated as equivalent to hypothetical truths about us (or about other possible observers). This was the manoeuvre of phenomenalism, which was *par excellence* the positivist theory of the external world. Phenomenalism tried to analyse all statements about the material world into statements about actual or possible experiences. Statements about observed objects were, under analysis, at least partly categorical: they recorded the actual observations. Statements about unobserved objects, on the other hand, were, when analysed, entirely hypothetical. But this conjunction of claims, as Berlin points out, cannot possibly be correct: the difference between what happens to be observed and what remains unobserved cannot possibly issue in a difference of *logical form*.

So, more generally, when Berlin takes up the question of a proposition's referring to an object presently unobserved, his line of argument can be seen as striking at the mixture of epistemology and logic which has marked the empiricist tradition. (The eventual consequences of rejecting the empiricist's epistemological notions of reference are radical, and are at the present time a major preoccupation of the philosophy of language.) One further thing that particularly comes across from Berlin's opposition to verificationism is a powerful sense (not shared by all philosophers) of the reality of the past, something which his metaphysical opinions join the whole body of his work in affirming.

Berlin did not accept positivism's view of meaning and knowledge, nor – above all – its view of philosophy itself as having the modest roles, up to its final retirement, of secretary to science and obituarist of metaphysics. His historical sense made him sceptical even of the more generous conception of philosophy held by post-positivist linguistic philosophy, which gave it the open-ended task of carefully and imaginatively charting the uses and implications of ordinary language, and diagnosing in those terms the origins of philosophical perplexity. Berlin claims, in 'The Purpose of Philosophy' and again in 'Does Political Theory Still Exist?', a larger task for it, in terms of an account, more perhaps in the spirit of Collingwood than of any analytical philosopher, of various models or presuppositions which men have brought to their experience, and which have helped, indeed, to form that experience. The understanding of these models, and the self-understanding of our own, are offered as one task of philosophy, and they imply others: for if the story of these various models gives a correct account of the constitution of human experience in different eras and cultural situations, then there are genuine questions about the objectivity of what is, at any given time or place, regarded as knowledge. The questions are not new, and have been explicit and pressing since (at the latest) Hegel. Linguistic philosophy had not much to say about questions of that sort and turned to other things; but the questions did not go away, or even change very much while neglected.

They can be pressed, in fact, even against natural science. Berlin has not himself done so, and indeed the one thing in these two essays that bears something of a positivist stamp is the account of science implied by his division between questions that are determinately answerable and those that are not, and the division, again, of the answerable questions into the empirical and the formal. But the activity of paradigms and models which Berlin invokes outside these domesticated areas can be detected in the development of natural science itself, as many present philosophers of science insist. Some of these philosophers, significantly, are committed to believing about scientific theories that they cannot properly be understood except in terms of their history — something which Berlin himself believes about anything that he finds really interesting.

Berlin himself has applied his concern with the role of models and presuppositions rather to the human sciences, insisting also, in 'The Concept of Scientific History' and elsewhere, on the peculiarity of those sciences in having a subject-matter which is of the same nature as the investigator. This feature of them, in Berlin's view, both permits and requires from the investigator a special insightful kind of understanding, not applicable to any other kind of subject-matter. This is of course the capacity which he salutes in those — Vico and Herder first among them — who have insisted that past ages, remote cultures, saw the world through different eyes from us and that an effort of identification is needed if their view is to be in any way recaptured. It is also a capacity which Berlin himself notably displays. It applies not only to understanding across time, but also to the very different outlooks, structures of understanding and preconception, which different kinds of thinkers can bring to the world in the same period.

These various structures or models, whether across time or contemporary, inevitably raise problems of relativism: whether there is any basis on which one such view can be seen as better, more adequate, in any absolute sense, than another. Berlin offers, so far as I know, no general theoretical critique of relativism, but he is certainly resistant to it — and he has a special reason to be so, in so far as his own account of human action and its intelligibility itself implies the falsehood of some ideologies and models of life which have been influential in the past and still remain so. In '"From Hope and Fear Set Free"' Berlin examines metaphysical questions about human freedom (questions which come before those issues of social and political freedom which he has discussed elsewhere), in connection with a very interesting and searching question, whether knowledge always liberates. He wants to stress the vast effect there would be on ordinary notions of action, purpose, praise, blame, regret, and so forth, if we really believed in a deterministic theory to the effect that our actions are the strict causal product of earlier states of affairs, stretching indefinitely back. The 'reconciling' hypothesis of self-determination, that we are free if among the causes of our action is our own choice, even though that choice itself be caused, Berlin joins Epicurus in finding not good enough, a form of 'semi-slavery'. Berlin does not himself argue directly against determinism, nor is his denial of the reconciling strategy, his insistence that the conceptual and moral costs of believing in determinism would be enormous, intended as an argument *in terrorem* against accepting determinism. But the principle of self-determination he sees as definitely mistaken, and the images of liberation that go with it, to that extent flawed: absolutely flawed, not merely relatively to another set of presuppositions. Indeed one suspects that he not only hopes but believes that determinism is false, and that the whole loaf of anti-determinist freedom which the libertarian craves is actually available.

In the account that he gives of philosophy, more than one sort of question is excluded from the realm of the determinately answerable. Among them are questions of value; and the fact that they should be so excluded, and that they should be, in that context, partly assimilated to questions of philosophy, are both facts characteristic of Berlin's outlook. That questions of value should be partly assimilated to questions of philosophy reminds us of the broad scope that Berlin gives philosophy. It also warns us that the reason why value questions are in his view ultimately contestable is not that they are 'subjective', or that their answers are merely expressions of opposed attitudes. Indeed, to read Berlin's discussions of conflicts between values in the context of a debate about subjectivism is to mislocate them and to miss their special force. The debate about subjectivism is characteristically concerned with conflicts of values between persons or societies ('Who is right?'). What above all concerns Berlin, on the other hand, is the tension between conflicting values in *one* consciousness.

Again and again, in these essays and elsewhere, Berlin warns us against the deep error of supposing that all goods, all virtues, all ideals are compatible, and that what is desirable can ultimately be united into a harmonious whole without loss. This is not the platitude that in an imperfect world not all the things we recognise as good are in practice compatible. It is rather that we have no coherent conception of a world without loss, that goods conflict by their very nature, and that there can be no incontestable scheme for harmonising them. There can, of course, be errors or limitations in thinking about values, whether in the particular case or in a more systematic way. For one thing, there can be the errors of omission and simplification, of succumbing to the illusion that one value can override all others and restructure everything. For Berlin, this is certainly a cardinal error, and it is in a special sense an absolute one — for it offends against something that is absolutely true about values. Yet the historical picture which Berlin also offers, the account of the different models of man and the world deployed at different times and in different societies, tells us also that it is the case — indeed, *must* be the case, in that Hegelian sense of 'must' which Berlin has so helpfully refused to dismiss — that not all values can be equally present to all outlooks. Moreover, intense consciousness of the plurality of values and of their conflict is itself a historical phenomenon, a feature of some ages (for instance, ours) rather than others. One thing, indeed, which can give us an insight into the point or claim of a certain value, its possible hold on our sentiments, is sympathetic understanding of a society which respected it with less pluralistic competition than it receives in ours.

The pluralism of values that Berlin advances is not *just* an application to ethics and political theory of the general anti-reductionist, anti-simplifying attitude in philosophy which he advances in the essay 'Logical Translation' (an essay which expresses very clearly some of the concerns of Oxford philosophy at that time). That general attitude appropriately gives way in the face of the demands of explanatory theory: it is obvious, indeed, that it has to give way in the face of theory, and the question in philosophy is how far explanation requires theory — a question to which present practice gives a much more positive answer than did the Oxford philosophy of the 50s. But the question in ethics, whether we should abandon the claims of some value which has force with us — abandon, for instance, considerations of loyalty or justice in the interests of general utility or benevolence – can hardly be a matter of *explanatory* theory. Philosophers have insisted, and still insist, that we encounter here the demands of another kind of theory, moral theory, which aims to systematise and simplify our moral opinions. But they rarely even try to answer a real question: what authority are theoretical tidiness or simplicity supposed to have against the force of concerns which one actually finds important? That question has no obvious answer, even after one has conceded considerable power (more, perhaps, than Berlin himself would concede) to philosophical theory in general.

It may be that there are no, or few, purely theoretical pressures to reduce the conflicts in our value-system. Berlin will say that there is a pressure to *not* reducing them, towards remaining conscious of these conflicts and not trying to eliminate them on more than a piecemeal basis: that pressure is the respect for truth. To deny the conflicts, indeed to try to resolve them systematically and once for all, would be to offend against something absolutely true about values. But then how are we to take the fact, already mentioned, that a high level of such conflict, and the consciousness of that, is a mark of some forms of life and some societies rather than others? Among the forms of life that support that kind of consciousness, a prominent position is needless to say occupied by the liberal society; and Berlin deploys the pluralism of values in defence of liberalism.

His defence of the liberal society is supported by the pluralism of values, I think, in more than one way. There is the obvious point that if there are many and competing genuine values, then the greater the extent to which a society tends to be single-valued, the more genuine values it neglects or suppresses. More, to this extent, must mean better. The point has strength even if we grant the important qualification that not all values *can* be pluralistically combined, and that some become very pale in too much pluralistic company. There are logical, psychological and sociological limits on what range of values an individual can seriously respect in one life, or one society respect in the lives of various of its citizens. (This is one thing that is being said by people who deny that liberal equality, for instance, is real equality – a point raised by the form that Berlin gives to equality in his discussion of it as one value among others.)

But there is a different kind of consideration, that the consciousness of the plurality of competing values is itself a good, as constituting knowledge of an absolute and fundamental truth. This is a good which, in the name of honesty, or truthfulness, or courage, may be urged against someone who recommends simplification of our values not, perhaps, as a theoretical necessity, but as a practical improvement. Here Berlin — *in the last analysis*, as thinkers of a rather different tendency put it — finds value in knowledge and true understanding themselves, and regards it as itself an argument for the liberal society that that society expresses more than any other does a true understanding of the pluralistic nature of values.

But what is that true understanding? What truth is it that is known to someone who recognises the ultimate plurality of values? In philosophical abstraction, it will be *that there are such values*, and, put in that blank way, it can be taken to speak for an objective order of values which some forms of consciousness (notably the liberal form) are better than others at recognising. But that way of putting it is very blank indeed. It is more characteristic of Berlin's outlook, and more illuminating in itself, to say that one who properly recognises the plurality of values is one who understands the deep and creative role that these various values can play in human life. In that perspective, the correctness of the liberal consciousness is better expressed, not so much in terms of truth — that it recognises the values which indeed there are — but in terms of truthfulness. It is prepared to try to build a life round the recognition that these different values do each have a real and intelligible human significance, and are not just errors, misdirections or poor expressions of human nature. To try to build life in any other way would now be an evasion, of something which by now we understand to be true. What we understand is a truth about human nature as it has been revealed — revealed in the only way in which it could be revealed, historically. The truthfulness that is required is a truthfulness to that historical experience of human nature.

We can see, then, that in Berlin's central conception of values and, connectedly, of humanity, there is an implicit appeal, once more, to historical understanding. We can perhaps see, too, how the development of his thought from general theory of knowledge to the history of ideas and the philosophy of history was not merely a change of interest; and that his complex sense of history is as deeply involved in his philosophy, even in its more abstract applications, as it is, very evidently, in his other writings, and in his life.

BERNARD WILLIAMS

The Purpose of Philosophy

WHAT is the subject-matter of philosophy? There is no universally accepted answer to this question. Opinions differ, from those who regard it as contemplation of all time and all existence — the queen of the sciences — the keystone of the entire arch of human knowledge — to those who wish to dismiss it as a pseudo-science exploiting verbal confusions, a symptom of intellectual immaturity, due to be consigned together with theology and other speculative disciplines to the museum of curious antiquities, as astrology and alchemy have long ago been relegated by the victorious march of the natural sciences.

Perhaps the best way of approaching this topic is to ask, what constitutes the field of other disciplines? How do we demarcate the province of, say, chemistry or history or anthropology? Here it seems clear that subjects or fields of study are determined by the kind of questions to which they have been invented to provide the answers. The questions themselves are intelligible if, and only if, we know where to look for the answers.

If you ask someone an ordinary question, say 'Where is my coat?', 'Why was Mr Kennedy elected President of the United States?', 'What is the Soviet system of criminal law?', he would normally know how to set about finding an answer. We may not know the answers ourselves, but we know that in the case of the question about the coat, the proper procedure is to look on the chair, in the cupboard, etc. In the case of Mr Kennedy's election or the Soviet system of law we consult writings or specialists for the kind of empirical evidence which leads to the relevant conclusions and renders them, if not certain, at any rate probable.

In other words, we know where to look for the answer: we know what makes some answers plausible and others not. What makes this type of question intelligible in the first place is that we think that the answer can be discovered by empirical means, that is, by orderly observation or experiment, or methods compounded of these, namely those of common sense or the natural sciences. There is another class of questions where we are no less clear about the proper route by which the answers are to be sought, namely the formal disciplines: mathematics, for example, or

I

logic, or grammar, or chess or heraldry, defined in terms of certain fixed axioms and certain rules of deduction etc., where the answer to problems is to be found by applying these rules in the manner prescribed as correct.

We do not know the correct proof of Fermat's Theorem, for example, —no one is known to have found it — but we know along what lines to proceed: we know what kind of methods will, and what kind of methods will not, be relevant to the answer. If anyone thinks that answers to mathematical problems can be obtained by looking at green fields or the behaviour of bees, or that answers to empirical problems can be obtained by pure calculation without any factual content at all, we would today think them mistaken to the point of insanity. Each of these major types of questions— the factual and the formal — possesses its own specialised techniques: discoveries by men of genius in these fields, once they are established, can be used by men of no genius at all in a semi-mechanical manner in order to obtain correct results.

The hallmark of these provinces of human thought is that once the question is put we know in which direction to proceed to try to obtain the answer. The history of systematic human thought is largely a sustained effort to formulate all the questions that occur to mankind in such a way that the answers to them will fall into one or other of two great baskets: the empirical, i.e. questions whose answers depend, in the end, on the data of observation; and the formal, i.e. questions whose answers depend on pure calculation, untrammelled by factual knowledge. This dichotomy is a drastically over-simple formulation: empirical and formal elements are not so easily disentangled: but it contains enough truth not to be seriously misleading. The distinction between these two great sources of human knowledge has been recognised since the first beginning of self-conscious thinking.

Yet there are certain questions that do not easily fit into this simple classification. 'What is an okapi?' is answered easily enough by an act of empirical observation. Similarly 'What is the cube root of 729?' is settled by a piece of calculation in accordance with accepted rules. But if I ask 'What is time?', 'What is a number?', 'What is the purpose of human life on earth?', 'How can I know past facts that are no longer there — no longer where?', 'Are all men truly brothers?', how do I set about looking for the answer? If I ask 'Where is my coat?' a possible answer (whether correct or not) would be 'In the cupboard', and we would all know where to look. But if a child asked me 'Where is the image in the mirror?' it would be little use to invite it to look inside the mirror, which it would find to consist of solid glass; or on the surface of the mirror, for the image is certainly not on its surface in the sense in which a postage stamp stuck on it might be; or behind the mirror (which is where the image looks as if it were), for if you look behind the mirror you will find no image there – and so on.

Many who think long enough, and intensely enough, about such questions as 'What is time?' or 'Can time stand still?', 'When I see double, what is there two of?', 'How do I know that other human beings (or material objects) are not mere figments of my own mind?', get into a state of hopeless frustration. 'What is the meaning of "the future tense"?' can be answered by grammarians by mechanically applying formal rules; but if I ask 'What is the meaning of "the future"?' where are we to look for the answer?

There seems to be something queer about all these questions – as wide apart as those about double vision, or number, or the brotherhood of men, or purposes of life; they differ from the questions in the other basket in that the question itself does not seem to contain a pointer to the way in which the answer to it is to be found. The other, more ordinary, questions contain precisely such pointers – built-in techniques for finding the answers to them. The questions about time, the existence of others and so on reduce the questioner to perplexity, and annoy practical people precisely because they do not seem to lead to clear answers or useful knowledge of any kind.

This shows that between the two original baskets, the empirical and the formal, there is at least one intermediate basket, in which all those questions live which cannot easily be fitted into the other two. These questions are of the most diverse nature; some appear to be questions of fact, others of value; some are questions about words and a few symbols; others are about methods pursued by those who use them: scientists, artists, critics, common men in the ordinary affairs of life; still others are about the relations between various provinces of knowledge; some deal with the presuppositions of thinking, some with the nature and ends of moral or social or political action.

The only common characteristic which all these questions appear to have is that they cannot be answered either by observation or calculation, either by inductive methods or deductive; and, as a crucial corollary of this, that those who ask them are faced with a perplexity from the very beginning – they do not know where to look for the answers; there are no dictionaries, encyclopedias, compendia of knowledge, no experts, no orthodoxies, which can be referred to with confidence as

3

possessing unquestionable authority or knowledge in these matters. Moreover some of these questions are distinguished by being general and by dealing with matters of principle; and others, while not themselves general, very readily raise or lead to questions of principle.

Such questions tend to be called philosophical. Ordinary men regard them with contempt, or awe, or suspicion, according to their temperaments. For this reason, if for no other, there is a natural tendency to try to reformulate these questions in such a way that all or at any rate parts of them can be answered either by empirical or formal statements; that is to say efforts, sometimes very desperate ones, are made to fit them into either the empirical or the formal basket, where agreed methods, elaborated over the centuries, yield dependable results whose truth can be tested by accepted means.

The history of human knowledge is, to a large degree, a sustained attempt to shuffle all questions into one of the two 'viable' categories; for as soon as a puzzling, 'queer' question can be translated into one that can be treated by an empirical or a formal discipline, it ceases to be philosophical and becomes part of a recognised science.[1] Thus it was no mistake to regard astronomy in, say, the early Middle Ages as a 'philosophical' discipline: so long as answers to questions about stars and planets were not determined by observation or experiment and calculation, but were dominated by such non-empirical notions as those, e.g., of perfect bodies determined to pursue circular paths by their goals or inner essences with which they were endowed by God or Nature, even if this was rendered improbable by empirical observation, it was not clear how astronomical questions could be settled: i.e. what part was to be played by observing actual heavenly bodies, and what part by theological or metaphysical assertions which were not capable of being tested either by empirical or by formal means.

Only when questions in astronomy were formulated in such a manner that clear answers could be discovered by using and depending on the methods of observation and experiment, and these in their turn could be connected in a systematic structure the coherence of which could be tested by purely logical or mathematical means, was the modern science

[1] The claims of metaphysics or theology to be sciences must rest on the assumption that intuition or revelation are direct sources of knowledge of facts about the world; since they claim to be forms of direct experience, their data, if their existence is allowed, belong, for our purposes, to the 'empirical' basket.

of astronomy created, leaving behind it a cloud of obscure metaphysical notions unconnected with empirical tests and consequently no longer relevant to the new science, and so gradually relegated and forgotten.

So, too, in our own time, such disciplines as economics, psychology, semantics, logic itself, are gradually shaking themselves free from everything that is neither dependent on observation nor formal; if and when they have successfully completed this process they will be finally launched on independent careers of their own as natural or formal sciences, with a rich philosophical past, but an empirical and/or formal present and future. The history of thought is thus a long series of parricides, in which new disciplines seek to achieve their freedom by killing off the parent subjects and eradicating from within themselves whatever traces still linger within them of 'philosophical' problems, i.e. the kind of questions that do not carry within their own structure clear indications of the techniques of their own solution.

That, at any rate, is the ideal of such sciences; in so far as some of their problems (e.g. in modern cosmology) are not formulated in purely empirical or mathematical terms, their field necessarily overlaps with that of philosophy. Indeed, it would be rash to say of any developed high-level science that it has finally eradicated its philosophical problems. In physics, for instance, fundamental questions exist at the present time which in many ways seem philosophical – questions that concern the very framework of concepts in terms of which hypotheses are to be formed and observations interpreted. How are wave-models and particle-models related to one another? Is indeterminacy an ultimate feature of sub-atomic theory? Such questions are of a philosophical type; in particular, no deductive or observational programme leads at all directly to their solution. On the other hand, it is of course true that those who try to answer such questions need to be trained and gifted in physics, and that any answers to those questions would constitute advances in the science of physics itself. Although, with the progressive separation of the positive sciences, no philosophers' questions are physical, some physicists' questions are still philosophical.

This is one reason, but only one, why the scope and content of philosophy does not seem greatly diminished by this process of attrition. For no matter how many questions can be so transformed as to be capable of empirical or formal treatment, the number of questions that seem incapable of being so treated does not appear to grow less. This fact would have distressed the philosophers of the Enlightenment, who were convinced that all genuine questions could be solved by the methods that had achieved so magnificent a triumph in the hands of the natural scientists of the seventeenth and early eighteenth centuries.

It is true that even in that clear day men still appeared no nearer to the solution of such central, indubitably philosophical, because apparently unanswerable, questions as whether men and things had been created to fulfil a purpose by God or by nature, and if so what purpose; whether men were free to choose between alternatives, or on the contrary were rigorously determined by the causal laws that governed inanimate nature; whether ethical and aesthetic truths were universal and objective or relative and subjective; whether men were only bundles of flesh and blood and bone and nervous tissue, or the earthly habitations of immortal souls; whether human history had a discernible pattern, or was a repetitive causal sequence or a succession of casual and unintelligible accidents. These ancient questions tormented them as they had their ancestors in Greece and Rome and Palestine and the medieval west.

Physics and chemistry did not tell one why some men were obliged to obey other men and under what circumstances, and what was the nature of such obligations; what was good and what was evil; whether happiness and knowledge, justice and mercy, liberty and equality, efficiency and individual independence, were equally valid goals of human action, and if so, whether they were compatible with one another, and if not, which of them were to be chosen, and what were valid criteria for such choices, and how we could be certain about their validity, and what was meant by the notion of validity itself; and many more questions of this type.

Yet — so a good many eighteenth-century philosophers argued — a similar state of chaos and doubt had once prevailed in the realm of the natural sciences too; yet there human genius had finally prevailed and created order.

> Nature and Nature's laws lay hid in night:
> God said 'Let Newton be!' and all was light.

If Newton could, with a small number of basic laws, enable us, at least in theory, to determine the position and motion of every physical entity in the universe, and in this way abolish at one blow a vast, shapeless mass of conflicting, obscure, and only half-intelligible rules of thumb which had hitherto passed for natural knowledge, was it not reasonable to expect that by applying similar principles to human conduct and the analysis of the nature of man, we should be able to obtain similar

6

clarification and establish the human sciences upon equally firm foundations?

Philosophy fed on the muddles and obscurities of language; if these were cleared away, it would surely be found that the only questions left would be concerned with testable human beliefs, or expressions of identifiable, everyday human needs or hopes or fears or interests. These were the proper study of psychologists, anthropologists, sociologists, economists; all that was needed was a Newton, or series of Newtons, for the sciences of man; in this way, the perplexities of metaphysics could once and for all be removed, the idle tribe of philosophical speculators eradicated, and on the ground thus cleared, a clear and firm edifice of natural science built.

This was the hope of all the best-known philosophers of the Enlightenment, from Hobbes and Hume to Helvétius, Holbach, Condorcet, Bentham, Saint-Simon, Comte, and their successors. Yet this programme was doomed to failure. The realm of philosophy was not partitioned into a series of scientific successor states. Philosophical questions continued (and continue) to fascinate and torment inquiring minds.

Why is this so? An illuminating answer to this problem was given by Kant, the first thinker to draw a clear distinction between, on the one hand, questions of fact, and, on the other, questions about the patterns in which these facts presented themselves to us – patterns that were not themselves altered however much the facts themselves, or our knowledge of them, might alter. These patterns or categories or forms of experience were themselves not the subject-matter of any possible natural science.

Kant was the first to draw the crucial distinction between facts – the data of experience as it were, the things, persons, events, qualities, relations, that we observed or inferred or thought about – and the categories in terms of which we sensed and imagined and reflected about them. These were, for him, independent of the different cosmic attitudes – the religious or metaphysical frameworks that belonged to various ages and civilisations. Thus, the majority of Greek philosophers, and most of all Aristotle, thought that all things had purposes built into them by nature – ends or goals which they could not but seek to fulfil. The medieval Christians saw the world as a hierarchy in which every object and person was called upon to fulfil a specific function by the Divine Creator; He alone understood the purpose of the entire pattern, and made the happiness and misery of His creatures depend upon the degree to which

7

they followed the commandments that were entailed by the differing purposes for which each entity had been created – the purposes that in fulfilling themselves realised the universal harmony, the supreme pattern, the totality of which was kept from the creatures, and understood by the Creator alone.

The rationalists of the eighteenth and nineteenth centuries saw no purpose in anything but what man himself had created to serve his own needs, and regarded all else as determined by the laws of cause and effect, so that most things pursued no purposes, but were as they were, and moved and changed as they did, as a matter of 'brute' fact.

These were profoundly different outlooks. Yet those who held them saw very similar items in the universe, similar colours, tastes, shapes, forms of motion and rest, experienced similar feelings, pursued similar goals, acted in similar fashions.

Kant, in his doctrine of our knowledge of the external world, taught that the categories through which we saw it were identical for all sentient beings, permanent and unalterable; indeed this is what made our world one, and communication possible. But some of those who thought about history, morals, aesthetics, did see change and difference; what differed was not so much the empirical content of what these successive civilisations saw or heard or thought as the basic patterns in which they perceived them, the models in terms of which they conceived them, the category-spectacles through which they viewed them.

The world of a man who believes that God created him for a specific purpose, that he has an immortal soul, that there is an afterlife in which his sins will be visited upon him, is radically different from the world of a man who believes in none of these things; and the reasons for action, the moral codes, the political beliefs, the tastes, the personal relationships of the former will deeply and systematically differ from those of the latter.

Men's views of one another will differ profoundly as a very consequence of their general conception of the world: the notions of cause and purpose, good and evil, freedom and slavery, things and persons, rights, duties, laws, justice, truth, falsehood, to take some central ideas completely at random, depend directly upon the general framework within which they form, as it were, nodal points. Although the facts which are classified and arranged under these notions are not at all identical for all men at all times, yet these differences – which the sciences examine – are not the same as the profounder differences which wearing

8

different sets of spectacles, using different categories, thinking in terms of different models, must make to men of different times and places and cultures and outlooks.

Philosophy, then, is not an empirical study: not the critical examination of what exists or has existed or will exist – this is dealt with by commonsense knowledge and belief, and the methods of the natural sciences. Nor is it a kind of formal deduction as mathematics or logic is. Its subject-matter is to a large degree not the items of experience, but the ways in which they are viewed, the permanent or semi-permanent categories in terms of which experience is conceived and classified. Purpose versus mechanical causality; organism versus mere amalgams; systems versus mere togetherness; spatio-temporal order versus timeless being; duty versus appetite; value versus fact – these are categories, models, spectacles. Some of these are as old as human experience itself; others are more transient. With the more transient, the philosopher's problems take on a more dynamic and historical aspect. Different models and frameworks, with their attendant obscurities and difficulties, arise at different times. The case of contemporary problems in the explanatory framework of physics, already mentioned, is one example of this. But there are other examples, which affect the thought not just of physicists or other specialists, but of reflective men in general.

In politics, for example, men tried to conceive of their social existence by analogy with various models: Plato at one stage, perhaps following Pythagoras, tried to frame his system of human nature, its attributes and goals, following a geometrical pattern, since he thought it would explain all there was. There followed the biological pattern of Aristotle; the many Christian images with which the writings of the Fathers as well as the Old and New Testaments abound; the analogy of the family, which casts light upon human relations not provided by a mechanical model (say that of Hobbes); the notion of an army on the march with its emphasis on such virtues as loyalty, dedication, obedience, needed to overtake and crush the enemy (with which so much play has been made in the Soviet Union); the notion of the state as a traffic policeman and night watchman preventing collisions and looking after property, which is at the back of much individualist and liberal thought; the notion of the state as much more than this – as a great cooperative endeavour of individuals seeking to fulfil a common end, and therefore as entitled to enter into every nook and cranny of human experience, that animates much of the 'organic' thought of the nineteenth century; the systems borrowed from psychology, or from theories of games, that are in vogue at present – all these are models in terms of which human beings, groups and societies and cultures, have conceived of their experience.

These models often collide; some are rendered inadequate by failing to account for too many aspects of experience, and are in their turn replaced by other models which emphasise what these last have omitted but in their turn may obscure what the others have rendered clear. The task of philosophy, often a difficult and painful one, is to extricate and bring to light the hidden categories and models in terms of which human beings think (that is, their use of words, images and other symbols), to reveal what is obscure or contradictory in them, to discern the conflicts between them that prevent the construction of more adequate ways of organising and describing and explaining experience (for all description as well as explanation involves some model in terms of which the describing and explaining is done); and then, at a still 'higher' level, to examine the nature of this activity itself (epistemology, philosophical logic, linguistic analysis), and to bring to light the concealed models that operate in this second-order, philosophical, activity itself.

If it is objected that all this seems very abstract and remote from daily experience, something too little concerned with the central interests, the happiness and unhappiness and ultimate fate of ordinary men, the answer is that this charge is false. Men cannot live without seeking to describe and explain the universe to themselves. The models they use in doing this must deeply affect their lives, not least when they are unconscious; much of the misery and frustration of men is due to the mechanical or unconscious, as well as deliberate, application of models where they do not work. Who can say how much suffering has been caused by the exuberant use of the organic model in politics, or the comparison of the state to a work of art, and the representation of the dictator as the inspired moulder of human lives, by totalitarian theorists in our own times? Who shall say how much harm and how much good, in previous ages, came of the exaggerated application to social relations of metaphors and models fashioned after the patterns of paternal authority, especially to the relations of rulers of states to their subjects, or of priests to the laity?

If there is to be any hope of a rational order on earth, or of a just appreciation of the many various interests that divide diverse groups of human beings – knowledge that is indispensable to any attempt to assess their effects, and the patterns of their interplay and its consequences, in order to find viable compromises through which men may continue to live and satisfy their desires without thereby crushing the equally central desires and needs of others – it lies in the bringing to light of these models, social, moral, political, and above all the underlying metaphysical patterns in which they are rooted, with a view to examining whether they are adequate to their task.

The perennial task of philosophers is to examine whatever seems insusceptible to the methods of the sciences or everyday observation, e.g. categories, concepts, models, ways of thinking or acting, and particularly ways in which they clash with one another, with a view to constructing other, less internally contradictory, and (though this can never be fully attained) less pervertible metaphors, images, symbols and systems of categories. It is certainly a reasonable hypothesis that one of the principal causes of confusion, misery and fear is, whatever may be its psychological or social roots, blind adherence to outworn notions, pathological suspicion of any form of critical self-examination, frantic efforts to prevent any degree of rational analysis of what we live by and for.

This socially dangerous, intellectually difficult, often agonising and thankless, but always important activity is the work of philosophers, whether they deal with the natural sciences or moral or political or purely personal issues. The goal of philosophy is always the same, to assist men to understand themselves and thus operate in the open, and not wildly, in the dark.

Verification

THIS paper is an attempt to estimate how far the principle of verification fulfils the purpose for which it is employed by many contemporary empiricist philosophers. The general truth of their doctrines I shall not call into question. The thesis which I shall try to establish is that the principle of verifiability or verification, after playing a decisive role in the history of modern philosophy, by clearing up confusions, exposing major errors and indicating what were and what were not questions proper for philosophers to ask, which has enabled it to exercise in our day a function not unlike that which Kant's critical method performed for his generation, cannot, for all that, be accepted as a final criterion of empirical significance, since such acceptance leads to wholly untenable consequences. I shall consequently urge that after due homage has been paid to its therapeutic influence, it needs to be abandoned or else considerably revised, if it is to be prevented from breeding new fallacies in place of those which it eradicates.

I propose to begin by assuming that what the principle sets out to do both can and should be done; and to consider whether it can do this alone and unassisted. I shall seek to show that it cannot, and that to maintain the opposite entails a view of empirical propositions too paradoxical to deserve serious notice.

As is well known, its supporters claim that the function which it fulfils is that of acting as a criterion for determining whether assertions of a certain type mean in fact what they purport to mean. The pressing need for such a criterion arises out of the view on which much modern empiricism rests, according to which all truly significant assertions must be concerned either with the facts of experience, in the sense in which they are the subject-matter of the judgements of common sense and of empirical science, or else with the verbal means used to symbolise such facts. The task in question is to find some infallible criterion by which to distinguish assertions of the first, i.e. experiential type, from all other possible modes of employing symbols. I must begin by making clear my use of certain essential terms: by a sentence I propose to mean any arrangement of words which obeys the rules of grammar; by a statement any sentence which obeys the rules of logic; and finally, by a proposition any sentence which conveys to someone that something is or is not the case. And this seems on the whole to accord with common usage. In addition I propose, at any rate in the first section of the argument, to mean by the term 'experience' only what phenomenalists say they mean by it, that is, only such actual or possible data as are provided by observation and introspection. I do not wish to assert that phenomenalism is self-evidently true. On the contrary, no method yet suggested of translating the propositions about material objects into propositions about data of observation and introspection seems wholly satisfactory. But for the purpose of my thesis it will be sufficient to confine myself to the latter, i.e. to propositions concerned solely with objects of immediate acquaintance; since if the verification criterion is inadequate in dealing with them it will *a fortiori* fail to apply to the much more complex case of statements about material objects. If this is true it will tend to show that the historical connection between phenomenalism and 'verificationism' is not a logical one and that the failure of the latter does not necessarily invalidate the former. This conclusion I should like to believe to be true, since the opposite would prove fatal to the view which seems to me to be true on other grounds, as I shall urge in the last section of this paper, that whereas the phenomenalist analysis of statements of common sense is fundamentally correct, and has not proved convincing more on account of insufficient ingenuity in the formulation of specific analyses, or of the vagueness of the *analysandum*, than because of some fatal defect in the method itself, the principle of verification, in spite of its undoubted efficacy in the past in detecting and destroying unreal puzzles, has now begun to yield diminishing returns, and even to create new spurious problems of its own. This, I shall argue, is due to the fact that it is not in principle capable of being applied to the whole field of empirical belief and knowledge, but only to a limited portion of it – a fact which is brought out particularly clearly by the examination of that version of it, sometimes called operationalism, according to which the different logical or epistemological categories to which a given proposition may belong are determined by the differences in the kind of tests normally employed to discover its truth or falsity.

The essence of the principle of verification will appear clearly if one considers its progressive modification in the face of difficulties. The bare assertion that all significant statements were concerned either with facts about experience or with the symbolic means of expressing them was too vague and excluded too little. Metaphysicians and theologians could claim that they, too, reported facts of experience, although facts of a very different order from those which were of interest to empirical scientists, arrived at by non-empirical processes of cognition, and thus wholly outside the range of any evidence drawn from the data of observation or introspection. A stricter criterion of significance seemed therefore to be required, at any rate in the case of propositions claiming to describe experience. To supply it (I do not vouch for the historical accuracy of this account) the principle of verification was adopted, a test which, so it is claimed, made it possible to determine without further ado whether a given collocation of words was or was not significant in the above sense. In its earliest and most uncompromising form it declared that the meaning of a proposition resided in the means of its verification; the questions 'What does the statement p mean?' and 'What must one do to discover whether p is true?' were logically equivalent – the answer to one was the answer to the other. The most obvious objection to this doctrine, which critics were not slow to urge, was that this formulation involved a glaring *hysteron proteron*; for before I could think of possible ways of verifying a given statement I first must know what the statement means, otherwise there could be nothing for me to verify. How can I ask whether a group of symbols asserts a truth or a falsehood if I am not certain of what it means, or indeed whether it means anything at all? Surely, therefore, understanding what the sentence means – what proposition it expresses – must in some sense be prior to the investigation of its truth, and cannot be defined in terms of the possibility of such an investigation – on the contrary the latter must be defined in terms of it. But this objection is not as formidable as it looks. A supporter of the theory may reply that what he means by the expression 'to know the means of the verification of p' is knowing in what circumstances one would judge the group of symbols 'p' to convey something which was or was not the case; adding that what one means by saying that one understands a given sentence, or that the sentence has meaning, is precisely this, that one can conceive of a state of affairs such that if it is the case – exists – the sentence in question is the proper, conventionally correct description of it, i.e. the proposition expressed by the sentence is true, while if it is not the case, the proposition expressed is false. To understand a sentence – to certify it as expressing a given proposition – is thus equivalent to knowing how I should set about to look for the state of affairs which, if the state of affairs exists, it correctly describes. To say that a sentence is intelligible, i.e. that it expresses a proposition, without specifying what the proposition is, is to say that I know that I could set about to look for the relevant situation without saying what kind of situation it is. It follows that any sentence such that I can conceive of no experience of which it is the correct description, is for me meaningless. The limits of what I can conceive are set by experience – that is, I can conceive only whatever is either identical with, or else in some respect similar to, the kind of situation which I have already met with or imagined; the possible is a logical alternative of, and conceivable only by reference to, the actual; whatever is wholly different from it is wholly inconceivable. The actual, on this view, consists of the data of observation, sensible and introspective, and what can be inferred from them. The logically possible is conceived only by analogy with it; sentences which purport to refer to something outside this are therefore meaningless. If nevertheless I claim that they mean something to me I am using the term 'meaning' ambiguously or loosely; I may wish to say that they suggest, or are evidence for, a situation, without formally describing it, as tears are evidence of distress without being a statement about it; or else that they evoke an emotion in me, convey or induce a mood or an attitude, stimulate behaviour, or even that no more is occurring than that I am acquainted with the normal use of the individual words in the sentences to which I attribute meaning and that they are grouped in accordance with the rules of grammar and of logic, as in certain types of nonsense verse. This seems prima facie plausible enough, and successfully eliminates whole classes of expressions as being meaningless in the strict sense because they seem to describe no conceivable experience, and can therefore, as Hume recommended, be safely rejected as so much metaphysical rubbish. Whatever survives this drastic test can then be classified exhaustively as being either direct statements about possible experience, that is empirical propositions, or second- or higher-order statements about the relations of types of such statements to each other, i.e. propositions of logic and other formal sciences. And this was as much as the anti-metaphysical party had ever claimed. It was soon seen however that as it stood this position was wholly untenable.

To begin with, the conception of 'means of verification' was far too narrow. If it was interpreted literally it always referred to the present or the immediate future in which alone sensible verification of what I was asserting could take place. This gave all statements about the past, and a great many about the present and future, a meaning which was prima facie very different from that which they seemed to have. Such a sentence for example as 'It was raining half an hour ago' had to be regarded as equivalent to one or more of such statements as 'I am now having a moderately fresh memory image of falling rain', 'My shoes look fairly, but not very, wet', 'I am looking at the chart of a recording barometer and observe an undulating line of a certain shape', 'I expect, if I ask you "Was it raining half an hour ago?", to hear the answer "Yes"' and the like. This is unsatisfactory on two grounds, equally fatal. In the first place, by translating all propositions about the past (and about the future) into propositions about experience in the present (which alone I can conclusively verify) it gives two senses of the word 'present'; the sense in which it is distinguishable from 'past' and 'future', i.e. the normal sense, and the sense in which it includes them; the second sense, being contrastable with nothing, adds nothing to any statement in which it occurs; to say in this sense that all significant statements refer only to the present is thus to utter a pointless tautology. Yet the sense in which alone it was relevant to say that all conclusively verifiable propositions were concerned only with the present, was the first, not the second, sense; the sense in which to speak of the present state of something is to distinguish it from past and future states. Moreover, the translation feels wrong. One does not usually mean by the sentence 'It rained yesterday' the present empirical evidence for it, not even the total sum of such evidence. For the relation 'being evidence of' not being that of logical implication, the evidential proposition may be true and the proposition which it claims to establish false; the two therefore cannot be equivalent. What I mean to assert is that it was raining yesterday, not that events which are now occurring make it unreasonable to doubt that it did: the rain I speak of is the rain of yesterday, whatever may or may not be happening today. To verify yesterday's rain conclusively (the *verificandum* being taken in a phenomenalist sense as a logical construction out of observation data), one has to have lived through yesterday and to have observed whether it rained or not. To do this now is in some sense of the word impossible: yet the meaning of the sentence is not seriously in doubt. It follows that either all propositions save those about the immediate present are meaningless: or that meaning cannot depend on conclusive verifiability.

To this the defenders of the theory can answer that in saying that the meaning of *p* resides (*liegt*) in the means of its verification they did not literally mean to assert any such equivalence: they meant only that '*p* is significant' entails that some means of verifying is possible. The proposition is never equivalent to the sum of evidence for it; but unless one can say that there could be a situation in which an observer could verify it, one cannot say that the sentence has any meaning. Thus 'p is significant' where p is empirical entails and is entailed by 'p is verifiable', but is not equivalent to any specific group of actual propositions cited as evidence for it. Moreover, by verifiability what is meant is verifiability not in practice, but in principle; this last being needed to eliminate not only the objection that some propositions, e.g. that there are mountains on the other side of the moon, are clearly significant and yet cannot be verified on account of technical difficulties which observers with more luck and skill than ourselves might overcome, but to secure plausible analyses of propositions about the past, which we are prevented from verifying by the accident of our position in time as well as space. We *might* have been born earlier than we were, and lived in countries other than those which in fact we inhabit; I cannot now, do what I will, verify the proposition 'Julius Caesar was bald' by direct inspection, but there is no *logical* reason why I should not have been born in ancient Rome in time to have observed Caesar's head; the reason is causal, unless indeed I define myself as having been born in the twentieth century, in which case some other observer could have carried out this observation. For there is no reason why 'p is verifiable' should mean 'p is verifiable by me.'[1] Solipsism even of the so-called methodo-logical variety is a wholly gratuitous assumption. I can conceive of other observers by analogy with my own self, however the notion of a parti-cular self is to be analysed. So much has been pointed out by Berkeley. To verify the proposition that such observers actually exist, and have experiences which are not ours, is of course a very different and much more difficult task. Thus 'p is significant' has now come to mean 'It is conceivable (i.e. there is no logical contradiction in supposing) that some-one should observe or should have observed what is correctly described by p.' In this watered-down form the principle does seem to acquire a much wider sphere of application and attempts at 'silly' analyses can be successfully foiled. But the position is still far from secured.

For all that can be accounted for on this hypothesis are such singular categorical propositions as are conclusively verifiable, at any rate in principle, by a suitably situated observer. This leaves three classes of propositions unaccounted for, and these by far the most commonly used: (1) propositions which are not singular; (2) propositions which are not categorical; (3) propositions which seem to be both singular

[1] See G. Ryle, 'Unverifiability-by-me', *Analysis* 4 (1936), 1–11.

and categorical, but not to be conclusively verifiable by observation.

1 General propositions offer the most obvious difficulty. No sentence of the form 'All s is p', whether taken in extension or intension, where s denotes an infinite set (or at any rate does not *explicitly* denote a finite one), can be verified by any finite number of observations. That is to say it is not conclusively verifiable at all. The same applies to all propositions containing 'any' or 'every' as components. The attempt made by Ramsey and those who accept his view to treat them as rules or prescriptions, logical or empirical, and therefore neither true nor false, cannot be defended since, as they are used, they are held to be refutable by a single negative instance, and it is nonsense to say of rules that they have instances or can be refuted. Yet they have clear empirical meaning, particularly when taken in extension, and cannot be left out of account. To meet this difficulty the principle of verification was revised and two types of it distinguished: the first, called verification in the strong sense, was the familiar version. The second, or 'weak' verification, was invented to apply to general propositions and to singular-seeming propositions about material objects, in so far as these were thought to entail general propositions about sense data – a view which it has proved far from easy to hold. Two versions of 'weak' verifiability are given by A. J. Ayer:[1] according to the first we ask about a given proposition 'Would any observations be relevant to the determination of its truth or falsehood?' If so the proposition is significant. This may well be true, but as it stands the suggested criterion is far too vague to be of use.[2] Relevance is not a precise logical category, and fantastic metaphysical systems may choose to claim that observation data are 'relevant' to their truth. Such claims cannot be rebutted unless some precise meaning is assigned to the concept of relevance, which, because the word is used to convey an essentially vague idea, cannot be done. Thus 'weak' verification, designed to admit only general, and material object, statements, cannot be prevented from opening the gates for any statement, however meaningless, to enter, provided that someone can be found to claim that observation is in some sense relevant to it. As a criterion for distinguishing sense from nonsense relevance plainly does not work: indeed to accept it is in effect to abrogate the principle of verification

[1] A. J. Ayer, *Language, Truth and Logic* (London, 1946), p. 38.
[2] On this see A. C. Ewing, 'Meaninglessness', *Mind* 46 (1937), 347–64, particularly 352–3.

altogether. Ayer, conscious of this perhaps, attempts to provide another far more rigorous formulation of 'weak' verification, which at first seems to fit our needs more adequately.[1] He says, "To make our position clearer, we may formulate it in another way . . . we may say that it is the mark of a genuine factual proposition . . . that some experiential [i.e. strongly verifiable] propositions can be deduced from it in conjunction with certain other premises without being deducible from those other premises alone. This criterion seems liberal enough.' Unfortunately it is a good deal too liberal, and does not guarantee us against nonsense any better than the previous test. What it appears to assert is this: given three propositions p, q, r, where r is conclusively verifiable in principle, then p is weakly verified, and therefore significant, if r follows from p and q, and does not follow from q alone. Thus 'All men are mortal' is 'weakly' verifiable, because 'Socrates will die' which does not follow from 'Socrates is a man' by itself, follows from the two in conjunction. It may be noted that 'verifiable' seems here to have lost its sense of 'rendered true' or 'established beyond doubt', and is equivalent to something much looser, like 'made probable' or 'plausible', itself an obscure and unexamined concept. However, even in this diluted form the principle will not do. For if I say

> This logical problem is bright green
> I dislike all shades of green
> Therefore I dislike this problem

I have uttered a valid syllogism whose major premise has satisfied the definition of weak verifiability as well as the rules of logic and of grammar, yet it is plainly meaningless. One cannot reply to this that it is put out of court by the confusion of categories which it contains, or some such answer, since this entails the direct applicability of a criterion of significance other than 'weak' verification, which makes the latter otiose. No criterion which is powerless in the face of such nonsense as the above is fit to survive. 'Weak' verifiability is a suspicious device in any case, inasmuch as it bears the name without fulfilling the original function of verification proper, and appears to suggest that there is more than one sense of empirical truth. The chief argument in its favour seems to be that unless it is valid, any theory which entails it must be false. Since the contrary instance cited above is fatal to it, this consequence must be accepted. Weak verification has thus failed to provide the needed criterion.

[1] op. cit., pp. 38–9.

By far the most ingenious attempt to solve the difficulty is that made by Karl Popper[1] who suggests that a proposition is significant if and only if it can be conclusively falsified by the conclusive verification of a singular proposition which contradicts it – as when a law is refuted by the occurrence of one negative instance. But while this may provide a valid criterion of significance for general propositions about observation data, it throws no light on whether the sense in which they are called true is or is not identical with that in which singular propositions are so called. The implication which one may be tempted to draw from this is that propositions of different logical types are true or false, verifiable and falsifiable, each in its own specific fashion: indeed that this is what is meant by saying that they belong to different categories; that is to say that the logical (and epistemological) character of a proposition is determined by the way in which it is verifiable (or falsifiable), the two being alternative ways of saying the same thing about it. This view, which if true would solve many difficulties, cannot, however, be accepted, as I hope to show in the next section of the argument. It should further be noted that Popper's criterion of falsifiability, while it may deal successfully with general propositions of observation, does not apply equally well to propositions about material objects, for whose benefit it was originally introduced. But as we have agreed to accept phenomenalism this is beside the issue, and the criterion may therefore be provisionally accepted.

2 The second type of proposition not covered by the original 'strong' verifiability criterion consists of those which are not categorical. These are highly relevant to the whole issue, and repay exceptionally close attention. It has too often been assumed by logicians that all hypothetical propositions are general, and all general propositions are hypothetical: 'All *s* is *p*' is equivalent to 'If *s* then *p*' and vice versa. Nothing could be further from the truth. While some hypothetical propositions are general, others are not. The commonest of all propositions which occur in the writings of contemporary positivists, the propositions indispensable to any discussion of meaning or verification, the familiar 'If I look up I shall observe a blue patch', are indubitably hypothetical, but in no sense general. To show this one need only point out that they are conclusively verifiable. Indeed it was because an attempt was made to reduce all other statements to verifiable propositions of this type that

[1] In his book *Logik der Forschung* (Vienna, [1934]) [now translated as *The Logic of Scientific Discovery* (London, 1959)].

absurdities resulted. I verify the proposition mentioned above by looking up and observing a blue patch: if conclusive verification ever occurs, it occurs in this case. It must be noted that I have actually proved more than I have asserted: not merely the hypothetical but a conjunctive proposition 'I shall look up and I shall see a blue patch' has been verified. This is unavoidable from the nature of the case. But although the conjunctive proposition entails the hypothetical, it is not entailed by it, and the two are therefore not equivalent. The conjunction is falsified if (a) I do not look up and see a blue patch, (b) I do not look up and do not see a blue patch, (c) I look up and see no blue patch. The hypothetical proposition is falsified by the occurrence of (c) alone. If either (a) or (b) is the case, the hypothetical proposition is rendered neither true nor false, and may be either. It is essential to note firstly that the relation between the protasis 'I shall look up' and the apodosis 'I shall see a blue patch' is not one of material implication, otherwise the whole would be verified by denying the protasis. Secondly, that it is not one of strict implication, since the antecedent may be affirmed and the consequent denied without a formal contradiction. Thirdly, that it is not necessarily causal: I may, of course, when I declare that if I look up I shall see a blue patch, say this because I believe that there is a causal connection between the two events, but equally I may not believe this, and decide to bet that this will happen because I am by temperament a passionate gambler, and all the more stimulated if I believe that the weight of inductive evidence is against me; or I may say it because it is an exception which disproves one causal law, without necessarily regarding it as being itself an instance of another law; or I may say it out of sheer contrariness, or any other motive whatever. My *rational* ground for saying what I do would doubtless take the form of a general causal proposition which entails the proposition on whose truth I am betting, but I may choose to behave irrationally, or use the proposition in an *ad absurdum* argument to prove its opposite: the general proposition 'Observers in conditions similar to these normally see blue patches if they look up' entails, but is not entailed by, the proposition 'If A looks up he will observe a blue patch'; the latter proposition, so far from being equivalent to the former, may be true where the other is false, and as was said above, may be conclusively verifiable – a condition which the general proposition is logically incapable of attaining. The proposition is therefore both singular and hypothetical, its subject being not a hypothetical variable, but a nameable particular. So far all seems clear. The difficulty arises when the antecedent is not fulfilled: when I assert, for example, that if I look up I shall see a blue patch, and then fail to look up. The proposition appears now to be no longer conclusively verifiable. The opportunity for that has been missed and cannot be recovered. I must now resort to the roundabout method of producing evidence for it, i.e. 'weakly' verifying the general causal proposition of which the proposition to be verified is an instance; nor can the instantial proposition be made more probable than the general proposition which entails it. But clearly the statement 'If I look up I shall see a blue patch', which now becomes 'If I had looked up I should have seen a blue patch', expresses a proposition which is still true or false in precisely the same sense as before, although the means of its verification have altered; yet clearly the statement cannot have changed in meaning because I did not in fact look up. Yet if it were true that the impossibility of strongly verifying a given proposition entailed that it had a logical character different from propositions which can be strongly verified, the proposition in question would alter in character solely because I did or did not choose to act in a certain fashion. This would mean that the kind of meaning possessed by singular hypothetical sentences or statements would depend on the empirical fact that their protases did or did not actually come true, which is patently absurd. It seems to me to follow that neither the meaning, nor the logical character, of a statement can possibly depend on what steps one would naturally take to ascertain its truth: and in so far as operationalists assert this without qualification, they are mistaken.

At this point someone might reply that although an unfulfilled singular hypothetical statement (or for that matter a hypothetical statement whose protasis is not known to be fulfilled) cannot be verified conclusively in actual fact, it can be so verified in principle. I did not in fact look up and so I cannot know for certain what would have happened if I did; but I might have looked up; or rather it is not self-contradictory to assert that an observer could or did look up; and such an observer, possible in principle, is in a position to verify the proposition conclusively. And so such propositions are, after all, no worse off than categorical statements about the vanished past: they too may not in fact have been verified conclusively; but they could have been so verified; and so are verifiable conclusively in principle. This argument, plausible though it is, is ultimately untenable, for the reason that were I situated favourably for verifying these unverified hypotheses, I should *ipso facto* not have been able to verify some of those which I in fact did: and I could not, in the logical sense of 'could not', have done both. An eternal

22

omnisentient being which is in all places at all times can, if it chooses, verify all categorical propositions about past, present and future phenomena: but even it cannot verify what did not occur; that which might have occurred had not that happened which in fact did. And if it is omniscient as well as omnisentient, and if there is any sense in which it could be said to know this too, it knows it by means other than sensible verification. A simple example will, I hope, make it clear. Suppose that instead of asserting one singular hypothetical proposition, I assert two such propositions in the form of the premises of a dilemma, such that the protasis of each is incompatible with the protasis of the other. For instance: 'If I remain here I shall have a headache. If I do not remain here I shall be bored.' Each of these propositions may itself be verifiable in principle: the conjunction of both cannot be verified conclusively, even in principle, since it involves me in the logical impossibility of being in a certain state and not being in it at the same time. Of course I can adduce the evidence of various observers for what would happen under these two logically incompatible sets of conditions. But such inductive evidence verifies only 'weakly' (whatever meaning may be attached to that unfortunate phrase). 'If I were now at the North Pole I should feel colder than I do' cannot in principle be strongly verified, since I cannot even in principle be simultaneously here and at the North Pole and compare the different temperatures. It is beside the point to say that this arises only if I am defined as capable of being situated here or at the North Pole but not at both; whereas I might have been a giant with one foot on the North Pole and the other in this room, in which case I might have verified the proposition conclusively. I could myself be defined differently, but the same problem would still arise whatever the defined scope and my powers; a proposition asserting an unfulfilled possibility can always be constructed to contradict whatever is the case, and this can be made the protasis of a second singular hypothetical proposition whose verifiability is incompatible with that of the first. To put it semi-formally: given that for every empirical proposition p at least one contradictory $not\text{-}p$ is constructable; then for every singular hypothetical proposition of the form 'If p then q' (let us call it pq) a second proposition 'If not p then r' may be constructed (let us call it $-pr$), where r may or may not be equivalent to q. Then it is the case that where pq and $-pr$ are propositions describing the possible data of a given observer, the conclusive verification of pq and $-pr$ is not compossible, and the truth of either is compatible with the falseness of the other. And yet each of the two alternatives of the disjunction is in its own

23

right a proposition which in suitable circumstances could be conclusively verified; either may be true and the other false, either probable and the other improbable; their only logical relation is that of un-co-verifiability – they cannot both be conclusively verified even in principle. And this plainly cannot alter the meaning which either has in its own right. If this conclusion is correct it follows that the meaning of a proposition need not be affected – let alone determined – by the fact that a given means of verification is or is not logically possible in its case. I have emphasised the case of singular hypotheticals because they seem to bring out particularly clearly that if meaning depends on the relevant type of verifiability, then in order to know what one of these conjunctions of propositions means one requires to know whether both the protases are true. And this is self-evidently false. Yet these are the very propositions which occur in all philo-sophical analyses of empirical statements, the stuff of which logical constructions are built, the basic propositions to which propositions about the public world are commonly reduced by phenomenalists of all shades and hues.

Perhaps another example will make this even clearer. Supposing that I have a bet with you that all persons seen entering this room will appear to be wearing black shoes. Let the term 'this room' be defined as anything recognised by both of us as being correctly described as this room in virtue of certain observable characteristics, such that if either of us certifies their disappearance from his sense field, the entity described as this room shall be deemed to have ceased to exist. Under what conditions can such a bet be lost or won? We may begin by affirming the truth of the analytic proposition that the room will last either for a finite time or for ever. In either case the set of persons observed to enter it is similarly either finite or infinite. Only if it is the case that the observed set of visitors is finite, that the room visibly comes to the end of its existence, and that each of the persons who are seen to enter appears to wear black shoes, can I win the bet. When, on the other hand, it is the case either that the room lasts for ever, or that the set of persons seen to enter it is without limit, or both these, but at least one person appears to wear shoes of some other colour than black, or no shoes at all, I lose the bet. There are however further possibilities: when, for example, either the room lasts for ever or the number of persons seen to enter is limitless, or both, and every person entering appears to wear black shoes, in that event the bet is undecided, since the proposition on whose truth or falsity it turns has been neither verified nor falsified

24

conclusively. In all possible cases it could in principle be falsified by seeing the arrival of a person not wearing black shoes. But whereas in some cases it could also be verified conclusively, in others it can not. Yet when we arrange the bet neither of us need know whether I am in principle capable of winning or not. Nevertheless the proposition in terms of which the bet is stated is not in the least ambiguous. It is not the case that the words 'All persons . . .' must if the proposition is to have a definite meaning be used to refer *either* to a finite set (in which case conclusive verifiability is possible), *or* to an infinite set (in which case it may not be), but not to both. Yet if the meaning of a proposition always depended upon the type of verifiability of which it is capable, the above would be systematically ambiguous: we should have to be regarded as having made two separate bets, one on the behaviour of a finite set, the other on that of an infinite one. Yet we are under the impression that only one bet had been made, because we attributed to the proposition beginning with the words 'All persons will . . .' not many senses but one, namely, that in which it is equivalent to 'No one person will not . . .'. And we are right.

Like the previous example this tends to show that if one wishes to understand a sentence which purports to express a proposition when it is asserted by someone, while it is doubtless generally useful to discover under what conditions he would consider its truth as established, to regard its meaning as dependent on what kind of conditions these would be is to hold a false doctrine of what constitutes meaning. Of course I do not wish to deny that in general I can only discover the difference between sentences of different kinds, e.g. between those used to refer to visual data and those concerning auditory ones, or between propositions concerning persons and propositions about physical objects or about sense data, by observing in what kind of experience verification for them is sought. But it does not follow from this that the kind of verification which a given proposition can in principle obtain determines the type of meaning which it possesses, and so can act as a principle of logical or epistemological classification, such that propositions belonging to two different classes, defined in this way, cannot for that reason belong to one and the same logical or epistemological category, or be answers to questions of the same logical type. And yet this is the fallacy which seems to me to underlie much that is said by upholders of theories of verification and operationalism. That significance is connected with verifiability I have no wish to deny. But not in this direct fashion, by a kind of one-to-one correspondence.

3 This brings us to the third type of proposition mentioned above: the apparently categorical, but not conclusively verifiable propositions, as for example those about material objects or other selves. The scope of this paper does not permit an adequate discussion of the merits and defects of phenomenalism; but even if we conceive it to be in principle correct, however inadequate all existing formulations of it, we must allow that among the experiential propositions into which a proposition asserting the existence of a material object must be analysed there must inevitably be some which describe how the object would appear to an observer, were conditions different from those which in fact obtain; if in other words he were not observing what he is. The proposition 'I am holding a brown pencil in my hand' may or may not entail propositions about past and future actual and hypothetical data presented to me; analysts differ on this point; some hold these to be part of what is meant by 'this pencil', others maintain them to be only evidence for the existence of, but not elements in the analysis of it. And this holds equally of the actual and hypothetical data of observers other than myself. What is common, however, to all phenomenalist accounts is that part, at any rate, of what I meant by saying that it is an actual pencil that is now before me, and not the phantom of one, is that the datum which I am now observing belongs to a group of visual, tactual, auditory etc. data some of whose members are the subject-matter of hypothetical propositions which describe what I should be experiencing if I were not at this moment in the circumstances in which in fact I am. These propositions are, as was shown above, not co-verifiable with the propositions which describe what I am actually observing, and this fact alone is quite sufficient to make propositions about physical objects not conclusively verifiable in principle, whether or not they are held to contain, telescoped within them, various causal and general propositions, as according to some philosophers they do. Indeed the assertion that general propositions enter into the analysis of prima facie singular propositions about material objects seems to me a good deal more dubious than that these last are not conclusively verifiable; if this seems certain, that is due to the un-co-verifiability of some of the singular propositions which are true of the object, not as it is in the past or in the future, but at any given moment. Indeed when anti-phenomenalists maintain that every suggested translation of a given common sense statement into sense datum language, however richly it is equipped with general and hypothetical propositions, fails to render in full the meaning of the original, because material objects possess attributes which

necessarily elude observation; when for example G. F. Stout,[1] in discussing what we mean by the solidity of material objects as conceived by common sense, observes that we think of it not as a permanent possibility but as a permanent impossibility of sensation, what gives such objections apparent plausibility, and Stout's epigram its point, is that there is indeed something which must for logical reasons elude verification by the most exhaustive conceivable series of observations, carried out by any number of possible observers, namely, propositions about what I, or some other given observer, could verify, were we not situated as we are. And this the most thoroughgoing phenomenalism must do justice to, however successfully it may have exorcised the last remaining vestiges of the concept of matter as an invisible, intangible, dimly conceived substratum.

If what I have urged above is true, verification whether 'strong' or 'weak' fails to perform its task even within the framework of pure phenomenalism, which must not therefore be so formulated as to entail it as its primary criterion of significance. And to establish this negative conclusion was the main purpose of my thesis. In conclusion I should like to add a few remarks on what this seems to suggest with regard to the question of the proper analysis of physical objects and other selves. If, following the view suggested by C. D. Broad,[2] we look upon our concept of a given material object as a finite complex of sensible characteristics (to be referred to as m) selected more or less arbitrarily and unselfconsciously from the wider set of uniformly co-variant characteristics n, then m, which is constitutive of the object for a given observer, will differ for different individuals, times and cultures, although a certain minimum of overlapping common reference is needed for the possibility of communication in the present, and of understanding records of the past. The set of characteristics m, if it is affirmed to have an instance, will turn out to render true a finite number of categorical and a potentially infinite number of hypothetical propositions; and the paradoxical fact often urged against phenomenalism that any given proposition or set of propositions recording observations may be false, and yet the relevant proposition about a material object which is 'based' upon them may remain true – that in other words the latter type of proposition cannot be shown either to entail or be entailed by the former – is

[1] *Studies in Philosophy and Psychology* (London, 1930), p. 136.
[2] Discussed by John Wisdom in 'Metaphysics and Verification (1)', *Mind* 47 (1938), 480–1.

explained by the fact that m is vague and n (for all we know) infinite, and consequently however much of m you falsify it will never demonstrate that n has been exhausted. But when m, which represents your personal selection out of n, is progressively falsified, a point will arise at which you will probably abandon your belief in the existence of the material object in question, since your experience does not present a sufficient number of characteristics defined as m. But where this point will arise for a given individual is a purely psychological or sociological question; and I, who carve an m which differs from yours out of the common totality n, will understand you only to the extent to which our respective ms overlap; and therefore what will seem to you evidence adverse to your proposition will seem to weaken mine at the very most only to the extent to which your m overlaps with mine. Even if 'A case of m exists' were far more precisely formulated than it ever is in ordinary life, as a collection of singular propositions, it would still not be conclusively verifiable because some of its components are hypothetical and un-co-verifiable; but as words are commonly used it is always fluid and vague, and so cannot be conclusively falsified either. Thus the verification criterion, which was intended to eliminate metaphysical propositions in order to save those of science and common sense, cannot deal with these even in its loosest and most enfeebled form.

Other selves are more recalcitrant still. The strict verification principle seems to demand a behaviourist analysis of selves other than that of the observer, introspection data being confined to, because conclusively verifiable by, him alone. Even if, as was argued above, this be rejected and the existence of other selves, conceived by analogy with the given observer's own, be conceded at least the same obscure status as is, in the present state of philosophical discussion, enjoyed by material objects, each self being allowed to verify at any rate its own experience, it still seems difficult to explain, even in terms of the falsifiability criterion, what could show that the sentences 'My toothache is more violent than yours' or 'Smith thinks faster than Jones' are not meaningless. Each observer, we say, can vouch for the occurrence or the non-occurrence only of events in his own experience. Whatever may be said about the meaning of such terms as 'privacy' and 'publicity' as applied to data which are evidence for material objects, introspected states must, as language is ordinarily used, be declared to be private in some sense in which material objects are not: an inter-subjective observer who perceives my thoughts and feelings as well as his own seems a self-contradictory concept: otherwise it would be no more absurd to say that he and I experience the same headache as that we see the same table. Here, once again, the verification principle does not apply in either of its forms; and yet the propositions comparing the experiences of several observers seem at once intelligible, empirical, and as often as not precise and true.

The conclusion which follows, if the above account of the matter is correct, is this: that the criterion provided by 'strong' verification at best applies to a very narrow range of observation propositions; while 'weak' verification either fails to act as a criterion of sense altogether or, if made equivalent to 'strong' falsification, and in that form made sole arbiter of meaning, entails a brand of phenomenalism which provides unsatisfactory analyses of propositions about material objects and other selves. It follows *a fortiori* that the criterion of types of verifiability cannot act as the basis of classification of empirical propositions into logical categories. For it can neither distinguish statements recording observations from other categories of empirical propositions, nor enable us to distinguish different types of observation statements from each other. In view of this complete failure to satisfy our demand for a criterion, are we to abandon our search for a criterion altogether, or even declare the demand itself to be senseless, saying that meaning is meaning – an unanalysable concept – that to understand is an ultimate form of activity like seeing or hearing, that 'empirical' is an ultimate category, and can not be explained or defined otherwise than ostensively, that is by examples? This is perhaps the case. But if so, statements like the above express the fact too baldly and obscurely. What one ought rather to say is that verifiability depends on intelligibility and not vice versa; only sentences which are constructed in accordance with the rules of logic and of grammar, and describe what can logically be conceived as existing, are significant, are empirical statements, express genuinely empirical propositions. The notion of the logically conceivable must not be misunderstood. It must not be confused with the view ultimately derived from Russell, and sometimes offered as a substitute for verification theories, according to which a sentence has empirical meaning when every variable which occurs in it is such that one at least of its values denotes an actual or possible object of sensible or introspective knowledge; or, as it is sometimes put, when all the concepts in a judgement are *a posteriori* concepts; or, if a more familiar formulation is preferred, when understanding a proposition entails actual or possible acquaintance with at least one instance of every universal which occurs in it. Even if we ignore the difficulties of the phenomenalism which this entails it can only be a necessary, never a sufficient condition of empirical significance, at most a negative test. For I can formulate a sentence, correct by the rules of logic and of grammar and containing as variables only the names of observable characteristics, which yet may turn out to be meaningless, as for example 'Red hours are not more passionate than his ambition': this would doubtless involve a glaring confusion of categories, but the criterion, like that of 'weak' verification and for the same reason, is powerless to prevent this. The notion of significance cannot be determined by any such mechanical test: to say of a sentence that it means something, that I and others understand it, in other words that it conveys a proposition, is to say no more and no less than that we can conceive what would be the case if it were true. As for the meaning of 'I can conceive', only that is conceivable by me which in some respect resembles my actual experience, as it occurs in observation or introspection, memory or imagination, or any other form of direct acquaintance, which can be described only by reference to it, as a determinate, however logically distant from its source, of some determinable with at least one of whose determinates I am acquainted; much as a man born blind may understand propositions of visual experience by analogy with the senses which he possesses. The proposition that what is conceivable is necessarily similar to actual experience is analytic, being part of what is meant by the word 'conceivable'. To speak therefore of conceiving an experience dissimilar in all respects, wholly different, from my own, is to advance a self-contradictory concept, suggesting as it does both that I can apply my habitual logical categories to it, inasmuch as it is called experience, and that I cannot do so, inasmuch as it is declared to be wholly and utterly different from it. Statements which are metaphysical in the bad sense are meaningless not because they are unverifiable, but because they purport, in the language which resembles that which we normally use to describe situations which we regard as capable of being empirically experienced, to describe something which is alleged to transcend such experience, and to be incommunicable by any kind of analogy with it. Since, so far as we mean anything by these words, the limits of what can be conceived are set by analogy to what we are acquainted with, to deny such resemblance is tantamount to saying that what the proposition affects to describe is inconceivable; and this is to say that it is not a genuine proposition but, in the empirical sense of 'meaning' as descriptive, and not, e.g., emotive or evocative, a meaningless statement, linguistically similar to significant ones. Such a statement is unverifiable because, when examined, it turns out to be meaningless, and not vice versa, and it is meaningless because although words are being used in it in accordance with the accepted conventions of logic and of grammar, they represent the result either of genuine confusion, or of a pursuit of obscurity from whatever cause or motive, since they are used in a fashion different from that in which words are used when they are intended to describe the experienced world. And so, while they may resemble genuinely descriptive expressions, whatever else they may or may not be doing, they literally describe nothing.

Empirical Propositions and
Hypothetical Statements

I T is becoming the fashion among empiricist philosophers to assume that phenomenalism is really dead at last. Provoked into existence by non-naturalistic notions of material substance, it successfully undermined them; but it shared a sufficient number of fundamental metaphysical assumptions with its defeated rival to perish with it when the system of thought which nourished both was destroyed, in the very act of victory. A better ontology than that of Descartes or Locke, but still an ontology, it is therefore now held to be obsolete; and doubtless this is how it ought to be. But if phenomenalism is dead, the memory of it still haunts the writings of modern discussions of the nature of the external world to a surprising degree; from Eddington's notorious two desks, to the more refined and penetrating analysis of better equipped philosophical authors, it makes its presence clearly felt, usually taking the form of a sharp distinction; now between observation statements and those concerning material objects; now between two or more senses of the verb 'to see'; at other times between 'basic' or 'protocol' sentences and those of ordinary speech; or between various 'modes' of speech; or between 'strong' and 'weak' verification. Such versions of it are almost always formally guaranteed to carry no 'metaphysical' implications; nevertheless their striking resemblance to the older discredited variety is hard to overlook. Hence, an examination of its latest manifestations is not such a flogging of a dead horse as at first it may seem to be; for if it is dead, its ghost walks, and should, if possible, be laid.

Two further assumptions are made in the course of the following remarks:

1 The argument against the phenomenalist analysis of commonsense statements leaves open the question whether the information provided by the exact sciences such as physics can be translated without loss into phenomenalist terms. Perhaps it can; and perhaps this demonstrates something of importance; it has always been considered that the

language of science could, with no alteration of its 'meaning', be translated into solipsistic terms; which, however, is not held to be an argument in favour of solipsism. But if such a 'translation' does not adequately render the empirical descriptions of ordinary language, this will affect the propositions of science only in so far as these claim to be an extension of ordinary language used to describe the world, and not a specialised method of referring to aspects of it for some narrower, predictive or other, purposes – a specialised use of words which may be susceptible to a phenomenalist analysis. In any case the answer to the question whether this is so is, I believe, logically independent of the rest of my argument.

2 Nor do I wish to deny the historical achievement of phenomenalism. Whatever its defects – and I shall wish to say that they are fatal – it has made less excusable any return to those ancient delusions which the philosophers of substance from Thales to G. F. Stout have done much to promote. But beneficent as its influence has been, it has overstayed its welcome; its continued presence does more harm than good; and the argument set out below is intended to provide additional reasons for consigning it finally to an honoured grave.

I

Many forms of modern empiricism, and in particular modern phenomenalism, rest on the view that expressions describing material objects must in principle be capable of being translated (without residue) into sets of sentences about the data of actual or possible direct sensible acquaintance, past, present and future, on the part of real or possible observers ('sensible' is here used in the widest sense – to cover all states, activities or dispositions capable of being studied by empirical methods). Any alternative theories of how material object propositions are to be analysed tend to be rejected out of hand by modern empiricists on the ground that this must at some stage involve belief in the existence of non-sensible or transcendent entities or characteristics, and this is ruled out for the familiar reasons advanced, for example, by Berkeley, which rest on his theory of words; according to this, no expressions purporting to describe material objects can have any meaning, let alone be true, unless all the entities or characteristics to which they refer are either found in sensible experience – in the sense of 'sensible' defined above – or can be analysed into entities or characteristics so found. Since most empiricists hold that any alternative analysis of material object propositions involves the possibility of acquaintance with non-sensible entities or characteristics – and this they hold to be an unintelligible suggestion – phenomenalism appears to follow automatically. Disagreement can arise only about the adequacy of this or that suggested analysis of how material object sentences are to be 'reduced' (without residue) to sentences describing both what the observer does, or did, or will observe, as well as what he would, or would have, might or might have, observed under appropriate conditions; and the provision of alternative analyses on these lines has taxed the ingenuity of some of the acutest philosophers of our day. But common sense and the philosophers who are in sympathy with it have always felt dissatisfied. The reduction of material object sentences into what we may, for short, call sense datum sentences seemed to leave something out, to substitute something intermittent and attenuated for something solid and continuous. To dispel this sense of discomfort, phenomenalists began to explain that it was due to a confusion; the view that they were advocating was neither a metaphysical nor a scientific theory of what things were made of, or how they behaved, but something less adventurous – no more than an alternative language capable of rendering all that could be described in the material object language, and recommended for its therapeutic properties as an antidote to metaphysical hankering after non-sensible substrata. If translation into the sense datum language still seemed to leave something out – what some philosophers have called the 'irreducible categorical element' of material object propositions – this missing element was labelled emotive – a psychological residue – with no descriptive function; or else it was (with somewhat greater insight) connected with the legitimate demand for the kind and degree of vagueness, indefiniteness, and rich ambiguity of speech needed by the plain man for his normal, everyday purposes. But it was claimed that at any rate the hard core of descriptive meaning could be successfully transplanted, as it were, into the new language. The phenomenalist equivalent of a material object sentence might, like a new shoe, seem uncomfortable at first, but continued use would presently dissipate this feeling. The discomfort was only 'psychological', due to linguistic habits harmless in themselves, but tempting philosophers to false doctrines about language and the world.

Common sense continued to experience a certain discomfort, but found it difficult to formulate it in words. G. F. Stout[1] complained that the opaqueness – the 'permanent impossibility of sensation' – of material

---

[1] op. cit. (p. 27, note 1 above), pp. 136–7.

objects had been unjustifiably eliminated. W. F. R. Hardie[1] found it puzzling that 'hypothetical' causes could be said to cause 'actual' effects – but this was held, e.g. by A. J. Ayer,[2] to be mainly due to a misunderstanding of the language which phenomenalists were trying to use or 'recommend'. What I propose to do is to try to articulate what the main source of the discomfort felt by common sense seems to me to be, since I think that in this case the doctor's diagnosis too often neglects the specific nature of the patient's complaint. For it seems to me to be more than a mere source of discomfort, namely a valid and fatal objection to the phenomenalist analysis. However, even if I am mistaken in this, the complaint itself still seems worth examining.

It may be worth adding that even if phenomenalism turns out to be unacceptable, some of the stock objections to it are not less so. For the familiar anti-phenomenalist theses are often, even when valid, formulated in such a way as to convey anxiety to salvage altogether too much from the ruins of the theory they are intended to destroy. Consider, for example, the four most familiar types of attack upon it.

1 One of the most familiar objections urged against, for example, Berkeley, or Mill or Russell, is that when converting sentences about material objects into sentences about sense data, they fail to 'convert the observer' who 'occurs' in the protasis of the hypothetical statement, into 'sense data' – he remains irreducibly 'material'. It has indeed been suggested[3] that to 'dissolve the observer' a second proposition could be constructed which, presumably, would describe the activities of a second 'observer' who actually or potentially observes the body of the original 'observer'; this 'observer' in his turn requires a third 'observer' to observe him; and so we should get a Chinese box series of possible observers – referred to by a logically similar series of propositions, which would progressively 'reduce' or 'dissolve' the residual material object content of the original protasis. This asymptotic process of gradual whittling would tend to the ideal limit of pure phenomenalism. Then by somehow integrating the series, one might represent the material

---

[1] 'The Paradox of Phenomenalism', *Proceedings of the Aristotelian Society* 46 (1946), 127–54.

[2] 'Phenomenalism', *Proceedings of the Aristotelian Society* 47 (1947), 163–96.

[3] This argument was first developed to the best of my belief by H. H. Price. A somewhat more complicated method of the progressive 'elimination' of material bodies is propounded by R. B. Braithwaite, 'Propositions about Material Objects', *Proceedings of the Aristotelian Society* 38 (1938), 269–90.

object as definable in terms of it. A criticism related to the original objection is that such ideal 'observers' and their behaviour could not be properly described without perpetual reference to material objects, e.g. those which determine 'their' position in space, movements etc. Each of which again, for its analysis, at every point presupposes yet other material objects, so that the attempted analysis cannot get going without breaking down at any and every point in the process. Some philosophers try to soften the force of this objection by saying that such theoretically infinite theories have pragmatic limits set by the context and the practical needs of the situation, and sometimes[1] hold that sufficiently painstaking analysis (and most analysts are too lazy or bored to do the plodding required) could go a long way towards achieving pure phenomenalism. What both these kinds of objection, whether they are valid or not, suggest is that if phenomenalism fails, it very nearly achieves its result – the unresolved residue can be got down to almost vanishing point – which is perhaps as much as one can reasonably hope for.

2 Another often heard objection is that the hypothetical propositions about the experiences of observers which are indispensable to the phenomenalist analysis seem to involve something like the existence or reality of 'hypothetical facts' or 'hypothetical sense data' or 'unsensed sensibilia'. For otherwise, what do hypotheticals describe? Surely not nothing? And these postulated entities, unknown and unknowable to science and common sense, are, so it is urged, at least as mythological as the Lockean substratum which they were invoked to exorcise. Phenomenalism is accused of breeding new metaphysical entities – with their own pseudo-problems; but if we could only get rid of these some-how, say by an improved, non-correspondence theory of meaning, all might still be well.

3 It has also frequently been asserted that the promised 'reduction' of commonsense language by such methods as those of Descriptions, Logical Constructions etc. cannot in fact be performed successfully. Phenomenalists are challenged to provide an equivalent in sense datum currency of propositions about material objects, and when they decline to produce the precise equivalent, they are accused of uttering counter-feit cheques: and this is said to hold even more obviously of scientific entities – the promise to construct 'many-storied'[2] logical constructions, with sense data as foundations, and gamma particles two or three floors

---

[1] See D. G. C. Macnabb, 'Phenomenalism', *Proceedings of the Aristotelian Society* 41 (1941), 67–90.   [2] ibid.

above – has not been kept. Phenomenalists are accused of maintaining that, although phenomenalist language might be intolerably clumsy and prolix, it could in principle always be substituted for the ellipses of common speech: that normal language has the character it has in order to serve the use that it serves; that sense datum language would doubtless be inconveniently precise and definite and intolerably lengthy and tedious, and would have its own unfamiliar 'grammar', but that in principle the translation could be effected, although by sacrificing so much customary vagueness, ambiguity, indefiniteness etc. as would render it useless for everyday purposes. Against this, the opposition maintains that it is only necessary to try to put this programme into practice to see that it is a labour of Sisyphus and will not work; vagueness, ambiguity etc. are inalienable properties of commonsense language; but for this, the programme could perhaps be carried out; but as it is, the claim to reduce – plausible enough prima facie – turns out to be hollow once the bluff is called. Yet the reason for this is still the comparatively weak one that we should lose too much in the way of nuances, range, implied meanings of words; the feeling remains that the 'hard core' of meaning might still be 'reduced' or translated.

4 Finally, there are the difficulties about dealing with propositions about other minds, communication etc. in the appropriate Humean manner, too familiar to be repeated; which theoretically leaves open the possibility of the programme advanced by Berkeley whereby phenomenalism works for material objects and breaks down only in the case of persons.

The above is a characteristic selection from the, by now traditional, array of anti-phenomenalist arguments. I should like to suggest that, formidable and indeed fatal as some of them may be, they are usually so formulated as to convey a misleading impression, for despite their anti-phenomenalist air they are all in effect so much concealed pro-phenomenalist propaganda. The suggestion implicit in all these criticisms is that, while the phenomenalist goal is and must be striven towards – for the alternative is a metaphysical morass – the particular avenues thus far offered by phenomenalists are unfortunately blocked by various types of logical or epistemological obstacles: in other words that some such operation is desperately needed if we are ever to eliminate unverifiable or indescribable entities, but that the techniques offered by various philosophers have all, so far, broken down. This position is not unlike the situation with regard to, say, Fermat's theorem: what the theorem asserts is considered as being very likely true, at any rate not demonstrably fallacious, and in any case as being the kind of assertion which should be capable of demonstration or refutation by normal mathematical techniques. Similarly all phenomenalist operations so far conducted have indeed ended in failure; but they, and only they, are the kind of processes which can, in principle, be applied. *Some* kind of phenomenalist analysis must be correct, for the only alternative is a return to Locke, or Descartes, or Kant, and that, in this enlightened age, is surely not a thinkable course.

This is the bogey used to drive philosophers back to make yet another gallant attempt to break out of the impasse – to find a 'viable' translation into the sense datum language. The impression conveyed throughout, possibly because of a faulty theory of meaning and truth, is that phenomenalism is, after all, the only possible valid view, beset though it may be by grave objections and exaggerations: the problem is one of technical skill: once it is reformulated with sufficient ingenuity the problem will be solved, or dissolved. My thesis is that phenomenalism is not even prima facie plausible – let alone indispensable – and minor improvements, i.e. tinkering, cannot make it more so. Instead, therefore, of re-examining the all too familiar current objections to phenomenalism, and the answers to them, I should like to suggest that it might be valuable to try to find out what it is that makes common sense so uncomfortable – in order to see whether this discomfort is merely 'psychological', and perhaps due to the relatively accidental properties of ordinary language, or whether it is a symptom of some fatal defect in the theory.

II

What common sense, from Dr Johnson onwards, finds paradoxical in all phenomenalist analyses is, I believe, this: I say 'There is a brown table in the next room.' This, I am told, should mean a set or range of propositions of the type 'If "a normal observer" were to go next door and look, he would, in normal light, other normal conditions etc., see such and such brown-coloured data etc.' I say 'But supposing no one goes next door, what have we then? Is the apodosis false? Are there no brown data and no table?' I am told 'Of course not. Nothing regarding the consequent follows from denying the antecedent. In a sense, nothing follows at all. It still remains true that *if* someone looked, etc., he *would* see brown data etc.' I accept all this and remain dissatisfied. If I believe that there was in prehistorical times a land bridge between Africa and

America, then I agree – and possibly this is analytic – that if there had been an observer at that time suitably placed, he would have seen the land bridge or a portion of it. But I may wish to assert that, in fact, no such observer existed, and that the land bridge was nevertheless there, whether or not this is true. What I think common sense and G. F. Stout wish to say is that the question of the existence of the land bridge, like the existence of the table next door, is one thing, and the question of the presence or absence, even hypothetically, of an observer, is another. The statement that if there had been (and there was not) any observer, he would have observed (and no one did observe) certain data, seems to them not equivalent to asserting the past existence of material objects. Categorical propositions about material objects are replaced by unfulfilled 'counter-factual' hypothetical propositions about observers, and what troubles the plain man is the thought that if the hypotheticals are unfulfilled, if no observers were in fact observing, then if the phenomenalist analysis is correct, there was – in a sense datum sense – nothing at all, and, moreover, that this sense of 'existence' is basic: because the alleged material object sense in which the non-existence of actual sense data nevertheless can be 'translated into' the existence of material objects, is not a sense in which the word 'exist' is commonly understood. So if he is told that to say there was a material object – the land bridge in prehistoric times – is to say something about data there would have been if . . ., he feels cheated. For these data appear to depend on the activity of observers; so that the material object becomes analysed into a series of either purely hypothetical, i.e. non-existent, or at best intermittent, data occurring and disappearing as the observer observes and ceases to observe. And this seems empirically a different picture of the world from that which he started by believing; and in no sense merely a description of the old picture though in different words.

I shall now try to make this clearer. To analyse material objects in terms of the hypothetical data of observers is, in effect, to turn the statements about them into statements about the dispositional characteristics of observers. 'The table next door exists' on this view means that you or I or x, who are in this room, are possible or potential table-data observers. This asserts the existence of a dispositional characteristic; but dispositional characteristics are so called in order to contrast them with non-dispositional characteristics, the 'grammar' of which is rightly said to be different. If I ask 'Does he look much the same when he is asleep?', that is a plain, empirical question, the answer

39

to which can be discovered by ordinary empirical means, i.e. by looking. But if I ask 'Is he clever even when he is asleep?' this sounds quite wrong – I am rightly told that I evidently do not understand how the word 'clever' is commonly used; surely, I am told, to say that someone is clever is to say something of the following sort: that if certain sorts of questions are put to him, he will easily and correctly answer them, or that he grasps certain types of data and makes inferences from them more successfully than most people, and so on. When he is asleep, these conditions do not occur and the question is therefore inappropriate to the situation. How does all this apply to the table next door? The assertion that there is a table next door is made equivalent to what the observer would see if he looked, etc., i.e. a collection of hypothetical, i.e. dispositional-causal propositions about the observer; but when the causes do not materialise, neither, as a rule, do their effects, and when neither exists, there is a gap in the series of sense datum events. We accept this quite naturally in the case of normal dispositional characteristics: 'x is irritable' is compatible with, indeed it is compatible only with, 'He flies into tempers on slight provocation, or sometimes when there is no provocation at all'; i.e. at other times there are no bursts of temper, no continuing real substratum – there does not literally exist, in the ordinary sense of 'exist', something called potential irritation going on like volcanic activity underneath the surface; we do speak of unconscious or suppressed irritation, but to take this literally is to confuse words with things, to confuse the mythology of psychoanalysis with the furniture of the real world, to fall into Locke's errors. But if I say 'The table is next door [or 'The table has a back to it' or 'The table was here two hours ago'] even with no one looking', do I mean 'There are table-data whenever people look; but at other times, when no one is looking, nothing at all'? This is precisely what common sense does *not* believe to be true about tables. Common sense endows them with 'actual', i.e. non-dispositional characteristics in the absence of observers. The table is seen intermittently or not at all: the intermittent presence or non-existence of observers is a part of the intermittent or unrealised series of causes or conditions of its being seen; but it – the table – is assumed to have some characteristics continuously; it differs from irritability precisely in this respect – that unlike irritability it is believed to exist continuously in the literal sense when there are no intermittent data, no glances directed at the table. To analyse material object statements as statements about dispositional characteristics of observers, therefore, is to represent the material object as being, at most, an intermittent series of actual data with the gaps filled by hypothetical 'non-actualised' entities, i.e. in the sense datum sense by nothing at all. This, for common sense, is tantamount to destroying the continuity of the table – its history before and after it is observed, its unseen portion, its presence next door. Of course, phenomenalists stoutly and indignantly denounce this conclusion as a confusion of two senses of 'existence', a crude misunderstanding of the very notion of logical constructions. Tables, we might be answered, are logical constructions as irritability is: in both cases, the essential task is to eliminate Locke's substratum and to substitute for it a set of intermittent and hypothetical data. The unobserved table, or its unobserved back, continue to be as someone's irritability continues to be. Yet common sense does not raise difficulties of this type about the analysis of irritability; it accepts easily enough that irritability does not exist in the same sense as an actual burst of temper is said to do, that to speak of irritability is to use a kind of shorthand for a complex of causal laws and observation propositions. But when I say 'There exists a table such as you describe', am I really saying that it exists in the same sense of 'exists' as someone's irritable temper? Some characteristics of tables may, of course, genuinely be described as dispositional; i.e. in speaking of them I am referring to certain causal laws and hypothetical or intermittent data – e.g. when I say a table is combustible or useful or expensive. But this only means something by contrast with those properties of the table which are not dispositional, and perhaps a good many intermediate properties which we do not think of as either definitely dispositional or definitely 'actual'. The suggestion that *every* characteristic of the table is merely possible or intermittent or depends on dispositions of observers – that *everything* is dispositional, nothing actual – is exactly what common sense and Dr Johnson revolt against, not as being untrue, but as coming close to being meaningless, and certainly as suspiciously approaching some kind of solipsism – and one not very easy to describe in empirical (or any other intelligible) language.

What common sense dislikes is precisely the crucial role played by hypotheticals in the phenomenalist analysis, and it seems to me to display a sound instinct in so doing.

For this is the central point of this entire issue: that the translation of categorical existential statements into hypotheticals (of whatever 'level') is a dangerous operation and cannot be left to the mechanical operation of 'syntactical' rules, because different types of sentence do have certain normal uses in ordinary language – at any rate in most modern European languages – which we ignore at our peril; Humpty-Dumpty's nominalism goes too far: words are sometimes masters if we are to communicate without perpetual recourse to redefinition, i.e. if we are to communicate at all; and as we use words, categorical sentences, on the whole, tend to convey that the object referred to has occurred or is occurring or will occur in time; existed, is in existence, will exist; they have a non-descriptive, existential, ostensive element; they seem to invite us to look for the entity they purport to be about, and only when there is none such in any normal sense, e.g. in the case of a sentence like 'Bad temper is unattractive', do we avoid pseudo-problems by turning to the hypothetical mode of expression as the more natural, as likely to elucidate what is being asserted in words better adapted to expressing it. Existential propositions expressed categorically – in indicative sentences – tend, as it were, to 'point' towards their 'objects'; and demonstratives which appear in existential propositions, like 'this is', 'there is', 'here we have' etc., often function as substitutes for such acts of pointing to things or persons or processes. The characteristic force of the categorical mode of expression is often exactly this – that it acts in lieu of a gesture, of an 'act of ostension': 'Here *is* the book' I say to someone looking for it, or I could point to it and say 'The book', and convey roughly the same information by both methods. But hypotheticals normally do the opposite of this. Hypotheticals, whatever they describe or mean, whatever they entail or convey or evince, in whatever way they are verified or fail to be verified, do *not* as a general rule directly assert that something has been, is being, or will be occurring, or existing, or being characterised in some way: this is precisely the force of the conditional mood, and it is realisation of this which probably led Ramsey, for example, to assert that causal propositions were not descriptive at all, but commands or rules. Ramsey's analysis can easily be shown to be unsatisfactory, since it seems to rest on a fatally false view of the nature of meaning; but the feeling which led him to so strong a separation of general and hypothetical forms of expression from, say, singular categorical sentences, did not altogether lead him astray. For this gulf does divide categoricals and hypotheticals in our normal usage: whereas the first is normally used to describe the furniture of the world – what is, was or will be – the second is not; consequently, whenever a categorical (indicative) form of expression is used, often quite idiomatically, to convey something other than what is, or was, or will be, it is easily and without resistance on the part of common sense replaceable by a hypothetical (conditional) sentence – as in the case of indicative sentences referring directly or indirectly to dispositions, or general propositions of the 'all', 'every', 'any' type. But even this is in need of a significant qualification. If the general terms are so used as to suggest that they possess extension of any kind, the hypothetical form is felt to be to that extent insufficient, and categorical expressions are required to complete the analysis. Thus 'Anyone who was there at three o'clock saw the meteor fall', because it is compatible with 'and no one in fact was', can be translated into 'If anyone was there, or had been there, etc., then he saw, or would have seen, etc.'; whereas 'He gave away his books to anyone who asked for them' is not equivalent to 'If anyone asked for, had asked for, etc., his books he was, or would have been given, etc.', but needs in addition 'and some persons did ask'. It seems clear that in this last instance a conditional or hypothetical sentence by itself tells us nothing about what in fact happened, and an indicative or categorical one is therefore required by ordinary usage to convey 'existential import' – to refer to actual events which are believed to have taken place.

All this may seem altogether too trite and obvious, but there is a corollary which is evidently less obvious, namely that no direct translation from categoricals into hypotheticals is, as a general rule, and as our language is today ordinarily used, a correct analysis of, or substitute for them. And this seems to me to destroy one of the indispensable foundations of phenomenalism. For it is this sense of the illicit substitution of hypotheticals for categoricals which is responsible for the obscure feeling on the part of common sense that something – an *ersatz* entity – is being palmed off upon it by phenomenalists. Such a categorical existential material object sentence as 'The table is next door' or 'There is a table next door' is used at the very least to describe something which is occurring or being characterised at the time of speaking, together (perhaps) with some sort of prediction (and what has been called retrodiction) about what has been or will be occurring or being characterised during unspecified periods of time before and after the period of speaking; and being characterised or occurring, unless the contrary is specifically stated or implied, not intermittently but continuously, and in any case not 'hypothetically'. For to say that something is occurring hypothetically is a very artificial and misleading way of saying that it is not, in the ordinary sense, occurring at all, but might or would occur if conditions were realised which in their turn may or may not be realised. Consequently, whatever common sense may mean by the sentence 'There is a table next door', it cannot accept as fully equivalent in meaning any sentence not asserting that something is now, or has been, or will be, occurring or being characterised. It may well be that categoricals systematically entail corresponding hypotheticals (or disjunctive sets of such) – that the proposition 'The table is next door now' in some sense entails that if either observer A or observer B or C etc. were to go next door, one or other of them could see or touch such and such data; for invisible or intangible tables are not what we normally mean by 'table'. Likewise, it may be that hypotheticals in some cases may be said either to entail, or else to state conditions for the truth of, or else 'sufficiently justify', the assertion of categoricals; in other words, that if it is true that a normal observer (i.e. one free from hallucinations, etc.) sees, or has seen, or will see, or would see, or would have seen, certain data, under the appropriate conditions, it follows deductively and not inductively that there is a table next door. Something like this may be correct, and perhaps this is all that the phenomenalist requires as against Locke's insensible substance, or attenuated versions of it such as 'physical occupants'.[1] For it is clear that if I am to explain under what circumstances I *should* normally assert material object sentences, I can do so only by invoking hypothetical observers and their cognitive states: if I am called upon to describe the conditions in which such and such sentences are appropriate, then I cannot fail to make use of hypotheticals. But to describe conditions in which alone I should be inclined to enunciate a sentence is certainly not equivalent to giving its meaning. For my point is that the hypothetical sense datum sentence cannot be equivalent to, or an analysis of, a material object sentence if the hypothetical (sense datum) sentence asserts only what would be, while the material object sentence sometimes asserts what occurs, occurred, or will occur in the world. Existential propositions about material objects assert what is, was or will be, and not what might be. Stout had every reason to be suspicious of the description of the material world in such dubious terms as 'The permanent possibility of sensation', because however modified and refined, it both suggests a kind of permanent grid-like world framework and denies it. Dr

[1] And this is, without doubt, the great historical service of phenomenalism – that for more than two centuries it has been pressing home the paradoxical consequences of simultaneously holding both that material objects, if they exist, 'must' possess certain characteristics (although no one has been able to identify them at all clearly) which cannot, in principle, be empirically observed, *and* that these are among the characteristics with which the natural sciences necessarily deal.

Johnson's well known attitude does not, after all, rest on such a very gross misunderstanding. That is the heart of the case against phenomenalism.

But what precisely, it may be asked, is it that such categorical existential sentences do that hypothetical ones fail to do? Certainly I wish to avoid saying that the former describe the facts while the latter do not, since the unhappy term 'fact' has been used in too many different senses to be illuminating in this connection. Nor do I wish to assert that hypotheticals and categoricals are never interchangeable and are mutually exclusive – as if the forms of propositions could be distinguished into natural kinds corresponding to 'ontological' or Kantian categories, or 'ultimate grooves in reality'. But I do suggest that systematic differences in verbal form are often pointers to differences in meaning which it is important not to obscure. Hence, as a tentative way of putting it, I submit that those categorical propositions which we seem to be unable to 'reduce' to other logical forms without doing apparent violence to normal usage tend to direct attention to – invite us to look for – things and events in a way in which other kinds of expressions do not. This is felt most clearly about expressions containing demonstratives like 'this', or 'that', or 'here', but applies no less to existential propositions without demonstratives which identify something in the time series. In the case of objects with some or all of which we claim to be acquainted by some kind of direct inspection, this relation – which for want of a better word I propose to call 'pointing' – can literally occur: in declaring that a particular table is here before me, a particular sound is now growing louder, a particular doubt is now tormenting me, I am pointing at, directing your attention to, something with which I am directly acquainted, an event or a thing. But if I say 'The table is next door', 'The cupboard has a wooden back which you cannot see', 'Napoleon wore a three-cornered hat', 'Napoleon felt a twinge of remorse before the battle', I cannot, of course, in the literal sense be said to be acquainted with, or point at, a thing or event, for it is, in the ordinary sense of the words, not present, not here, not before me, not within my ken. And this is perhaps what lends such plausibility as it seems to have to the phenomenalist procedure of offering me hypotheticals intended both to describe unobserved characteristics and to indicate methods of observing, i.e. in some sense verifying them. But this will not do, for whereas the difference between categoricals and hypotheticals is one of logical form, whether syntactical or semantic, the difference between being able and not being able to observe a given object is empirical or causal. I cannot point to the table next door, or at a point beneath its surface, because it is invisible: there is the intervening wall or surface which makes this act unhelpful. In saying 'There is a table next door' I am, as it were, trying to refer to the table 'through the wall' – or to the back or inside of the table as if it were not concealed but before me, in my sense field. If the wall becomes transparent the relevant difference between the table here, in front of me, and the further table next door disappears, for the only relevant difference between the two types of case is that I was originally in a better position in space (or time) to describe the table in front of me. There may be important semantic differences, e.g. in learning the use of symbols for present as opposed to absent entities,[1] but there is no logical difference dividing sentences which describe things in my field of vision from those which describe things beyond the horizon.

The kind of communication which a demonstrative, categorical sentence, which purports to be true, seeks to perform in respect of unobserved objects and events may fail to achieve its object in at least one of two ways: the entity may not exist or possess the characteristics in terms of which it is denoted; or the failure may be due to some defect in my technique – if the relevant entity is not, for whatever reason, recognised by my audience; my effort to communicate is thwarted, but only by such empirical circumstances as physical walls, or the shape of the earth, or the limitations of my senses or imagination, or the date of my birth; thwarted by that and not by something incurably hypothetical, non-existential about the sentence itself. Let me give an example: when I say that Napoleon wore a three-cornered hat, or that on the evening before the battle of Borodino he had a twinge of remorse, I do not mean (though this is not strictly relevant to the argument) that one man and one man only was called Napoleon, and whoever was so called wore a three-cornered hat, or had a twinge of remorse. Proper names are not usually mere definite descriptions. My use of the word 'Napoleon' is, among other things, a substitute for a wave of the hand, an inclination of the head etc., because I cannot point in a literal sense, if only because I was born too late; and this is ultimately an empirical obstacle like the wall of a room or the nature of light or the structure of my brain. I am inviting you to direct your attention to Napoleon, or to physical or mental events in his history, and there is a non-descriptive and existential force in my use of the relevant words – and

[1] I owe this point to F. Waismann.

in particular of proper names – because I suggest or believe or know that such events have happened – that they are part of the collection of what was and is and will be. Certain types of categorical sentences in this way direct attention to things and events which therefore are taken to exist whether or not they are observed. The fact that they are in some sense capable of being directly observed, or verified, or that their existence can be supported by sense datum evidence, may be part of the meaning of such concepts as 'thing' or 'event', but it is not what is asserted when I say that they occur here or now, or have such and such characteristics; and the reason for this is that the hypotheticals which I am being offered in exchange for categoricals do not, even misleadingly and fatally, invite anyone (except it seems some philosophers) to look for any 'thing' or event in the time series. Whatever is being asserted by 'If it rains, I shall take my umbrella' or 'If Hitler had not wanted it, there would have been no war', it will not be found in the inventory of events, in the historical annals of the actual world, nor am I under any impression that I am being invited to look for any such entity. (Only philosophers have gone to the length of searching for or inventing ontological 'referends' of hypothetical propositions.) Hypothetical sentences do, of course, like other empirical expressions, involve the use of words which, to have any meaning, must themselves be capable of occurring in true ostensive sentences which do in some sense 'point' – words like 'rain' or 'umbrella' or 'Hitler', but in themselves hypotheticals do not 'point'; otherwise they would cease to be hypothetical, they would lose their conditional, non-actual-fact-asserting force.

At this point a critic might say (as A. J. Ayer did say to me in discussion) something like this: 'You rest your case on the generally felt distinction between what is dispositional and what is non-dispositional in the material world, and say that the latter cannot be described by hypotheticals, as the former can, without doing violence to normal usage. But this is not so. In the first place, many expressions which do not seem dispositional at first, turn out to be so on further analysis: for example, if we say that the table is heavy and six feet long, that seems at first categorical enough, but of course "heavy" means "if weighed according to a recognised technique, the instrument will record etc." and "six feet long" refers to the possible application of a ruler and so forth: these apparently categorical statements turn out, therefore, to need translation into hypotheticals to make them clear: from which it follows that the categorical form of statement by itself gives no sort

c

of indication of how sentences mean.' But this argument establishes less than it appears to do. I should not dream of maintaining that verbal or grammatical form is an infallible guide to logical form, i.e. kinds of ways in which sentences mean. Indeed, that is the whole point of exposing the dispositional character of expressions which prima facie appear non-dispositional. But because some or many categoricals are in this sense concealed hypotheticals (i.e. their meaning is made clearer, or certain errors are prevented, by the substitution of hypotheticals), because language is flexible and the frontiers shifting and vague, it cannot follow that the distinction does not exist at all, that the frontiers are invisible – for if that were so, such words as 'dispositional' and 'hypothetical' (there being nothing with which to contrast them) would not signify anything at all. And this is not what phenomenalists or defenders of the theory of logical constructions, if their own words are to mean anything, want to say. At this point the critic may say: 'But this is a sheer travesty of my position. Of course I do not wish to blur the useful distinction between hypotheticals and categoricals. What I am asserting is that all descriptive statements can in principle be translated into sense datum language: all material object statements will be transposed into hypothetical statements about sense data, and these are what they are by contrast with the only true ultimate, irreducible categoricals, those describing someone's actual sense experiences, e.g. Russell's basic propositions, Carnap's protocol sentences, etc. As for your distinction between dispositional and non-dispositional characteristics of material objects, or between hypothetical and categorical statements as applied to material objects, the sense datum language is perfectly well able to reproduce it in its own terminology: categorical material object statements will be translated into hypotheticals about sense data; hypotheticals about material objects will be rendered by hypotheticals about hypotheticals: thus to say that a given table looks brown is to say something about the dispositions of certain observers; to say that it is fragile is to say something about the dispositions of dispositions of these same observers; the distinction is one of degree of complexity of hypotheticals; but the whole pyramid of them only has descriptive force if they are about – if their ultimate subject is – the actual sense data of actual observers, about which all material object sentences, whether categorical or hypothetical, are in the end hypotheses or theories. For what else is there in the world but what people see and hear and imagine and do and suffer?' We are there at last: this really is what phenomenalism boils down to: that the only irreducibly

48

categorical propositions, by contrast with which alone hypotheticals are what they are, are statements about immediate experience, capable of direct, strong, 'knock-down' verification. These are basic. All else is theory and speculation about their behaviour and incidence. We have returned to the many-tiered logical constructions, with material objects and perhaps their more obvious causal properties on the floors immediately above the 'basic' ground floor (or should it be basement?), and the upper levels occupied by positrons, nerve impulses, super-egos, and possibly vectors and non-Euclidean spaces and numbers too, as well as the *Zeitgeist*, and the British Constitution and the national character. In a sense, this position seems almost too academic in character: if phenomenalists find difficulty, in fact, in producing the sense datum equivalents of even plain categorical material object statements, their claim to produce two or more storeys of such – simple hypotheticals and over these rows of complex ones – hypotheticals about hypotheticals – seems somewhat unreal; but even if we do not press for cash in the form of basic sentences against phenomenalist cheques (as being unfair and against the spirit of the conventions in use of language) the argument still remains fallacious. For what this view comes to is that material object sentences – including existential ones – are so many general propositions or hypotheses or theories about the behaviour of sense data. And this is precisely what common sense finds so repugnant. For a general proposition or theory may be interpreted purely intensionally – i.e. irrespective of whether or not instances of the concepts involved in fact occur; whereas such a sentence as 'The table next door is brown' is existential and as such has extensional import, and asserts that something *is* occurring in a sense in which general or hypothetical propositions proper do not normally assert anything of this sort; if such general propositions are taken extensionally as well as intensionally, i.e. if general propositions about sense data are to be understood to assert more than a mere logical or causal nexus between the possible experiences of possible observers, namely the existence or occurrence of something or other which the nexus connects, then, to perform this task, unsensed sensa or sensibilia must be introduced: and these are rightly as much taboo to phenomenalists as Lockean substances or physical occupants, and a good deal odder in character. The point is that existential material object propositions directly assert that something exists in a sense in which theories or hypotheses do not directly assert this. One can bring out this point most sharply (at the cost of some exaggeration) by asserting baldly that all theories, hypotheses, general and hypothetical propositions

49

etc. may be true and yet nothing exist at all; for if the protases are unfulfilled, the apodoses have no application; whereas the proposition that some existential material object propositions are true is not compatible with the proposition that nothing exists at all.[1] What this oversimple paradox serves to bring out is that the essence of hypothetical or conditional sentences is to be in a peculiar way non-committal – in the sense in which, let us say, singular (empirical) existential categoricals normally commit the speaker to something which in principle can be directly verified. Now it is notoriously impossible directly to verify unfulfilled conditionals: but all conditionals must entail at least one such unfulfilled conditional, and consequently in this respect cannot be equivalent to statements asserting only what is directly verifiable by an act of observation. Existential categoricals on the other hand commit us, because there is normally an ostensive (pointing) property about existential categorical material object propositions.[2]

The same point may be brought out in yet another way. According to the phenomenalist analysis, sentences describing material objects will differ in logical type according to the presence (to my senses) or the absence of the object in question. If it is present, I am said to be acquainted with actual seen data, and my sentence is at least partially analysable into irreducibly categorical ('basic') propositions: if it is absent, it is wholly analysable into hypotheticals. But this is surely not the case: if I say that there is a brown, wooden table in this room, I can, if I like, go on to say that among the propositions which I can assert of it, some are obviously categorical, some plainly hypothetical, some perhaps of neither kind; and then it cannot make a logical difference, i.e. a difference of principle, whether the table is before me in the room, or hidden behind a wall: whatever is hypothetically true, i.e. dispositional, about the present table (or its visible portion) is doubtless equally hypothetical

---

[1] This is, of course, not literally true, since theories presuppose the existence of theorists with all that they need by way of a universe in order to fix the 'grammar' of their words, but this is not part of what the theories themselves assert, nor is it logically entailed by them.

[2] It may be worth adding that such demonstratives as 'there is' or 'this is' are seldom employed to refer to 'sense data' – for that is a term which is rarely of use in ordinary experience, and is more properly applicable to that aspect of things which concerns physiologists or oculists or impressionist painters, and is useful precisely because it contrasts that which interests these specialists – purely sensuous qualities – with material objects – things – the furniture of ordinary life.

(dispositional) about the one next door (or its visible portion): but whatever is categorical about the first is categorical about the other – absent – one too. The actual steps which I am obliged to take in order to *verify* propositions about a given table will, of course, vary with circumstances: if the table is moved out of my ken, or someone blindfolds me, I cannot do what I could have done had this not happened; but the *meaning* of the sentence which I utter does not alter with the movements of the table or the condition of my eyes: the meaning of the sentence 'There is a brown table in my study' does not swing forwards and backwards from partially categorical to wholly hypothetical as I move around it, or saw it in half, or walk in and out of my study, or as the walls of my study change from opaque to transparent, and neither does it wholly consist of a cluster of hypotheticals compatible (if their antecedents are unfulfilled) with the non-existence of any experiences whatever. Perhaps we now see more clearly the confusion from which these odd consequences spring: namely the confounding of the meaning of what we are saying with the varying conditions under which we feel inclined to say it.

III

At this point, some uneasiness may be felt about the attribution to our language of a capacity to 'point to' objects in absence – as if the transition from pointing to objects directly perceived to this semi-metaphorical sense of pointing may not be quite legitimate. It is here that the phenomenalist may wish to play one of his strongest cards, for one of the most tempting advantages which his theory appears to offer is that by substituting logical constructions for inferred entities, he promises to describe the world solely in terms of the so-called data of immediate acquaintance. He undertakes, in effect, to describe everything by means of logical or linguistic rules, including rules for the use of conditional particles like 'if' and 'provided that', and otherwise confine himself solely to what we can directly and literally point to in our everyday experience. And to speak of the ostensive function of a sentence which purports to point towards, direct attention to, something – the table – real enough, indeed, but not here and not now, something unobserved, i.e. outside the field of direct acquaintance – is this not to go beyond and against the principle of not importing unfamiliar and dubious entities, to contravene the rule of the definability ostensively of all empirical terms? Are we not introducing something not met with face to face, not directly verifiable, and consequently not directly descriptive, perhaps altogether non-empirical? And this may at first unnerve the strict empiricist; but his anxieties will be groundless. For the notion of 'not here', 'not observed', must in any case be introduced into language seeking to describe the world sooner or later, and how this is accomplished is a psychological rather than an epistemological question. It is one thing to admit that whatever in one's descriptive language is not governed by syntactical rules must be capable of ostensive elucidation: and a very different one to say that I may not refer to anything unless I can establish the meaning of the variables of my language in terms of what I am actually experiencing here and now; if I adopt the latter principle, I become unable to refer to the past or the future or to the experiences of others in order to identify by contrast 'here' and 'now' and 'observed by me' and so on – that way lies the kind of verification theory of meaning which has more than once been shown to lead to an extravagantly solipsist analysis of the meanings of words, ending literally in nonsense. The meaning of such 'basic' words as 'here', 'now', 'observed', depends on the existence of an equally 'basic' use for 'not here', 'not now', 'not observed', in contrast with which alone the meanings of 'here', 'now' etc. can be established. There is no need to go on with this line of argument – such comparatively primitive notions as 'not now', or 'beyond the horizon', cannot be 'constructed' without circularity out of sense fields occurring in 'specious presents'; but without such notions classification, and therefore language, in the ordinary sense, is demonstrably impossible. Hence, this kind of objection to the possibility in principle of pointing to objects in absence cannot be considered seriously, for it rests on the assumption (ultimately perhaps traceable to Aristotle's doctrine of actual versus potential being) that what is not here does not exist in the same sense of 'exist' as that which is here, which rules out all possibility of descriptive symbolism. For what exists but is not here exists and is not here in exactly the same sense of 'exists' as what is – does exist – here. Without this, all words would lose their function of discriminating and classifying.

IV

There is one more objection to be met. Supposing someone were to ask, 'But how can we say anything about the table apart from the hypothetical sentences describing what an observer would see if he walked round it etc.? Is the table round or oval, dark or light brown,

52

light or heavy? Surely the sense datum school of philosophy, if it has established nothing else, has made it clear beyond any doubt that these properties in some sense depend on the observer, his physical position, his physiological and psychological condition etc.? Surely the argument from illusion, for example, cannot be dismissed as showing nothing at all because of logical considerations of how different types of sentences are used? Does the gramophone play tunes in a desert, or to an audience which is stone deaf? How does the view advanced here differ from the most untenably naïve of all forms of naïve realism?' This rejoinder rests on a serious and important confusion which may in part be responsible for the desperate feeling that only phenomenalism can somehow, in the end, be true. The theories advanced by physiologists, say about the indispensability of the mechanism of the ear to the hearing of sounds, are empirical theories, corroborated by observational and not linguistic tests: and to say, therefore, that a particular kind of hearer is necessary is to assert a causal, i.e. empirical, and not a semantic or logical proposition. I am saying that the event described as the hearing of a sound emitted by a gramophone depends on certain necessary conditions, and amongst these the structure of the hearer's brain or ear occurs in the same sort of way as, let us say, the physical properties of the needle attached to the sound box of the gramophone. But when I analyse propositions about the meaning of sentences, I am certainly not asserting, and need not necessarily be implying, propositions stating causes or conditions of the events which they describe. There may very well in particular cases exist a causal nexus between the person of the observer and a given material object – what this nexus is, it is the task of the natural sciences to investigate. But this causal nexus is precisely what the phenomenalist[1] claims *not* to be discussing when he offers a reduction of categorical material object sentences to hypothetical sense datum sentences – if he were, his theory would amount to a queer kind of occasionalism, metaphysical or empirical, according to his view of connections in nature, whereby the observer who figures in the protasis of the phenomenalist hypothetical could destroy a table by averting his gaze as surely as by setting it on fire.[2] When I say that a material object exists or has certain characteristics, I am not, it seems to me, committing myself necessarily to any specific theory about the

[1] For example, A. J. Ayer, op. cit. (p. 35, note 1 above).

[2] This is one of the notorious absurdities of which Berkeley is at times guilty, and on which beginners in philosophy are often taught to practise their critical powers.

necessary or sufficient conditions of the existence or character of the object. Hence, the question of when, or for how long, the table next door is coloured brown need not in principle ever affect the answer to the question 'What do I mean when I say "There is a brown table next door"?' This, of course, needs qualification: the meanings of words *are* affected, and often very deeply affected, by our explicit or implicit causal beliefs, and the analysis of what is meant by an expression may very well reveal all kinds of physical or social or psychological beliefs or assumptions prevalent in a given society, a change in which could affect the meaning of words. The degree to which the dispositional character- istics of observers, treated as persons in time and space, enter into the way in which we employ material object words will vary widely: thus, it seems to me reasonably clear that when we say that there is a table next door, we are *not* implying any particular beliefs about the presence or dispositional characteristics of the normal human observer, beyond the fact that if it is a table at all, it must be not wholly invisible, intangible to him etc. – since otherwise it would not be what we mean by a material object. It seems a little less obvious that I can today say that it is coloured brown when not observed, for perhaps by now rudimentary physiological knowledge is sufficiently widespread to have imported into the notion of being coloured certain causal beliefs about the effects in the visual field of changes in our nervous system, etc. It seems very much less clear that I can say that roses smell sweet when no one smells them, or that winds howl when no one hears them, and it seems clearly eccentric to say that heard melodies are sweet, while those unheard are literally sweeter. And all this is doubtless useful in throwing light on our normal usage with regard to such words as 'smell sweet', or 'howl', or 'sweet melodies', some of which do, while others do not, imply the presence of persons with certain psychological, physiological etc. attributes as observers. I am merely concerned to show that a quite sufficient number of material object sentences do *not* presuppose such dependence on the existence or behaviour of observers of this kind, that the relation of observers to material objects is more properly to be called an empirical and not a semantic question, however deeply verbal usage and empirical beliefs may be interconnected; and that consequently the view that nothing can in principle be significantly said to occur without explicit and implicit reference to observers is a major fallacy which rests on failure to distinguish between the causal propositions of natural science or common sense and propositions about meaning.

I return to my original point that phenomenalism, or at any rate the most prevalent modern form of it, seems to rest on a mistaken analysis of what normal existential material object statements state; they state that things or events existed, or exist, or will exist, or were, are, or will be, characterised by this or that characteristic; and not that something might exist or would exist, or would have existed, the truth (if not the assertion) of which is logically compatible with the non-existence of anything whatever. Even if hypothetical propositions alone describe the conditions without which we should not assert or be justified in asserting the relevant categoricals, yet the meaning of the former is not the same as the meaning of the latter. And this is so even if we go further and hold, as some do, that the two types of proposition strictly entail one another; since whatever the sense in which mutual entailment is regarded as tantamount to, or identical with, logical equivalence (as it is by some logicians), it is clearly not the same as the sense of identity of meaning in which two or more descriptive sentences can be said by common sense to mean the same; yet it is this last sense of 'meaning the same', as between the *analysans* and the *analysandum*, and it alone, that the best known variants of modern phenomenalism seek to establish and, if the above thesis is correct, seek in vain.

Logical Translation

THERE is a cluster of problems which have formed the traditional subject-matter of philosophers, in particular of logicians and epistemologists – problems which may be said to form the heart of their inquiries. I refer to such time-honoured questions as those which derive from the classification of judgements or propositions into various types – negative and affirmative, categorical and hypothetical, general and singular; judgements about the past or the present or the future; judgements about material objects or persons, about the data of perception or of memory or of the imagination. Every student of philosophy is all too familiar with the type of question I mean: e.g. are hypothetical judgements properly described as being true or false, and, if so, how is this determined? Is there a particular kind of 'fact' which establishes the truth or falsity of modal judgements in the way in which certain kinds of categorical judgements are said to be verifiable or falsifiable by ordinary 'facts' or 'events'? What do judgements about the past or future describe? Do there exist past and future facts for them to describe and, if so, in what sense of 'exist'? Do negative judgements describe 'negative facts', and if not, what function do they perform? Can sentences about material objects be translated into sentences about the actual or possible sensible experience of observers, or are material objects not, in this sense, 'reducible' to sense data? Are general propositions about 'classes' containing an infinite number of members, and are there such classes and in what sense of 'are'? Or, alternatively, are empirical general propositions perhaps not 'really' propositions at all but 'rules' or 'prescriptions' (and is this particularly true of causal judgements?), or are such statements descriptions, not indeed of infinites of some sort, but of actual or recommended habits or dispositions to behave in certain ways or to perform various operations of a theoretical or practical kind? Or perhaps not so much statements about, as concrete examples of, these tendencies at work, not descriptions or rules but exercises of verbal habits in accordance with certain rules? Every student of philosophy will recognise that much writing, both modern and ancient, has been devoted to giving answers to these questions, and an immense amount of ingenuity has been used in the elaborate defence of this or that theory against logical or epistemological objections. The purpose of this paper is to indicate that some forms, at any rate, of this discussion, illuminating as they may be in various unintended ways, rest upon at least one fundamental fallacy which has vitiated the topic from its earliest beginnings in Greek philosophy, and still obsesses the thought of many distinguished contemporary philosophers.

I

The most persistent symptom of the fallacy I have in mind is the desire to translate many prima facie different types of proposition into a single type. This process is so ingrained a practice on the part of philosophers, and in particular logicians, that we hardly stop to ask what the motive for this operation is. Thus the traditional Aristotelian doctrine of the syllogism strongly suggests that the first mood of the first figure, *Barbara*, is the ideal pattern of scientific knowledge, and that a science is defective unless it is, at any rate in principle, capable of being set out in this form. Similarly, propositions embodying 'clear and distinct ideas' occupy a uniquely privileged position in the Cartesian theory of knowledge; as ideas of this type are to the rationalists, so empirical statements expressing 'simple ideas' or 'impressions' of direct experience are to the British empiricists, and 'basic' or 'atomic' propositions to Russell and his followers, 'atomic' and 'protocol' propositions to the early Viennese school, and so forth. All these schools of thought, differing and indeed sharply opposed as they may be on many other crucial issues of principle, have at least one thing in common: they clearly favour one type of proposition or statement before all others; they treat it as possessing a virtue which other types conspicuously lack; it seems to them untouched by the problems and difficulties which afflict other modes of expression which are represented as being defective or likely to lead to paradoxes from which the model propositions are commendably free. Indeed, the possession of such logical defects and difficulties is identified with failure to approximate to the ideal model of the 'good' proposition. The stock example of the logic books, 'The cat is on the mat', is an example of just such a 'good' proposition. This is a proposition which seems to offer no difficulties, and to need no theory to 'explain' it, provided that it is true and easily verified – e.g. if there occurs before the eyes of the speaker a cat which is in fact sitting on a mat. The relation between the symbols and what they symbolise is then assumed to be one of simple correspondence: the sentence is like a cap so constructed as to fit its particular object; the object is present and the cap fits it precisely; 'difficulties' arise only when the object is not of the type required, or not present, or indeed not existent at all. So long as the cat is on the mat the sentence 'The cat is on the mat' is obviously true and offers no difficulties. But if the cat leaves the mat, the sentence suddenly begins to bristle with difficulties: it is still perfectly intelligible, but what does it now describe? It is false, but how are false propositions related to a world which, *ex hypothesi*, verifies only propositions which are true? If the cat had not moved, the sentence would still have been true; what kind of 'facts' does this kind of hypothetical sentence describe? And if it entails 'The cat is no longer on the mat', is the relation of this true negative proposition to the world analogous to that of the corresponding, no longer true, affirmative one? Is *not* being on the mat a 'feature' of 'reality'? Are there negative facts? Are there hypothetical facts? Are there false facts? If not, is the relation of these 'difficult' sentences to their subject-matter of a kind radically different from that apparently simple and direct correspondence which seemed to govern the relation of the selected 'straightforward' sentences to theirs? Or were we altogether too simple and naïve in the first place when we took these straightforward sentences to consist of symbols in direct correspondence to external reality? The reader will recognise here a world of long familiar problems and the classic solutions of them – simple correspondence, complex correspondence (early Russell), coherence, intuition, the various solutions of pragmatism, operationalism, strong and weak verifiability etc. Underlying this type of approach to the subject there is the common assumption that there are certain propositions (or sentences) of the simple, straightforward, 'good' kind, which offer no problems, with the implied corollary that if all propositions were only of this type, no difficulties would arise, and the elaborate and never quite satisfactory theories advanced to remove them would not be required. There is a kind of latent dualism which permeates this method of treating the descriptive use of words, whereby propositions are almost instinctively divided into straightforward and problem-raising, tractable and troublesome, good examples of their kind and eccentric or degenerate species requiring special remedial treatment, good and bad, sheep and goats. The selected ideal model of what a 'good' proposition should be will naturally differ according to the philosophical outlook of the logician and his school: Cartesians, after a formal bow to theology and ethics, inclined to place those of mathematics and

58

mathematical physics foremost; Locke, Berkeley, Hume, Mill, Russell, and modern empiricists pursue the ideal of empirical propositions, purified of everything which could make them erroneous, as being alone immediate, incorrigible, and simple, and for this reason 'fundamental'. My purpose is, however, not to contrast the competing candidates for this privileged status, but to draw attention to the phenomenon of competition itself. For it seems to me that its goal is illusory, that this entire way of looking at the subject rests upon a gigantic fallacy, perhaps almost as old as logic itself, and that acceptance of it has lured philosophers into seeking two familiar roads out of the difficulty, each of which leads into its own dead end. The reason for this is that the 'difficulty' is unreal, and the methods of dealing with it consequently neither solve nor fail to solve any genuine question.

II

The situation is this: we begin by taking some harmless statement, say 'It is 3 p.m., and the book is on the table', as a fair example of an informative proposition. This, if true, does not at first appear to give rise to any philosophical difficulties: there is something reassuring about being able to observe the hands of a clock and the presence of the book on the table, and to report this in language appropriate for this purpose; the symbols for it fit their subject-matter like caps specially designed to do so, or like arrows which satisfactorily hit the target at which they are aimed, or whatever metaphor conveys the same notion. This is evidently one of the most fundamental conceptions – or metaphors – of how language functions: on the one hand I have the symbols, on the other the world. The former are fashioned to describe or express or convey or symbolise the latter. The relationship is, as it were, ostensive. If I am asked what the symbols mean I can point, or think I can point, at something which I have used the symbols to mean. Difficulties begin as soon as the possibility of such direct pointing breaks down. If I infer from the above propositions that 'If the book is on the table, it is not on the chair' and am asked what this means, I find that I cannot point in the same simple and expressive fashion. The apodosis – '[the book] is not on the chair' – raises a difficulty since obviously absence is not to be pointed to in the way that a specific position in my vicinity can be. Moreover, the hypothetical proposition is not equivalent to the negation of the conjunction 'The book is on the table and the book is on the chair.' The 'meanings' of conditional sentences cannot be pointed to as, perhaps, the 'meanings' of some categorical ones can, and this is part of what we mean by calling them conditional. And if I further go on to meditate upon the fact that books, as a rule, are not as large as tables, I am again unable to point to something in my environment as the 'referend' of my symbols. By this time some minutes have passed, and if I am now asked whether it is true that the book was on the table at 3 p.m., I cannot in any literal sense of the word point to this 'fact' either, since it is past, gone, not before me. This suggests strongly that there is some fatal gulf which divides the original sentence, which 'fitted' its portion of the real world so neatly, from these more troublesome sentences, which, meaningful though they obviously are, are like so many collections of displaced symbols in search of their proper places in the real world – homeless names vainly seeking for their unfindable owners.

The problem of how symbols mean has now emerged in its crudest and most uncompromising form, and to solve it two expedients have been adopted. Each of these has for many years formed the nucleus of much interesting speculation; nevertheless each of them turns out upon examination to be equally desperate and futile. The first takes the form of what we may call, for want of a better label, the deflationary method. It assumes that the only genuine, fully formed proposition is that of the favoured kind (and this will differ for the different philosophical schools) and that all other types of proposition derive their logical force solely from some type of traceable relationship to it. In the case we have selected, the favoured model is affirmative, singular, categorical, and empirical. Since it is conjunctive in form and conjunctive 'facts' are not easy to find in nature, it seems best to make it 'simpler' still, and split the complex into two 'simple' propositions: 'The book is on the table'; 'It is now 3 p.m.' But this, as it stands, will not quite do. If the criterion of meaning on the part of a symbolic expression is the existence before its user of something at which he can point, books and tables and even times of day make this process no easier for they cannot be simply pointed at. The entire panoply of phenomenalist armament is here brought into play. I am told that I cannot point at tables, but only at tabular appearances or data, nor at books as reposing upon them, but only to bookish data as standing in certain visual, tactile etc. relations in my visual, tactile etc. fields to the tabular data. '3 p.m.' is even less capable of being pointed to, and an elaborate translation of its meaning is offered again in visual, tactile, etc., terms as being that to which my symbols ultimately refer. The ideal proposition gradually emerges as requiring a minimum of certain definite properties. Thus, at the very least, it must be:

1 Affirmative, for how am I to point at what is not there?

2 Categorical, for how am I to point at the something that only might be; or, in the case of unfulfilled hypotheticals, that cannot in principle be?

3 Singular (or a finite collection of singulars), since it must be something or other, particular and specifiable, for what would it be like to point to something in general, belonging to no particular time and place, discoverable in no one's specific sensible field?

4 Logically simple, for how can I point at something which is disjunctive, i.e. a this-or-that, but neither specifically this nor that? Nor can it be conjunctive, for how can I point to something which is both-this-and-that?

5 Not only particular but about the present: it must refer to something in my sense field, here and now; for how can I point to something not here, or in the past, or in the future? If the 'object' of the sentence is elsewhere or already over, or not yet arrived, it is not 'actual', the arrow has no target, the cap has nothing upon which to fit (or not to fit).

6 It must refer to something 'immediately given', for unless it does this, the 'object' is again not here, not now etc., and the fatal difficulties recur in another form.

7 It must be true (although this is a desideratum of an altogether different order, and one which the theory, so far from insisting upon it, does its best to circumvent), for if it is false what does it point to? If a proposition is false, it describes nothing, it only misdescribes, but misdescription is only another kind of failure on the part of the arrow to hit its target; and if meaning is a sort of target-hitting, then what is false is also meaningless.

This is not, of course, intended to be an exhaustive catalogue of the minimum of properties required by the 'good' propositions – those which give no trouble, the model statements whose relation to their subject-matter is so clear and so simple that if no other statements were in use, no logical or epistemological problem would arise. It seems but a short step from this to that 'immediate' contact with reality in which thought and being are one, the realm of the Hegelian Absolute, where there are no problems and no mental pursuit of unattainable goals, because there are no minds, and nothing to pursue.

Leaving aside for the moment what would constitute representative examples of such 'good' sentences or propositions (we shall return to this later since clearly this is the heart of the matter), it seems clear that if we set about the subject in this way we are committed to looking upon sentences or propositions which do not conform to the ideal either as being wholly meaningless, or else as precariously saved by being shown to have some kind of logical relationship to the ideal propositions, which may yet confer some kind of status upon them, although necessarily a somewhat inferior one. For we may still rescue such imperfect propositions by looking upon them as possessing meaning in proportion as they contain 'sound' elements; i.e. can be analysed as complexes, some elements in which are meaningful in the approved sense, i.e. through being affirmative, categorical, simple, singular, true, about what is here and now before the speaker etc. – so many grains of pure gold embedded in a baser medium. This medium can then be removed from them, and upon examination will turn out to mean nothing at all, but perhaps, at best, to perform some other logical or psychological function. This is the sort of view which lurks at the back of such theories as those of Logical Constructions, whether in the older Humean version, or in the later, more elaborate form developed by Russell and his disciples. If we practise this kind of analysis, we start by asking about any given sentence whether it is genuinely descriptive; and if this claim has been made on its behalf, we require that the sentence shall be so analysed into its constituents that the truly descriptive elements in it shall be revealed in the form of 'basic' or 'atomic' propositions which have the properties required of the 'good' propositions, i.e. direct correspondence with experience in the sense adumbrated above. The proposition analysed is then revealed as a complex of irreducible simple statements, with logical constants acting as links and determining formal properties. Everything not so analysable is relegated to a non-descriptive realm and labelled as emotive, or expressive, or a psychological residue etc. – a kind of linguistic slag heap, from which the precious ore has been extracted – useful enough in some respects, and more than this, perhaps biologically or psychologically indispensable, but liable to land us in metaphysical or theological confusions if we mistake it for an informative or fact-affirming use of words. Descriptive language emerges as a 'construction' logically built out of the 'basic' bricks, consisting of the 'good' propositions only; whatever is left over is to be relegated as being non-propositional. What, on this view, is to become of all such *soi-disant* propositions as hypothetical or general propositions, statements about the past and future, about material objects, about other persons etc.? There are no two ways about it: in so far as they give genuine information they are *not* hypothetical, *not* about the past etc., and if it is desired to retain them unimpaired, they will have to be expelled from the class of genuine propositions altogether. This predicament is by no means confined to empiricists or positivists. So faithful a disciple of Aristotle and Descartes as Cook Wilson, when he asked himself what singular hypothetical propositions were about, convinced himself that reality consisted of what is and was and will be, and not of what might be or might have been; consequently, hypothetical propositions could not be real propositions at all (for what did they describe?), but something to do with connections between questions; for questions, being neither true nor false, do not assert or describe, and so are free from the requirements exacted of all claimants to true propositional status. It is true that the connections turned out to hold not so much between the questions as between the answers to them; and 'answers' are in fact the old familiar propositions scarcely disguised at all; and so the problem had not been solved after all. But the very oddity of this effort to show that hypothetical propositions were not properly propositions at all is symptomatic of the effects of the doctrine which made this odd procedure seem worth attempting. Again, when F. P. Ramsey suggested that causal propositions were perhaps not propositions at all, he did so because causal statements were obviously general, and if interpreted extensionally (and what is it to ask for the meaning of a symbol if not for its extension?) could not be pinned to anything that could be pointed to; because general statements did not seem to point to — be knock-down verifiable by — anything which was sensed or introspected, or described as so many items in somebody's experience. Indeed the very ideal of an entirely extensional logic — the rigidly extensional interpretation of meaning — the almost superstitious horror of intensional analyses as a relapse into the darkness of metaphysics, is symptomatic of this attitude. Language was viewed as a kind of system of verbal credit, where descriptive sentences functioned like cheques which, to be used at all, did not indeed need to be immediately converted into bullion, but retained their value only so long as they were in principle so convertible. The gold cover of such sentences consisted in the facts of direct experience, 'objects' of 'knowledge by acquaintance', and the degree of meaning which any such expression possessed depended directly upon the amount of such cover in terms of the basic or 'good' propositions —

themselves directly convertible into the bullion of 'facts' – which it turned out to have. In so far as it was not so covered, it was liable to be exposed as in the strict sense not descriptive; and if to have meaning was to describe, meaningless. This naturally led to intolerable paradoxes too familiar to be rehearsed here. It was difficult, for instance, to maintain that general propositions, or propositions of science, were non-descriptive (but, as some declared, merely matrices for the generation of meaningful sentences), since they were obviously refutable, i.e. falsifiable by negative singular propositions, and if they could be false, they were propositions after all. All the notorious difficulties which beset rigorous versions of phenomenalism (or the early, uncompromising kinds of logical positivism) emerged in their acutest form in the course of the attempt to force propositions of various types into the Procrustean bed of the chosen model – the 'atomic', not further analysable, incor-rigible proposition. Paradoxes began to accumulate; propositions about the past were required by the more uncompromising among the early positivists to become ('in some sense') propositions about the future – or else to be eliminated. Propositions about the present underwent the same drastic treatment, and this, incidentally, was soon seen to provide two senses of 'about the future' – the normal sense in which propositions about the future were distinguished from those about the present and the past, and an abnormal sense in which all propositions were 'in some sense' or 'for methodological purposes' propositions about the future; in this sense 'the future' could no longer be contrasted with the past or present, or indeed with anything else, and so in the end turned out to be devoid of meaning. Similarly, propositions about other selves turned out to be a sub-class of propositions about the observer's own data, and the words 'my own data' or 'the observer's data' were robbed of meaning with the same fatal inevitability; for now all data were 'in some sense' the observer's own, and a solipsism followed which, there being no statable non-solipsism with which to contrast it, also turned out to describe nothing. It gradually became clear that what was being demanded was the relegation to the limbo of 'non-propositional' language of everything which was not categorical, affirmative, singular, about the speaker himself, about his immediate experience, here and now etc., but since these attributes could not *ex hypothesi* be contrasted with anything beyond (for the statement of it was logically prohibited), the deflationary programme of 'reducing' all propositions to a selected type of proposition, certified as genuine (as well as the milder versions which accorded significance to 'imperfect' propositions, but only in so far as the blood royal of the genuine propositions flowed through some portion of their complex structures), turned out to be one of the worst mares' nests of modern philosophy. It was evident that the deflationary method led into an *impasse* and had to be abandoned.

The other or inflationary route was the precise inverse of the first. It began again with the assumption that the only genuine propositions were categorical, true, singular, etc.; but since there obviously did exist expressions clearly not of this kind, e.g. statements normally called hypothetical, or general, or about the past or future of other persons, or false, or unverifiable, or not clearly classifiable as either empirical or *a priori*, to which it was unplausible to deny all descriptive power, it was decided to cut the knot by boldly accepting the fact that they were, after all, what they seemed to be, i.e. perfectly valid and intelligible, propositions as descriptive as any others, unjustly suspected of being defective only because they were assumed to be about the same kind of entities as those dealt with by the 'good' non-trouble-giving propositions with which they were so unfavourably contrasted. Once it was grasped that they were concerned with entities different in kind from the favoured propositions, they might be rescued, and even accorded equal status with the latter. This doctrine maintained that hypothetical propositions, for example, were not at best partly categorical, partly not propositions at all, but that they were perfectly good propositions in their own right, but concerned with a special class of entities – 'hypothetical facts', or 'real possibilities', or 'essences', or the like. General propositions, similarly, presided over a perfectly genuine kingdom of their own, populated by entities called 'universals'. Propositions about the past and future dealt with past facts and future facts respectively, unfulfilled hypotheticals dealt with 'unactualised possibilities', and the categorical, singular etc. propositions originally set up as ideal models no longer represented a superior species, but were assigned their place as equals among their peers, governing as they did, not indeed all facts, but only some among them, i.e. those which were actual, present, particular etc.

Worlds upon worlds of new entities suddenly became unfolded. Regions inhabited by mathematical or logical entities were revealed to the view – unchanging Platonic forms, connected in queer ways with the 'real world', or else detached from it and secure in their own serene and beautiful universes. Realms of 'subsistent' entities, inhabited by immortal essences, came into being to correspond to the many forms of the imagination, scientific, mathematical and poetical, capable moreover of accommodating games, Utopias, mythological and heraldic creatures, and every other form of logically coherent fiction. These theories, which grew more and more fantastic, provided for everything which had been or could be thought of, true and false, reasonable and nonsensical; the world of ordinary life was somewhat vaguely treated as a species of the curious genus 'entity', and distinguished by the pseudo-attributes 'actuality' or 'existence', which ignored the lethal force of Kant's refutation of the ontological argument. It was a process of uncontrolled inflation, and it operated on a very simple principle: that all genuine propositions were *au fond* categorical, singular, true, etc.; but instead of trying, as the deflationists had done, to extricate only what was genuinely categorical, non-hypothetical, non-general etc. out of the unsifted mass of what, prima facie, looked like propositions, it boldly proceeded as if all these statements were already categorical and singular and all that was required of genuine propositions, and set about discovering entities to correspond with them. Thus if, let us say, hypothetical propositions were in the last analysis categorical, what were they categorical about? Plainly about hypothetical entities. If general propositions were *au fond* singular, what kind of things did they describe? Individual things – 'ingredients of facts' called 'universals'. General propositions were in truth singular propositions, and their subjects were universals much as those of more routine singular propositions were the events or 'facts' of 'direct experience'. Propositions about the past were about 'timeless' entities qualified by the attribute 'pastness' exactly as propositions about the present were about similar entities qualified by 'presentness'. False propositions were true about 'possibilities' while true propositions were true about 'actualities'. It was very simple; all propositions as such were categorical about something or other, and the task of metaphysics and the theory of knowledge was to establish the 'status' of what in any given case this something was. These timeless 'entities' or 'essences' with their many curious attributes were now the targets which the propositional arrows struck, the shapes in the real world which the linguistic caps precisely fitted. Their relations to one another – the 'structure of reality' – was the province of a new metaphysical discipline called variously phenomenology, logic etc.; and a special intellectual faculty was postulated (or discovered) whose business it was to fix the unalterable 'ontological status' of mathematical, historical, psychological, scientific, fictional etc. entities to each other. The question always took the same form: what kind of categoricals were hypothetical propositions, what species of singular propositions were general ones; what did negative propositions affirm, what did false propositions state truly?

The vice of the inflationary method was the precise opposite of the deflationary one: if the latter prohibited the saying of much that could intelligibly be said, the former encouraged speculation and description of much that did not exist and could not be related to the real world because there was nothing to relate. The first method used Occam's razor to eliminate too many necessary entities; the second set no limit to their multiplication. The inflationary method was not a straitjacket like its rival, but it led to consequences which were more ludicrous because it manufactured entities which grew increasingly fantastic. The proliferation of bogus 'objects' proved too much even for their creators: the free play of the imagination cannot indefinitely be represented as discovery. Formal methods can be made use of to expose the absurdity of this method. According to the theory of 'subsistents' a true statement corresponds to 'existent' entities, while a false one, to have any meaning at all, must correspond to non-existent, 'subsistent' entities (or propositions). What relation, if any, occurs, on this view, between existent and subsistent entities? Any proposition describing such a relation must itself, to be meaningful, necessarily correspond to something or other, not a 'subsistent' or collection of 'subsistents' in the ordinary sense, but to something or other – a 'super-subsistent' at some 'higher level'. But this is tantamount to converting relational propositions into subject-predicate propositions about entities; all of these entities will require relations to other entities if they are to be described at all, but no sooner are such relations provided than they turn into particulars requiring their own relations, etc., and this is a vicious infinite regress of the most obvious kind. On a representative theory of language things in the real world are like so many islands connected with or kept apart from each other by gap-like entities which correspond to relations. The Midas touch of any Meinongian theory fills these gaps with subsistent entities, and thus makes impossible the description of any particular object; for objects can be described only in terms of their relations to other objects, or of the relations of their own internal parts to one another, while here relational propositions, as in the similar system of Leibniz, are treated as if they did not exist; where all relations function like terms, there are no relations. The situation is that of Bradley's nightmare; all relations are converted into terms, and new relations are perpetually needed to relate the new terms; but no sooner are they created than they turn into terms themselves, calling for relations to relate *them*:

these, as soon as invoked, harden into terms themselves. But terms cannot be related by terms; this fallacy, common to Bradley and Russell in his middle period, which turns logic into an extravagant ontology, can go no further.

III

Oddly enough, the fallacy which underlay the inflationary method was identical with that which vitiated the reverse process of deflation. For in each case what was demanded was forcible assimilation of all propositions to a given type; in one case non-categorical, non-singular, non-veridical etc. propositions were considered *pro tanto* as not propositions at all, in the other they were all, in principle, looked upon as categoricals, but concerned with peculiar entities the description of which involved intolerable paradoxes. In both cases what was not categorical, or singular, or veridical etc. was regarded as peculiar, problematic, needing special explanation. In one case this was done by condemning all but one type of proposition as vicious, although partially redeemable in inverse proportion to the distance from the ideal type. In the other case all propositions were pronounced equally virtuous, and the curse was taken off the suspected types by transferring it to the object itself. Provided the entities to which propositions corresponded were sufficiently variegated, the propositions could be pressed into the same logical uniform, i.e. all propositions were *eo ipso* categorical, singular, affirmative, true etc. The deflationary method gave the impression that only 'good' propositions stood, as it were, face to face with the real world; all others were forms of squinting at it from the side, or of purblindness, or indeed, in extreme cases, of total blindness. The inflationary theory represented all propositions as being equal *vis-à-vis* their objects, but endowed many of these objects with exceedingly queer logical and metaphysical properties to whose existence lack of imagination, or excessive respect for commonsense notions, had too long rendered philosophers blind or inattentive. (The analogue in the case of the more fanciful theories of perception will readily come to the mind of the students of this branch of philosophy.) What is common to both methods and equally fatal to either is, of course, the correspondence model. For it leads to the view that one class of propositions, and one only, is properly so called; and by the simple expedient of eliminating all its rivals *a priori*, leaves the victorious class without attributes. Properties with which there is nothing to compare cannot be described; consequently all genuine propositions cannot, in principle, and literally,

68

be of the same logical type, for there is then no way of indicating what it is.

This fatal dichotomy ('either categorical or not a proposition') is not confined either to a particular province of philosophy or to a particular school of thinkers. In ethics, for example, it sometimes takes the form of claiming to detect specific ethical characteristics, whether *a priori* or empirically, as being 'inherent' in objects or persons, characteristics as many and as various as may be wanted to meet all the apparently irreducible distinctions between the various ethical predicates which occur in sentences expressing moral judgements. Alternatively, if the deflationary method is adopted, it may take the form of a ruthless axe, with which all ethical statements which cannot be translated into the favoured type of proposition (or whatever in them remains obstinately unreduced after they have been subjected to this treatment) are lopped off and consigned to Hume's bonfire as devoid of the right kind of significance, or anyhow insusceptible to philosophical analysis; and the same treatment is meted out to aesthetic, political, or historical judgements, and other recalcitrant material. Nor is this method confined to empiricists: Plato and Aquinas, Descartes, Leibniz and their modern disciples merely represent the obverse of this outlook: which considers sense perception or other sources of empirical evidence to be so many inferior, confused 'modes' of cognition, lower forms of mental activity, condemned in proportion as they are thought to fall short of the ideal model of the kind of *a priori* knowledge, and the type of combination of words, which the particular rationalist philosopher happens to favour as the paradigm of clarity or infallibility. In this respect there is relatively little to choose between the fundamental attitudes that govern these apparently deeply opposed schools of thought: each condemns the ideals and practices of the other for failing to satisfy criteria which are drawn from the same sort of misleading mythology. Their criticisms of one another's theories are often valid enough; it is only when their positive grounds for this are revealed that we receive a sudden shock. For the case sometimes resembles nothing so much as that of a man who with great cogency demonstrates the lunacy of another man who claims to be Napoleon, and then adds as a clinching argument that he is Napoleon himself.

IV

So much for the merits of the inflationary and deflationary methods, with their apotheosis of the favoured mode of expression: it might not be without interest to consider the nature of one of the most persistently recommended types of such model propositions – the 'basic' propositions of the analytical school of modern empiricism. What are the unique properties of these propositions in virtue of which they represent, we are told, the lowest level, the ground floor of the many-storied buildings called logical constructions? They must be the ultimate, not further reducible, 'foundations of knowledge', upon which all else must rest; hence they must be simple, indubitable, and somehow reflect the nature of reality more directly and infallibly than any others; for otherwise they will lose their privileged status, and cease to be the bullion in terms of which all other expressions claiming to be intelligible can be certified as philosophical legal tender. What, then, do they require in the way of characteristics if they are to be, as it were, face to face with reality? One property they must have, and that is of being capable of being known in a way which precludes their ever being false; they must be absolutely safe. Their occurrence in ordinary speech may be infrequent, and they may look or sound unwieldy or barbarous when articulated; they may turn out to be thoroughly jejune and uninteresting, and they may be of little use in normal communication; but they will have one enviable attribute which no other type of expression will be in a position to boast – they will in some sense be ultimate, reducible to nothing else; they, and they alone, will be wholly 'testable' by any rational being who chooses to entertain them, and they will serve as the foundation of all other knowledge – which surely should be a reward enough for any amount of dullness and platitudinousness. It might be as well to inspect one of these humble but indispensable entities: let us return to our earlier example and assert 'The book is on the table.' This will not do; we have obviously said too much; the sentence is not 'safe' and 'basic' in the sense required. It is certainly not incorrigible, for we may be labouring under an illusion of one or more of the senses. What we see before us may not be a book nor its pedestal a table. In accordance with time-honoured practice, to use the scrupulous methods taught to us by the sense datum philosophers a quarter of a century ago, we start the process of 'reduction' which is to lead us to the discovery of what can be whittled down no further. We must not say that there is a book on the table, we must say 'There are bookish data surrounded by tabular ones' – all the rest is inductive and uncertain. But this will not do either, for what do we mean by 'bookish', and what do we mean by 'tabular', and where are these data occurring, and when, and for how long, and to whom are we saying these words, and how do we know that they are conveying

70

the information we mean them to convey? To fulfil the programme everything that is uncertain (i.e. might turn out to be false) must be remorselessly pruned away, however poverty-stricken the remainder may turn out to be; for truth and, above all, infallibility are what is required rather than richness of content. Consequently we continue the whittling process. We are at some point obliged to say that by 'bookish' and 'tabular' we mean something sufficiently resembling a standard model or models in terms of which these terms are, or could be, defined. Do the data before us sufficiently conform to this standard to be properly described as tabular or bookish? How can we tell? Must we assume that our memory is infallible? But does not this bring about what of all things we most wished to avoid, the necessity of referring to the existence of entities in the past, past experiences on our part, which are not 'here', not 'before us', as those data must be which basic sentences are invented to describe? So we must continue to cut away; our memory may be fallible and the alleged past data not have occurred; if we are to give 'bookish' and 'tabular' their proper meanings we must no longer have recourse to occurrences as the standard models for these words, but only to the belief, whether true or false, that such data did once actually occur. By 'bookish' and 'tabular' we mean no longer what resembles standard book-like or table-like appearances, but only what we believe may so resemble. But alas, even this heroic act of self-denial will not suffice. For even in order to believe that this or that occurred in our past, if only for the purpose of providing a minimum point of reference for symbols, such words as 'before' and 'after' must refer to something not now present. Once we abandon the mythological region of the 'point-instant', of the 'immediate' present, we become theoretically liable to the risk of error, for what we are referring to is in some sense not before us, and may turn out to be different from what we think it to be. In this academic sense there is no empirical statement we cannot doubt: we are not sure that there are other selves capable of understanding our words; we do not know that the words themselves are performing the task of classifying our immediate data, since classification includes assimilation to other members of a given class, but this has been ruled out, since we cannot be certain, in the sense required, whether they — the other members of the class — in fact possess the model characteristics attributed to them, since *ex hypothesi* they must be absent and not available for inspection. By this time it should be becoming plain that we are marching with rapid strides towards a logical absurdity. We are trying to say at one and the same time that we are attributing certain

71

characteristics to our data by means of the infallible propositions which report direct acquaintance, and yet also that we can only name these characteristics by contrast or comparison to other characteristics which, being absent, cannot be infallibly known, and so cannot guarantee us against error when invoked for the purpose of comparison or contrast. Yet to say that something is true or false is at the very least to compare it with the past or the future, with entities not here and not now, that is, to relate it to a field wider than the object under review. We can escape this only by saying that we are not asserting, only naming, only christening. But it is doubtful whether even this can be done without calling in what is absent and therefore theoretically dubitable; and in any case to name is not to describe and therefore not to say anything true or false; the act of christening is not the uttering of a proposition, however basic, however trivial, however non-informative. Our basic propositions are gradually becoming names for the phenomena of what used to be called 'pure sensation'. Whether such phenomena occur or not is relatively immaterial; the point is that in a world which consists of nothing else, description, language, true and false propositions, are terms which cannot be given any interpretation.

v

What is this but, under another name, the quest for the absolute immediacy desiderated by Bradley, the pure manifold of Kant, the pure 'given' – not yet 'distorted' or 'mutilated' by categories and concepts of 'discursive thought' – Bergson's unbroken continuum of pure duration, which appears in more sophisticated forms as the search for logical particulars or for the referends of logical proper names – for the ultimate constituents of the world which alone are real but cannot, owing to the generalising character of words, ever be described?

It should by now be clear that the search for basic propositions in this sense leads nowhere, since it proceeds from a fatal misconception; but what is of greater interest is not whether such propositions can in fact be formulated, but why so many thinkers have felt so desperate a need for their existence and have expended so much ingenuity upon a task so inevitably doomed to frustration. In other words, why did philosophers look for answers (at times heavily disguised as metaphysical investigations of various kinds) to so odd a series of questions as: 'When we utter a hypothetical proposition, what kind of categorical proposition are we uttering?' 'When we make a general statement, to what class of singular statements does it belong?' 'When we speak of the past or the future, which portion of the present are we referring to?' 'When we speak about objects far away, what are the objects in our vicinity with which they are identical?' 'When we ask questions about the lives of other persons, which incidents in our own autobiography are we referring to?' 'When we speak of the external world, which of our "inner" sensations are we describing?' Yet this is what the demand for a purely extensional logic comes to; and such ingenious notions as, for example, the concept of material implication to some extent derived from this attitude; it acted as perhaps the strongest single motive for the employment of this weapon in the attempted transformation of hypotheticals into conjunctions or disjunctions of categoricals. And although it can be shown easily enough that the promise to 'reduce' all contingent hypothetical propositions by this means cannot be fulfilled, it is worth inquiring why such desperate efforts were expended upon seeing how much could be translated by this unpromising method. One obvious reason was of course the need, particularly acutely felt after the excesses of idealist metaphysics, to discover a criterion for the exclusion of what was literally nonsense. The coherence theory of truth seemed to destroy, or at any rate to blur, the differences between the intelligible and the meaningless use of words, and any test of significance possessing initial plausibility appeared welcome to those who were struggling to build a dyke against the torrent of sometimes inspired, but largely unintelligible, writing. Moreover, there was the desire to arrest what I have called inflation. Too many metaphysicians behaved as if differences in types of expression were pointers to differences of 'types of fact', and this led to a view that there were as many metaphysically irreducible kinds of entity in the world as there were different modes of expression in use; and the systematic demonstration that this was not so, that nouns did not necessarily 'correspond' to things, nor adjectives to characteristics, is one of the major glories of modern empiricism and modern logic. Sentences previously thought to be logically independent were shown to be translatable into one another, and this did, no doubt, have the effect of an automatic check upon the indiscriminate multiplication of entities, showing much metaphysical discussion to be baseless and due to verbal confusions. And although the search for infallible criteria of significance proved a wild goose chase, because significance is not determinable by a specific set of rules, yet this approach did mark a great philosophical advance which it will take more than such maxims as 'Every sentence has its own logical grammar' to discredit. But the method is obviously being pushed to fantastic lengths when we are invited to judge all statements in terms of their logical relation to the selected model, and as a result either to reject a number of meaningful sentences on the ground that they are not 'basic' or 'atomic', nor molecules constructible out of such atoms (not suitable bricks for the *Logischer Aufbau der Welt*), or, alternatively, to manufacture entities which would enable all propositions to be represented as categorical, singular, atomic, basic etc., or combinations of these; and this when the so-called 'basic' or 'atomic' propositions themselves turn out on examination to approach the limits of meaninglessness – not to be recognisable forms of descriptive human utterance. And yet it is clearly not some unaccountable love of the odd and the fanciful which has driven so many distinguished thinkers towards this eccentric remedy;[1] it must correspond to some permanent tendency on the part of philosophers, some very deeply rooted metaphors which govern the thought of logicians and epistemologists. Perhaps, therefore, attention to the psychology of philosophical thinking of this kind may throw some light upon this curious state of affairs.

VI

As a tentative hypothesis about some possible causes of this attitude, I should like to mention three fundamental fallacies which by their interplay may have contributed to bring about this result.

1 *The correspondence theory of language*

There is nothing prima facie very unnatural or surprising about the assumption that words are names, and that it is not truth, so much as meaning, that is a form of correspondence between symbols and things. After all, we learn language to some degree by being shown things, or made to touch or hold them, and then told what words to use; and many words are in fact names, class names, but still names, labels attached to classes of objects absence of which makes the use of these names inappropriate. Berkeley, who showed such genius in refuting the fallacy of *unum nomen, unum nominatum,* and discredited, one hopes for

[1] Perhaps the first explicit account of it occurs in Plato's *Theaetetus*, in which Socrates describes it as an opulent dream. The resemblance between the Platonic simile and the doctrine of, e.g., Wittgenstein's *Tractatus Logico-Philosophicus* (London, 1922) is most striking.

ever, the notion that because there were general terms, therefore universals were among the real inhabitants of the universe, himself fell into the converse fallacy of supposing that although general terms did not stand for entities which are general (because there could be none such) they could, if they were to be meaningful, be translated into other terms which did stand for entities. This led in time to the doctrine that a language could be discovered or invented which was free from, and proof against, logically misleading expressions; such a language would be 'logically perfect', and it would consist exclusively of words which did directly correspond to things and their properties, and otherwise only of logical words – constants, transformation rules and the like, whose very form would clearly show that they made no claim to describe or refer to anything whatever. From this it naturally seemed to follow that it was possible, provided one took enough trouble, to arrive at combinations of words which were closer to – stood in a more face-to-face relation with – reality than those in ordinary use; this was the purpose of the whittling operation mentioned above. Even if some meaning could be given to the 'fundamental' or 'basic' sentences which represent the ideal goal of this process, the fallacy did not stop there but directly involved its perpetrators in the entire Procrustean programme. For it held out the alternatives of either eliminating all but basic propositions and combinations of them from the logically perfect language, leaving the untranslated and untranslatable portions of hypothetical, general etc. propositions to fend for themselves as best they could, as psychological attitudes, dispositions or states, emotional residues etc.; or of stretching the basic propositions to cover (as we are told Procrustes did with the legs of his shorter guests) whatever one required to say, which led to the production of fanciful worlds populated by Meinong's queer entities. The theory is fallacious because all words are not names, and meaning is not a species of correspondence with a triadic or any other unique, formally analysable, structure (with unconvincing *ad hoc* adjustments to explain away, say, the obvious difficulties created by false propositions); yet neither is it an utterly absurd theory of meaning; many words or sentences can, in a sense, be said to 'correspond'; this metaphor, if it throws darkness on some, clarifies other ways in which words are used. But when what has significance solely because and in so far as it characterises a particular part of a whole is predicated about the whole, a logical fallacy is generated; and the result turns out to be meaningless. This is precisely what occurs when the effort is made – however unavowed – to represent every species of proposition as combinations of one single species. This is logical translation at its most misguided.

2 *The Ionian fallacy*

A related tendency is the extension of what may be called the Ionian fallacy of asking what everything is made of. The Ionian philosophers themselves may be wholly guiltless of this, since what they were probably asking were questions of physics, from which metaphysical ones were perhaps not clearly distinguished in their day. But the form which this inquiry has taken in later times, from Aristotle to Russell, is a search for the ultimate constituents of the world in some non-empirical sense. Does it really make sense to ask whether the universe consists of events, or point-instants, or sense data, or occurrences? These terms are considered an improvement on such entities as substances, or forms, or unknowable substrata, or Hegelian ideas, since prima facie they wear a more empirical look. But this is a mere deception. For what kind of answers are these questions designed to elicit? If everything consists of 'occurrents' or 'occurrences', what would it be like for something not to be an occurrent or occurrence? How could we know, by what species of empirical or metaphysical inspection, if it were not? And if we could not know this, what significance can we attach to the positive assertion that everything is so composed? What evidence can we have for it or its contradictory? In making it, what are we denying, what alternative are we ruling out, and how can we know when we are and when we are not justified in doing this? A sentence of the form 'Everything consists of . . .' or 'Everything is . . .' or 'Nothing is . . .', unless it is empirical, i.e. states what might be, and only *de facto* is not, otherwise, states nothing, since a proposition which cannot be significantly denied or doubted can offer us no information. And although this is a truism which need not be further laboured, yet notable philosophers have been trapped into thinking that they can significantly ask what everything is made of, very much as if the question were answerable in the way in which empirical questions are answered, save only that the answers are given in terms of such ultimate constituents as occurrents or sense data or atomic facts, as if such entities existed and had characteristics and histories of their own; such thinkers are naturally committed to the view that the propositions which describe such 'ultimate constituents' are basic in the sense required. And since the world consists of these basic ingredients, language cannot do better than mirror them – reproduce the 'structure of reality'. Atomic propositions are the names of such ultimate constituents, molecular ones of combinations of them. This is indeed a metaphysic with a vengeance, without any of the virtues of the more interesting metaphysical systems, which have at times embodied illuminating historical or psychological or poetical insights in the guise of logical or metaphysical discoveries. This strange ontology combines all the vices of the correspondence theory of meaning with everything that positivists have justly urged against synthetic *a priori* judgements; for what are these judgements which purport to analyse the universe into its ultimate constituents, so ultimate that there can be nothing to contrast them with, but synthetic, *a priori*, and meaningless into the bargain?

3 *The search for security*

Finally, there is what Dewey once called the quest for certainty. Plainly one of the most powerful of philosophical stimuli is the search for security – the infallible knowledge of incorrigible propositions. As we have said above, no matter how dry, dull, uninformative such propositions may turn out to be, or how difficult to formulate, all our efforts and austerities will be most richly rewarded if we really secure unassailable certainty at last, reach islands, which may be small and arid and isolated, so long as they constitute dry land in an uncertain and uncharted sea. All the doctrines which look upon belief and opinion as capable of being distilled until they yield up their granules of certain knowledge (which, we are informed, they 'presuppose'), all the doctrines which hold out the goal of clear and distinct ideas whose certainty nothing could cloud, or speak of simple substances, or of simple ideas, not compounded of parts and therefore indestructible and undistortable, or of such ultimate prime matter as impressions, or bundles of sensations, or 'basic' or 'atomic' facts, or 'protocol sentences'; what are all these but an attempt to convey the view that at some time we must reach the last stage of our journey, beyond which it is logically impossible to go, for surely even the weariest river of analysis must somewhere wind safe to the sea of 'the ultimate stuff' of which everything is made? It is as if we were told that logical security could be had, but only at the price of extreme modesty; if we ask for too much, as ambitious metaphysicians have done, our treasures will melt into thin air, but if we ask for little – lowering the scale of our demands as the chances of their being wholly satisfied look more and more remote – we may go away not altogether empty-handed after all. A little is better than nothing; our foothold will be very precarious, but if we take sufficient care we need never slip; by contracting our claims to an absolute minimum we may be able to obtain a logical guarantee for the little that is left; the results may be humble but at least they will be safe; and that is surely worth any sacrifice. Or, to use another image, the ever-narrowing circle of light may reveal little of interest or importance, but that is more comforting than to be left in total darkness. Yet the truth is that even humility and self-denial cannot help; a claim may be modest, but it is still a claim; and the guarantee we seek, however qualified, is still a guarantee and consequently a logical impossibility. Whatever the psychological causes of this pursuit of security, it leads to fatal consequences, for it leads to the belief that there must be a group of propositions, tested and found indestructible, which forms the minimum gold reserve without which intellectual currency cannot be exchanged. It is one thing to maintain that sometimes we believe, and at other times know; sometimes we doubt legitimately, and sometimes we only think that we doubt, because it is thought philosophically proper or logically possible to do so, when in fact we are as certain (in the sense of 'certain' in which that word is normally used) as it is possible to be in the context in which we should normally say this. It is one thing to say this, which is true, and another to look for, and affect to find, incorrigible propositions, and worse still to maintain that they are indispensable to all descriptive language. For there is no reason to suppose that any empirical proposition is literally incorrigible in the sense that it cannot in principle be false. This kind of guarantee (which Kant made the most interesting of all attempts to obtain) is not to be had; not because nature is hostile and unwilling to yield up her secrets, but because upon examination the notion of such a guarantee turns out to be meaningless. This must surely follow from what has been shown about the delusiveness of the very notion of basic propositions. To say anything significantly about the world we must bring in something other than immediate experience (whatever 'immediate' may mean), namely the past and the future, and absent objects, and other persons, and unrealised possibilities, and general and hypothetical judgements, and so forth. And if these, because we cannot certify them as certain, are cut away, in the end literally nothing will be left. We cannot speak without incurring some risk, at least in theory; the only way of being absolutely safe is to say absolutely nothing; this is the goal towards which the search for 'fundamental' propositions asymptotically tends. Why are we so bent upon retaining these incorrigible propositions? Because we have been told that if these cannot be discovered everything will for ever remain uncertain, and that this is not merely discomfiting but in some way philosophically 'unsatisfactory'. But this is only another case of the fallacy of uttering 'Everything is . . .'; for the word 'uncertain' can only be given interpretation by being contrasted with 'certain', of which we must consequently have had, or be able to imagine, at least one characteristic example, if we are to attach any significance to the word. The fallacy is to suppose that the proposition 'The word "certain" has at least one application' entails the proposition 'What is certain is incorrigible.' And those who are betrayed into supposing that certainty entails incorrigibility will naturally look upon propositions guaranteed as being incorrigible with especial favour, as foundations upon which all else rests. We have returned once again to the privileged class of basic propositions, and to the desire either to translate all other propositions into them or combinations of them, or else to represent them as being poor relations dependent upon the privileged class – and so partly propositional and reputable, partly non-propositional and denizens of some inferior realm; or at the worst altogether non-propositional, to be relegated to some waste-paper basket vaguely defined in pejorative psychological terms.

These three fallacies, interconnected as they obviously are, at any rate psychologically, while they may not be sufficient by themselves to afford a complete explanation of how those fatal twins, the processes of inflation and deflation, pursue their disastrous careers, nevertheless do serve to throw some light upon the major fallacy involved; namely the belief or assumption that all propositions must in principle be either translatable into, or at any rate in some way connected with, the approved type of sentences (which alone fully reflect 'the structure of reality'), or else suffer from defects which must either be explained away or palliated by special logical 'treatment', or, if they prove too recalcitrant, removed with their owners beyond the logical pale.

What moral are we to draw from this? Not, certainly, that no translation at all is possible between types of proposition – if only because successful reductions of this type are a salutary psychological check upon the tendency to inflation and multiplication of entities, and indeed indispensable as a method for precluding certain types of nonsense; nor yet that metaphors should not be used by philosophers in explaining the relations of propositions among themselves as well as their function in speaking about the world. Words mean, not by pinning down bits of reality, but by having a recognised use, i.e. when their users know how and in what situations to use them in order to communicate whatever they may wish to communicate; and for this there are no exhaustive formal rules. But because there is no single criterion of meaning and no single method or set of rules for testing it, it does not follow that there are in principle no criteria at all, no methods and no rules which may apply in differing types of context and situation. But neither, on the other hand, does the fact that many metaphors have proved fatal, or at least misleading, tend to show that all metaphors can or should be eliminated as such, and speech rendered absolutely literal. For the ideal of 'literalness' in this extreme sense is merely another instance of the fallacy of 'basic' sentences, with their false claim to fit 'the facts' precisely and completely, against which my argument has been directed. The development of language is to a large extent the development of metaphors, and to attempt to discriminate between the metaphorical and non-metaphorical use of words, where metaphors are either embedded in normal speech, or a source of genuine illumination, would be absurdly pedantic, and, if pushed to extremes, unrealisable. To translate, reduce, deflate, is philosophically laudable so long as there is a real gain in clarity, simplicity, and the destruction of myths. But where it is obvious that types of proposition or sentence cannot be 'reduced' or 'translated' into one another without torturing the language until what was conveyed idiomatically before can no longer be conveyed so fully or clearly or, at times, at all in the artificial language constructed to conform to some imaginary criterion of a 'logical perfection', such attempts should be exposed as stemming from a false theory of meaning, accompanied by its equally counterfeit metaphysical counterpart – a view of the universe as possessing an 'ultimate structure', as being constructed out of this or that collection or combination of bits and pieces of 'ultimate stuff' which the 'language' is constructed to reproduce. Unless this is realised, logical translation continues to be misused, particularly when attempts are made to force propositions, on pain of degradation or even elimination, to conform to some uniform model, and so to rob them of their most important uses and differences. Of all philosophical obsessions this is almost the most persistent, and has thrown too much dust in the eyes of philosophers in the form of insoluble, because illusory, philosophical problems.

Equality

'EVERY man to count for one and no one to count for more than one.' This formula, much used by utilitarian philosophers, seems to me to form the heart of the doctrine of equality or of equal rights, and has coloured much liberal and democratic thought. Like many familiar phrases of political philosophy it is vague, ambiguous, and has changed in connotation from one thinker and society to another. Nevertheless it appears, more than any other formula, to constitute the irreducible minimum of the ideal of equality. Moreover it is not self-evident in the sense in which many simple empirical propositions seem so; it has not been universally believed; and it is not uniquely connected with any one philosophical system. The notion of each man counting for one and only one does not depend on belief in rights, either natural or positive, either divinely bestowed or adopted by convention. The statement that each man is to count for one may, of course, be conceived as flowing from the recognition of natural rights possessed by all men as such — rights 'inherent' in being a man at all — whether innate, or conferred at birth by a divine act — and so an 'inalienable' element in the 'ultimate structure' of reality. But equally it can be held without any metaphysical views of this kind. Again, it may be regarded as a rule, whether universal or confined to certain defined classes of persons, deriving its validity from a system of rights based on specific legal enactments, or custom, or some other identifiable source of human authority. But again, it need not depend on this. One can perfectly well conceive of a society organised on Benthamite or Hobbesian lines, in which rights did not exist, or played a small part, and in which the principle of 'every man to count for one' was rigorously applied for utilitarian reasons, or because such was the will of the despot, or of the majority, or of the legislator or whoever held sovereignty in a given society. It is doubtless true that the most ardent champions of equality were, in fact, believers in human rights in some sense. Some were theists who believed that all men had immortal souls every one of which possessed infinite value and had claims which consequently must not be set aside in favour of objectives of lower value; some of these in addition believed in absolute

81

standards of justice, divinely sanctioned, from which the doctrine of equality was directly deducible. Others were liberals and democrats, some of them deists or atheists or others ignorant of, or opposed to, the Judaeo-Christian tradition, who believed in the principle of equality *a priori*, as being revealed by natural light or whatever other source or method of knowledge was regarded as being the most certain. This was the foundation of the faith of the framers of the declarations of human rights in the American and the French revolutions; and has indeed been perhaps the strongest single element in egalitarian doctrines from the days of the Gracchi to the socialists and anarchists of modern times. But the connection between 'counting for one' and the doctrines of Christian theology or the French *philosophes,* or this or that view of reason or of nature, is rather more historical and psychological than logical. At any rate it is not one of mutual entailment. For this reason it may be of some use to inquire what this principle will look like if it is detached from its normal historical and psychological setting – whether it possesses any inherent plausibility of its own, and whence it derives its universal and perennial appeal.

I should like to suggest that there is a principle of which the egalitarian formula is a specific application: namely that similar cases call for, i.e. should be accorded, similar treatment. Then, given that there is a class of human beings, it will follow that all members of this class, namely men, should in every respect be treated in a uniform and identical manner, unless there is sufficient reason not to do so.[1] But since more than a finite degree of social and personal uniformity is in practice difficult or impossible to achieve, the principle ordains that the rule should be applied in, at any rate, important respects – those respects in which the type of treatment accorded to each other by human beings makes a great deal of difference to them, affects them deeply, forwards or frustrates their desires or interests in a significant degree. The assumption here seems to be that unless there is some sufficient reason not to do so, it is 'natural' or 'rational' to treat every member of a given class (in this case, men) as you treat any one member of it. To state

[1] In this formulation the principle will cover both of the forms of equal rights to property distinguished by Richard Wollheim ['Equality', *Proceedings of the Aristotelian Society* 56 (1956), 281–301], i.e. both absolute equality of property, and equality conditional upon specific qualifications, say, sufficient means to enable a man to buy it, or legal rights of inheritance, and the like. The notion of 'sufficient reason' can be made to cover almost any type of situation, and is suspect for that very reason.

the principle in this way leaves open crucial issues; thus it may be justly objected that unless some specific sense is given to 'sufficient reason', the principle can be reduced to a trivial tautology (it is reasonable to act in manner *x* save in circumstances *y*, in which it is not rational, and *any* circumstances may be *y*); furthermore that since all entities are members of more than one class – indeed of a theoretically limitless number of classes – *any* kind of behaviour can be safely subsumed under the general rule enjoining equal treatment – since unequal treatment of various members of class A can always be represented as equal treatment of them viewed as members of some other class B, which in extreme circumstances can be so constructed as to contain no more than one actual member; which can reduce this rule to vacuity. There obviously can exist no formal method of avoiding such reductions to absurdity; they can be rebutted only by making clear what reasons are sufficient and why; and which attributes are alone relevant and why; and this will depend on the outlooks and scales of value of different persons, and the purposes of a given association or enterprise, in terms of which alone general principles can retain any degree of significance – whether in theory or practice. In concrete cases we distinguish good reasons from bad, central characteristics from irrelevant ones. Some inequalities (say, those based on birth) are condemned as arbitrary and irrational, others (say, those based on efficiency) are not, which seems to indicate that values other than equality for its own sake affect the ideals even of passionate egalitarians. A part of what we mean by rationality is the art of applying, and combining, reconciling, choosing among general principles in a manner for which complete theoretical explanation (or justification) can never, in principle, be given.

To return to the principle in the form in which it is normally applied: if I have a voice in settling the destinies of my society I think it unfair that all other members of it should not also have a similar voice; if I own property, it is unfair that others (situated in relevant respects as I am) should not do so too, and if I am allowed to leave it to my children in my will it is unfair that others should not have a similar opportunity; if I am permitted to read or write or express my opinion freely it is wrong, unjust, unfair etc. that others should not be permitted to do so too. If someone is not to be allowed to do these things, or have these advantages, then sufficient reasons must be given; but no reason need be given for not withholding them, i.e. for an equal distribution of benefits – for that is 'natural', self-evidently right and just, and needs no justification, since it is in some sense conceived as being self-justified.

A society in which every member holds an equal quantity of property needs no special justification; only a society in which property is unequal needs it. So too with the distribution of other things – power or knowledge, or whatever else can be possessed in different quantities or degrees. I can justify the fact that the commander of an army is to be given more power than his men by the common purposes of the army, or of the society which it is defending – victory, or self-protection – which can best be achieved by this means; I can justify the allocation of more than an equal share of goods to the sick or the old (to secure equality of satisfactions), or to the specially meritorious (to secure a deliberately intended inequality); but for all this I must provide reasons. If I believe in a hierarchical society, I may try to justify the special powers or wealth or position of persons of a certain origin, or of castes or classes or ranks, but for all this I am expected to give reasons – divine authority, a natural order, or the like. The assumption is that equality needs no reasons, only inequality does so; that uniformity, regularity, similarity, symmetry, the functional correlation of certain characteristics with corresponding rights of which Wollheim speaks, need not be specially accounted for, whereas differences, unsystematic behaviour, change in conduct, need explanation and, as a rule, justification. If I have a cake and there are ten persons among whom I wish to divide it, then if I give exactly one tenth to each, this will not, at any rate automatically, call for justification; whereas if I depart from this principle of equal division I am expected to produce a special reason. It is some sense of this, however latent, that makes equality an ideal which has never seemed intrinsically eccentric, even though extreme forms of it may not have been wholly acceptable to either political thinkers or ordinary men throughout recorded human history. There seem to me to be at least two conceptions which are involved in this love of order, each of which Wollheim has touched upon (although not by name or directly). These are the notions (1) of rules, and (2) of equality proper. I should like to say something about each of these.

1 *Rules*

All rules, by definition, entail a measure of equality. In so far as rules are general instructions to act or refrain from acting in certain ways, in specified circumstances, enjoined upon persons of a specified kind, they enjoin uniform behaviour in identical cases. To fall under a rule is *pro tanto* to be assimilated to a single pattern. To enforce a rule is to promote equality of behaviour or treatment. This applies whether the rules take the form of moral principles and laws, or codes of positive law, or the rules of games or of conduct adopted by professional associations, religious organisations, political parties, wherever patterns of behaviour can be codified in a more or less systematic manner. The rule which declares that tall persons are permitted to cast five times as many votes as short ones creates an obvious inequality. Nevertheless, in the framework of this inequality it ensures equality of privilege within each of the two discriminated classes – no tall man may have more votes than any other tall man, and similarly with short men. This is Wollheim's first sense of 'equality', in which, although the commodities or liberties, be they power or property or status, may not be owned in equal quantities or to an equal degree by everyone, yet every member of each class has an equal right to that which has been accorded to the class as a whole. This type of equality derives simply from the conception of rules as such – namely, that they allow of no exceptions. Indeed what is meant by saying that a given rule exists is that it should be fully, i.e. equally fully, obeyed by those who fall under it, and that any inequality in obedience would constitute an exception, i.e. an offence against the rules. In so far as some minimum degree of prevalence of rules is a necessary condition for the existence of human societies (and this seems to be an almost universal, but still empirical, law), and in so far as morality, both personal and political, is largely conceived of in terms of rules, the kind of equality with which obedience to rules is virtually identical is among the deepest needs and convictions of mankind. In this sense equality is coextensive with social morality as such – that is to the degree to which social morality is conceived as a system of coherent, i.e. not internally contradictory (and, according to some moralists, mutually entailing), sets of rules. A plea for equality in this sense is therefore a plea for life in accordance with rules as opposed to other standards, e.g. the *ad hoc* orders of an inspired leader, or arbitrary desires. In this sense, then, to say that inequality is wrong is, in effect, to say that it is wrong to obey no rules in a given situation, or to accept a rule and break it; and a situation in which some men, for no stated reason, and in accordance with no rule, consistently obtain more than other men with the same, or sufficiently similar, relevant characteristics (however this is determined) is then described as being unfair. To provide no reasons for breaking a rule is described as irrational; to give reasons for obeying rules – save in terms of other rules – is regarded as unnecessary: rules are their own justification. In a moral system which consists entirely of rules, and is definable in terms of them, adequate reasons for breaking rule x must take the form of rule y, which in certain circumstances may come into collision with rule x, and, in accordance with rule z, will then cancel or modify it or, at any rate, be allowed to do so. A society which accepts a morality, whether personal or social and political, analysable into sets of rules of varying orders of stringency, some independent of each other, some connected by relations of entailment or mutual exclusion, may then be open to at least three kinds of criticism.

(*a*) I may accept the rules, and complain that too many exceptions are being made without specific rules to back the exceptions. If I merely object to the exceptions as such, I am merely complaining of the infringement of moral or social laws, as such. If the exceptions fulfil the desires of some people to the detriment of the fulfilment of the desires of others – for example where the desires are for some commodity in scarce supply, be it property, or power, or status, or the fruits of civilisation, then if there is no rule governing such distribution (or if there is a rule but exceptions to it are made arbitrarily, i.e. without being deducible from, or justifiable in terms of, other accepted rules) I complain, in addition, of unfairness, i.e. that similar cases are being treated dissimilarly, when the whole essence of the rules is that this should be avoided.

(*b*) I may complain that the rules themselves are bad or iniquitous. This complaint may take several forms. I may complain that a given rule offends against some other rule or principle which seems to me more important or morally superior. A rule consistently favouring the tall as against the short would offend against the rule which I regard as superior, according to which physical characteristics must not be considered in, let us say, the distribution of honours; or against a rule which lays it down that all men, or all Englishmen, or all members of the Aristotelian Society, must be treated as being equal in this regard. Then again someone may say that equal treatment only for members of the Aristotelian Society offends against equal treatment for all Englishmen, or that equal treatment for all Englishmen offends against the principle of equal treatment for all Europeans, or all men. In short, a rule may be condemned as offending against some wider rule to which it is then regarded as forming an irrational exception. Or it may be attacked on the ground that it conflicts with some rule not necessarily wider but merely incompatible with it; in cases of such conflict, egalitarianism seems to entail that any rule which includes under it a larger number of persons or a larger number of types of persons[1] shall always be preferred to rules which ensure identical treatment only for smaller numbers or a smaller number of types; and a society will fail to be egalitarian to the degree to which in the formulation of its rules, or in its system of deciding which rules win in cases of conflict, it is influenced by principles other than those of the intrinsic desirability of identical treatment of the largest possible number of persons or classes of persons; for example if it is bent on the maximisation of happiness, which may well entail gross inequalities.[2] And of course there are many other goals or values which may deflect the course of strict egalitarianism, as, for instance, the desire to encourage the arts and sciences, or a predominant desire to increase the military or economic power of the state, or a passion for the preservation of ancient traditions, or a strong taste for change and variety and new forms of life. All these may or may not breed rules that conflict with the principle that every man is to count for one and only one. This principle will indeed be preserved by the mere existence of rules within each area dominated by the rules themselves; but rules cannot guarantee its extension beyond their own field. For the rules themselves may create inequalities, and the conflict between the rules still greater ones. To say, as we often do of a rule, that it is itself unfair is, in effect, to say that it contradicts some other rule with a wider area of equal treatment – a rule which, if obeyed, will ensure that a larger number of persons (or classes of persons) shall receive similar treatment in specified circumstances. But to say of the

[1] A policy of equal treatment for the largest number of persons may easily conflict with a policy of equal treatment of the largest number of classes of persons. Thus a reformer bent on abolishing discriminatory legislation may find himself faced with a choice between incommensurables, e.g. of emancipating either one large class of 'inferiors', say the poor, or several such classes, say religious or racial minorities, which between them contain fewer members than the single large class. The first policy will give equality to more human beings; the second will abolish a greater number of class distinctions. Since either course can correctly be said to increase equality, and both cannot (for some practical reason) be adopted, the choice of a conscientious egalitarian will depend on the type of equality preferred. As it stands the question before him cannot be answered.

[2] With the exception, I suppose, of those societies in which the desire for equality is itself so much stronger than all other desires that inequality automatically breeds greater misery than any other possible arrangement.

rule that it is bad or iniquitous need not mean this; it need mean only that it is in conflict with some other rule or principle not necessarily itself tending towards greater equality. In case this seems too abstract, let me illustrate: although Bentham's doctrine about each man to count for one was in fact embodied by him in his utilitarian teachings, it seems plain that equality is not itself entailed by utilitarian principles, and might, indeed, on occasion conflict with them. Thus it can be argued that societies organised hierarchically, certain types of medieval society for example, or theocratic societies or even societies founded on slavery, may conceivably offer their members a greater degree of happiness (however this is calculated) than societies in which there is a greater degree of social or economic equality. When Montesquieu or Rousseau, for example, declare that the objection to slavery is not that it makes men unhappy – for it may not: the slaves may prefer to remain slaves – but that it is slavery, that men have no right to enslave other men, that it is unworthy of human beings to create such forms of life, they are pleading for equality for equality's sake. They are in effect saying that any society which has rules or laws enjoining or permitting slavery, even though its members may be happier than if they had been free, and even though Aristotle may be right and men exist whose faculties are realised best in slavery, is yet a society to be condemned, not for breaking the rules under which it lives, but for obeying the wrong kind of rules, pursuing the wrong kind of values. And this implies that equality, that is to say, the rule that each man is to count for one and for no more than one, whether in the distribution of property or in the number of votes he has in the sovereign assembly, or in the opportunities for education or pleasure, or in whatever respect, is an end in itself, in possible conflict with other ends, but higher than they and, in cases of conflict, to be preferred.

(c) Finally, someone may attack a society not indeed for breaking the rules that it affects to respect; nor yet for living by rules that are bad, or in conflict with some other ends or ideals which the critic regards as of greater moral authority; but on the ground that it lives by rules at all, that it is rule-ridden. And if it is pointed out to him that a certain minimum of rules is an empirical necessity for the preservation of any degree of human organisation, then he may retreat to the position that the rules in use go far beyond this minimum, and that a morality not compounded out of rules, but consisting of the pursuit of some ideal in a spontaneous and imaginative way, analogous to the creative activity of a painter or a composer, or to even less disciplined forms of self-expression, where both the use and recognition of rules is at a minimum, is to be preferred. It is salutary to be reminded that moral and political outlooks are not coextensive with systems of moral or political rules. The romantic attack upon the moral systems both of rationalists and empiricists at times took precisely this form of denunciation of the propositions and imperatives of the classical ethical systems, not because they were mistaken or deleterious, but because they were general. The romantic philosophers, particularly in Germany,[1] assailed their predecessors for imposing rules, amalgamating cases, whether individual characters or moral situations or moral actions, that were necessarily unique and incommensurable under the umbrella of some universal formula. They attacked all those who seemed to them bent on forcing the teeming multiplicity and variety of human activity into a Procrustean bed of symmetrical sets of moral rules which, precisely because they were rules, tended to represent differences as being relatively unimportant, and similarities as being alone relevant; and especially those who, so it was maintained, by following a false analogy with the natural sciences ignored or misrepresented vital individual differences, in virtue of which alone things and persons possessed their unique value, and did this in order to achieve an egalitarian society, dominated by rules – a society directed against the existence of all those elements which the romantics regarded as alone worth preserving.

All three types of attack upon a given social or political order are, to say the least, relevant to the belief in equality. Let me recapitulate them: they take the form of saying

(*a*) that rules are broken for no sufficient reason; or
(*b*) that the rules are themselves bad or iniquitous or otherwise inadequate; or
(*c*) that the rules are deplorable simply because they are rules.

Of these (*a*) represents the most direct demand for equality, for any protest against exceptions because they are exceptions is a genuine plea for equality; (*b*) springs from a demand for equality only if the rules are attacked on the ground that they are in conflict with other rules aimed at producing a greater degree of general equality; (*c*) is a direct attack upon the ideal of social equality as such. It is clear that this ideal is not solely the equality which all rules entail as such (even though it may

---

[1] This, or something like it, was also advocated by Bergson in one of his last works, *The Two Sources of Morality and Religion* (London, 1935).

derive much force from an intimate connection with moral systems to which universality, order, rules, laws etc. are central), since otherwise rules could not themselves be criticised as leading to inequality, as we have seen that they can be. What then is this ideal?

II

2 *Equality proper*

In its simplest form the ideal of complete social equality embodies the wish that everything and everybody should be as similar as possible to everything and everybody else. It may serve to make this concept clearer if we try to conceive of some of the characteristics of a world in which no type of egalitarian would have anything to complain of. I doubt whether anyone has ever seriously desired to bring such a society into being, or even supposed such a society to be capable of being created. Nevertheless, it seems to me that the demands for human equality which have been expressed both by philosophers and by men of action who have advocated or attempted the reform of society can best be represented as modifications of this absolute and perhaps absurd ideal. In the ideal egalitarian society, inequality – and this must ultimately mean dissimilarity – would be reduced to a minimum. The greatest single cause of complaint has been disparity in the possession, or enjoyment, of characteristics or commodities which have been strongly desired by men at most times – such as property, political or social power, status, opportunities for the development of faculties or the obtaining of experiences, social and personal liberties and privileges of all kinds. And the attack has taken the form of maintaining that a society in which some men are much richer or stronger or freer than others; in which some men possess the power of acquiring what they want and of preventing others from acquiring these same things or other things which they in turn want; or in which some men are paid homage and deferred to and permitted to live as they wish in ways and degrees which set them off from other men; all these are societies which offend either against the principle of natural rights, which according to those who hold this principle belong to all men as such; or against some rational principles whereby these differences may indeed be justified, but only by the provision of sufficient reasons for instituting or maintaining them. Disputes occur about what these rights are; or what reasons are sufficient or good; and whether such characteristics as differences of birth or of colour or of religion of or wealth are true sources of unequal rights, or furnish good reasons for instituting political or social or other similar inequalities. There is, of course, a significant difference between these two ways of approach. Those who believe in natural rights differ mainly in establishing what these rights are, how their existence can be verified, whether all of them belong to all men, or only some to all, or only some to some; and whether equality is desirable in fields other than those covered by the claims created by the existence of natural rights. The other school – those who appeal to reason (though historically their views have overlapped with and become inextricably mingled with those of the believers in natural rights) – if they are to be consistent, must believe that equality should stretch over the entire field of human relations, and be modified only when there is sufficient reason to do so. Then disagreement may arise as to what constitutes a sufficient reason, and how great a modification a given reason justifies, and so forth. The first school, if it is consistent, will not object to inequalities, providing these do not infringe natural rights. But the second must protest against any inequality, unless a sufficient reason for it is produced. It is the latter, therefore, who go further, and are nearer to the extreme ideal which I should now like briefly to mention. Apart from the crucial question of what are and what are not sufficient reasons in such cases, it seems plain that inequalities of wealth or power are merely some among the possible inequalities which can excite opposition; they tend to be so prominent because they matter – affect human lives – more deeply, as things are, than other forms of inequality. But this is not always necessarily so. Even the most convinced social egalitarian does not normally object to the authority wielded by, let us say, the conductor of an orchestra. Yet there is no obvious reason why he should not. And there have been occasions – few and far between – when this has actually happened. Those who maintain that equality is the paramount good may not wish to be fobbed off with the explanation that the purpose of orchestral playing will not be served if every player is allowed equal authority with the conductor in deciding what is to be done. Inequality in the organisation of an orchestra there patently is; the reason for it is the purpose of orchestral playing – the production of certain sounds in certain ways which cannot, in fact, be achieved without a measure of discipline which itself entails some degree of inequality in the distribution of authority. But a fanatical egalitarian could maintain that the inequality of the players in relation to the conductor is a greater evil than a poor performance of a symphonic work, and that it is better that no symphonic music be played at all if a conductorless orchestra is not feasible, than that such an institution should be allowed to offend against the principle of equality. To be more serious, the unequal distribution of natural gifts is a well-known obstacle to economic equality: in societies where there is a high degree of equality of economic opportunity, the strong and able and ambitious and cunning are likely to acquire more wealth or more power than those who lack these qualities. The fanatical egalitarian will look on this with horror; and because differences of natural talent will always tend towards the creation of inequalities, if only of prestige or influence, he will consequently wish – if equality is the paramount goal – to root out the evil at the source. He will tend to wish so to condition human beings that the highest degree of equality of natural properties is achieved, the greatest degree of mental and physical, that is to say total, uniformity – which alone will effectively preserve society, as far as possible, from the growth of inequalities of whatever kind. Only in a society where the greatest degree of similarity between the members occurs – where physical characteristics, mental endowment, emotional disposition, and conduct are as uniform as possible – where people differ as little as possible from each other in any respect whatever, will true equality be attainable. Only in such a society will it be possible to reduce to a minimum those differences of treatment, or of power, or of position, or of natural or acquired characteristics, that are liable to lead people to complain that they have not what others have, and to ask for reasons why this should be so. It may be that the creation of so uniform a society, whether or not it is intrinsically desirable, may not, in fact, be feasible. It may also be that even the attempt to approach it as closely as is humanly possible requires a degree of radical reorganisation which cannot be carried out without a highly centralised and despotic authority – itself the cause of the maximum of inequality. Some convinced egalitarians have, as everyone knows, in practice accepted this as unavoidable, and have defended the institution of violent inequalities and the total suppression of many normal human claims as a necessary prerequisite for the creation of an ultimate equality. The moral and practical value of this is not relevant to the issue before us. What seems worth emphasising is that so long as there are differences between men, some degree of inequality may occur; and that there is no kind of inequality against which, in principle, a pure egalitarian may not be moved to protest, simply on the ground that he sees no reason for tolerating it, no argument which seems to him more powerful than the argument for equality itself – equality which he regards not merely as an end in itself, but as *the* end, the principal goal of human life. I do not suppose that extreme equality of this type – the maximum similarity of a body of all but indiscernible human beings – has ever been consciously put forward as an ideal by any serious thinker. But if we ask what kinds of equality have in fact been demanded, we shall see, I think, that they are specific modifications of this absolute ideal, and that it therefore possesses the central importance of an ideal limit or idealised model at the heart of all egalitarian thought.

To examine some of these modifications. There are those who believe that natural human characteristics either cannot or should not be altered and that all that is necessary is equality of political and juridical rights. Provided that there exists equality before the law, such normal democratic principles as that of one man one vote, some form of government arrived at by consent (actual or understood) between the members of the society, or at any rate the majority of them, and, finally, a certain minimum of liberties – commonly called civil liberties – deemed necessary in order to enable men freely to exercise the legal and political rights entailed by this degree of equality, then, according to this view, no interference in other regions of activity (say, the economic) should be permitted. This is a common liberal doctrine of the last century. If it is complained that in a society where a large degree of political and legal equality is ensured, the strong and the clever and the ambitious may succeed in enriching themselves, or acquiring political power, 'at the expense of' – that is to say, in such a way as to keep these goods from – other members of the society, and that this leads to patent inequalities, liberals of this school reply that this is the price for ensuring political and legal equality, and that the only method of preventing economic or social inequalities is by reducing the degree of political liberty or legal equality between men. This amounts to an admission that we must choose one of several ways of treating men as counting for only one; that they can be 'counted for one' only in some respects, but not in others. For we are told, with considerable empirical evidence, that to count men for one and only one in every respect whatever is impracticable, that the full degree of, let us say, legal and political equality often results in economic and other forms of inequality, given the different endowments of men, and that only in an absolutely uniform, robot-like society, which no one wants, can this be effectively prevented. Those who believe this commonly maintain that the only inequality which should be avoided is an inequality based on characteristics which the individual cannot alter – unequal treatment based, for instance, on birth, or colour, which human beings cannot alter at will. Given that all human beings start off with equal rights to acquire and hold property, to associate with each other in whatever ways they wish, to say whatever they will, and all the other traditional objectives of liberalism, and with no special rights or privileges attached to birth, colour and other physically unalterable characteristics, then even though some human beings, by skill or luck or natural endowment, do manage to acquire property or power or ascendancy which enables them to control the lives of others, or to acquire objects which the others are not in a position to acquire, then, since there is nothing in the constitution of the society that actually forbids such acquisitiveness, the principle of equality has not been infringed. This is a pure form of *laissez-faire* society which its proponents freely admit may lead to inequalities, but defend upon the ground that it gives an equal opportunity to all, a career genuinely open to all the talents – whereas any attempt to secure a greater degree of ultimate equality can only be obtained by interfering with this initial equalisation of opportunity for all. In effect this is, of course, tantamount to a plea for liberty at the expense of total equality; for it is only pure anarchists who believe that the maximum degree of liberty is wholly compatible with the maximum degree of equality in all important respects, and are called mistaken or Utopian to the degree to which this proposition has in fact been falsified by experience. The distinction between general rights and special rights of which H. L. A. Hart has spoken[1] and to which Wollheim refers, seems to be relevant to this kind of belief. One could easily conceive of a society in which all special rights (rights based on contract or on paternity, for example) will be instances of general rights – particular cases of them – because in such a society, at least in theory, any member can enter into a contract, any member can be a father, any member can enrich himself. There are no rights which belong to individuals in virtue of some characteristics – birth or blood or colour – which other members cannot in principle possess. In this schema certain types of traditional inequality have certainly been ruled out. But to maintain that this is the kind of society that true egalitarians desire would be disingenuous; for if one asks why some types of equality are protected in this case, initial equality whereby all men start off theoretically equal, while other types of equality are not protected, e.g. economic or social equality – equality in respect of whatever men can acquire by their own efforts – the answer is that the

[1] H. L. A. Hart, 'Are there any natural rights?', *Philosophical Review* 64 (1955), 175–91.

criterion of equality has plainly been influenced by something other than the mere desire for equality as such, namely desire for liberty or the full development of human resources, or the belief that men deserve to be as rich or as powerful or as famous as they can make themselves – beliefs which are not connected with the desire for equality at all.

It is at this point that it becomes clear that in considering what kind of society is desirable, or what are 'sufficient reasons' for either demanding equality or, on the contrary, modifying it or infringing it in specific cases, ideals other than equality conspicuously play a vital role.

This is clearly noticeable even in the writings of the most impassioned champions of the widest possible equality. Almost every argument favourable to equality, and in particular the assumption that everything that is scarce should be distributed as equally as possible unless there is strong reason against it, is to be found in the writings of Condorcet. The doctrine of equality in the Declaration of the Rights of Man and Citizen which heralded the French Revolution owes at least as much to him as it does to Rousseau or other thinkers. Yet even Condorcet contemplates the necessity for the government of human beings by men of enlightenment, above all by experts, men versed in the new, not yet created sciences of the behaviour of man – sociology, anthropology and psychology – who alone can create an organisation in which the greatest number of the desires of rational men will not be frustrated, as they have been hitherto, by prejudice, superstition, stupidity and vice. Yet this élite is plainly to have greater powers than those whom they are to govern disinterestedly. And the reason for this is not merely that, without this, true equality cannot be achieved for the majority of men, but also that certain other ends must be striven for, such as happiness, virtue, justice, progress in the arts and sciences, the satisfaction of various moral and spiritual wants, of which equality, of whatever kind, is only one. Condorcet does not himself seem to be troubled by the problem of whether the quest for equality will clash with the need to seek these other ends, for, in common with many thinkers of his day, he took it for granted all too easily that all good things were certainly compatible, and indeed interlocked, with each other. We need not go into the reasons for this peculiar belief, which has dominated much western thought at all times. The principal assumptions which underlie it are, firstly, the view that since political and moral questions are factual in character, they can each be answered by one true proposition and one only (otherwise they are not genuine questions), and secondly, that no true propositions can be inconsistent with one another; from this it must follow that all the propositions which describe what should be done must at the very least be compatible with one another; and in the perfect harmony which nature is thought to be, not merely compatible, but mutually entailing and entailed – for that defines a system, and nature is known *a priori* to be such a – indeed *the* – harmonious system.

Whether or not this is the correct explanation of this central assumption, Condorcet did not allow the possibility of a collision between various human ends. It was left to others to emphasise the fact that in life as normally lived the ideals of one society and culture clash with those of another, and at times come into conflict within the same society and, often enough, within the moral experience of a single individual; that such conflicts cannot always, even in principle, be wholly resolved; that this can be traced to empirical causes, and does not entail either such theological doctrines as those of original sin, or the relevant beliefs of Buddhist doctrines, nor yet such pessimistic views of human character as those of Hobbes or Schopenhauer, or the ideologies of modern irrationalism. It follows that when the pursuit of equality comes into conflict with other human aims, be they what they may – such as the desire for happiness or pleasure, or for justice or virtue, or colour and variety in a society for their own sake, or for liberty of choice as an end in itself, or for the fuller development of all human faculties – it is only the most fanatical egalitarian that will demand that such conflicts invariably be decided in favour of equality alone, with relative disregard of the other 'values' concerned.

III

Equality is one value among many: the degree to which it is compatible with other ends depends on the concrete situation, and cannot be deduced from general laws of any kind; it is neither more nor less rational than any other ultimate principle; indeed it is difficult to see what is meant by considering it either rational or non-rational.

Yet the principle that every man shall count for one and no more than one demands a little more consideration before we finally abandon it as one of the ends pursued by men, needing neither explanation nor justification, being itself that which explains other rules or ethical principles. It seems, as we have seen above, intimately bound up with the belief in general rules of conduct. This belief may rest upon religious or metaphysical or utilitarian grounds, or derive from the love of order or system as such. However that may be, it often takes the form of a demand for fairness. The notions of equality and fairness are closely bound up: if as a result of breaking a rule a man derives benefits which he can obtain only so long as other men do not break but keep the rule, then no matter what other needs are being served by such a breach, the result is an offence against a principle best described as that of fairness, which is a form of desire for equality for its own sake. If I enter a bus and do not pay for my ticket, and conceal this fact from the conductor and the other passengers, and give the sum withheld to a pauper whose situation is thereby improved materially, it may be argued that at any rate from a utilitarian point of view I have done what is right. The bus company will not know of its loss; nor would so small a loss noticeably decrease 'its' happiness; I possess a strong will and shall not fall into bad habits; the conductor has not noticed that he was not paid, and will not even so much as suffer from a sense of failure to carry out his duties; the passengers in their ignorance will not be led into temptation and demoralisation, nor will there ensue any weakening of confidence between the persons concerned in the transaction, leading in the end to the discontinuance of the bus service. The general sum of happiness – in this case via that of the subsidised pauper – will surely have gone up to a greater degree than if I had paid my fare to the bus conductor. Nevertheless, quite apart from the morally relevant fact that, having entered into a quasi-contractual obligation to pay, I have broken my promise, my act would be condemned as unfair, for it would rightly be maintained that I can only gain advantage (or the pauper can only gain advantage) so long as the other passengers continue to behave as they did before – since if my act were generally followed no one would pay, and the buses would stop running. So long as my advantage directly depends on the fact that others continue to obey the rule which applies to me as much as to them, so that I alone profit by the exception which I have made in my own favour, such a relaxation of the rule for my benefit would be rightly stigmatised as unfair (as well as dishonest); and although critical situations can be easily imagined in which it would be morally better that I should act in this way and break my contract, or cheat, yet it is clear that a person of normal moral sensitiveness would cheat in this manner only with considerable qualms – qualms derived not merely from the fact that he has broken a contract, but from the sense of the unfairness of what he was doing. Indeed liability to such qualms is among the very criteria of what we call moral sensitiveness. If, despite them, a man resolved to commit such an act, his moral justification would necessarily take the form of invoking, and attempting

97

to balance the claims of, ends or values other than those of equality. He would be drawn in one direction by such considerations as the sanctity of promises; the social need to keep one's word and preserve the rule of law and the social order; the intrinsic desirability of avoiding unfairness; and so on. These factors he would have to weigh against such others as the desirability of increasing happiness (in this case of the pauper) or of avoiding the creation of misery; the claims, say, of scientific curiosity; the desire to follow some romantic impulse or vision of life, and so on. And the same kind of considerations will apply when exceptions are made to rules for 'good' or 'sufficient' reasons. The goodness of the reasons will depend upon the degree of value or importance attached to the purposes or motives adduced in justifying the exceptions, and these will vary as the moral convictions – the general outlooks – of different individuals or societies vary. I may consider it right to reward ability and achievement, and not, for example, honesty and kindness when they are accompanied by stupidity or ineptitude or failure. But others may well think this wrong, and the opposite morally right. I may think it right to reward the bearers of celebrated names or the descendants of famous families as such; or to deny certain rights to Negroes which I grant freely to Englishmen; and may try to defend this policy by maintaining that a society in which this is the normal practice seems to me intrinsically better, or more stable, or to accord more closely with some pattern sanctioned by my religion, or my metaphysical beliefs about the structure of the universe, or the laws of history; whereas you will reject a society dedicated to such practices as iniquitous because, let us assume, you reject my religion, or my metaphysics; or because you believe me to be interpreting them falsely, or think that a society constructed on such principles is intrinsically bad, or politically precarious; or simply because you believe so passionately in equality for its own sake that you are not deterred by the realisation that the consequences which I (and perhaps you too) wish to avert may well be brought about by opposing my policies. There are many ways in which such basic disagreements can manifest themselves: one man or sect or political party may desire equality in one sphere of life, say in social or in legal relationships or legal status, and ignore the economic consequences; another may regard economic relationships as being supremely important, and be prepared to tolerate lack of social or legal equality for the sake of a given economic structure. Some may regard exceptions made in favour of specific gifts or genius as justifiable by social results. Others may regard this as unfair, but, in their turn, believe in some natural social hierarchy, like Burke, and demand full equality of treatment upon each rung of the ladder – the only 'true' equality – but bitterly oppose as being contrary to the natural order any attempt to deny the existence or relevance of such rungs or hierarchies, with its accompaniment of demands for equal treatment for all.[1] Consequently when, as often happens, a man admits that a law is administered fairly – that is to say with due regard to the principle of equality – but complains that the law itself is bad or iniquitous, we cannot always be clear about what is meant. The critic may wish to say that the more fairly the law in question is administered, the more this frustrates a principle of wider equality in which he himself believes, as when a law based upon the principle of discrimination between coloured and white men is administered fairly, i.e. with scrupulous regard to equal treatment within each category, but is thereby itself the cause of inequality between coloured and white men. But the critic may have other reasons for complaint. He may attack this law because it offends against some value other than equality – because it promotes misery, because it frustrates talent, because it makes for social instability, because it insists upon equality in what the attacker thinks unimportant matters, but ignores equality in what he regards as more important aspects of human life (the scale of importance being decided in terms of values other than equality itself); because it ignores the claims of a religion; because it fulfils the claims of religion; because it is obscure or vague or too difficult to obey; and for an infinity of other possible reasons – very commonly because, as in the instance given above, it permits one kind of equality at the expense of another, which can be a matter of fine nuance. In Wollheim's very ingenious example, where all the members of a community have equal rights and one vote per head, and each votes for some end different from those of the others, but two members by constantly voting in the same way are enabled theoretically to overrule all the others, what we object to is not the inequality of such a system, for in legal and even in political terms complete equality is clearly ensured. The unfairness of which Wollheim speaks is caused by our recognition that in this situation too great a majority of the voters find themselves permanently frustrated; we desire to see some degree of equality not only of choices but of satisfactions,

---

[1] Or, like Plato and Aristotle, insist only on the natural hierarchy and appropriate differences of treatment at each level, without apparently caring whether there is social or economic equality between inhabitants of the same level, implying clearly that within each class unbridled competition can take place. Classical thought seems to be deeply and 'naturally' inegalitarian.

and would regard it as 'fairer' if some system of chance, e.g. lot, were adopted, which by equalising the chances of success, would prevent at any rate this type of systematic dissatisfaction. We should regard a system in which each person were permitted to have 'his day' as fairer still. This is a typical clash between two systems incompatible in practice, each of which can claim to promote equality; one in the matter of the machinery of self-government, the other in the matter of the distribution of rewards. Similarly there is a conflict between those for whom equality means non-discrimination in fields of human activity deemed important (however these are identified) on the basis of unalterable characteristics, e.g. origins or physical characteristics and the like, and those who reject this as an inadequate criterion and desire equality of treatment to remain unaffected even by such 'alterable' attributes as religious or political views, personal habits and the like. We seem to choose as we choose because one solution seems to us to embody a blend of satisfaction of claims and desires (or to contain or omit other factors) which we prefer as a total pattern to the blend provided by the other solution. Indeed the intervention of considerations of equity in the rigorous workings of some deductive legal system are due to a desire for justice that we are not always able to analyse too closely, into which the principle of 'every man to count for one' does indeed enter, but without any clear understanding whether he is to count for one in the sphere of legislative rights, or of responsibility for action, or in the receipt of benefits, or in other respects, between any of which conflict all too easily occurs. And, of course, even in matters of equity the 'counting for one' principle is, as often as not, modified by other ends and beliefs, in whatever combination they occur in a given culture or ethical system or within the outlook of an individual thinker.

Finally, those must not be forgotten who, as was said above, object to all rules as such and desire a society, whether this is practicable or not, governed in an unsystematic manner by the will of an inspired leader, or by the unpredictable movement of the Volksgeist, or the 'spirit' of a race, a party, a church. This amounts to rejection of rules, and of equality as an end valuable in itself, and it is as well to recognise that this attitude is not as rare or as ineffective as liberal and socialist thinkers have sometimes assumed. In its conflicts with the traditional western principles of equality or justice or natural rights, or that minimum of civil liberties which is required to protect human beings from degradation and exploitation, romantic irrationalism has at times won easily enough. I cite this only as a warning against the thesis that the commandment to treat all men alike in like situations needs no independent argument to support it, and that the proper criteria for what constitutes likeness cannot be doubted or conflict with each other, but are something taken for granted by reasonable men, a form of the working of natural reason which needs no justification, but is as self-evident as the principle of identity or that red is different from green. This is far from being so; and the vicissitudes of liberal principles in the last, and especially this, century, seem partly due to the unwarranted assumption on the part of their defenders that those who reject these principles only do so through ignorance or intellectual indolence or mental perversity or blindness.[1] Belief in equality – fairness – the view that unless there is a reason for it, recognised as sufficient by some identifiable criterion, one man should not be preferred to another, is a deep-rooted principle in human thought. It has been assimilated into many systems, those of the utilitarians and the theories of natural right, as well as various religious doctrines, but can be isolated from them, and has entered them less by way of logical connection, than by psychological affinity or because those who believed in these utilitarian or religious or metaphysical doctrines also in fact – perhaps from a craving for symmetry and unity that is at the root of all these views – believed in equality for its own sake, and therefore considered any society which did not make sufficient room for this principle to be to that degree worth less than

[1] As, for instance, by Locke, when in *The Second Treatise of Government* (chapter 2, section 4) he says there is 'nothing more evident, than that Creatures of the same species and rank promiscuously born to all the same advantages of Nature, and the use of the same faculties, should also be equal one amongst another'. This is the equality that 'the Judicious *Hooker*' is then praised for regarding as 'evident in it self, and beyond all question'. This, of course, is the pure doctrine of Natural Law, which Locke himself questioned (in the same year [1690]) in the *Essay* (book 2, chapter 2, section 4) where he tells us that '*there cannot any one moral rule be proposed whereof a man may not justly demand a reason*' and contrasts 'that most unshaken rule of morality and foundation of all social virtue, "That one should do as he would be done unto" ', which can 'without any absurdity' be questioned and 'a reason why?' demanded – with such genuinely senseless questions as '*why* "it is impossible for the same thing to be and not to be" '. Locke's hesitations and confusions mark the beginning of the breakdown of the notion that at least some moral or political principles are as self-evident as those of logic or that 'red is different from blue'. An excellent discussion of this and related topics is to be found in Morton White's article on 'Original Sin, Natural Law, and Politics', *Partisan Review* 23 (1956), 218–36.

one that did. In its extreme form egalitarianism requires the minimisation of all differences between men, the obliteration of the maximum number of distinctions, the greatest possible degree of assimilation and uniformity to a single pattern. For all differences are capable of leading to irregularities of treatment. If this ideal is on the whole rejected in actual political doctrines, this seems mainly due to the fact that it conflicts with other ideals with which it cannot be wholly reconciled; indeed most ethical and political views are forms of less or more uneasy compromise between principles which in their extreme form cannot coexist.

Equality is one of the oldest and deepest elements in liberal thought, and is neither more nor less 'natural' or 'rational' than any other constituent in them. Like all human ends it cannot itself be defended or justified, for it is itself that which justifies other acts – means taken towards its realisation. Many policies and views of life, themselves not particularly wedded to the ideal of equality, have been surreptitiously smuggled in under its cover, sometimes, as Wollheim suggests, with a certain measure of disingenuousness or hypocrisy. To isolate the pure ore of egalitarianism proper from those alloys which the admixture of other attitudes and ideals has at various times generated is a task for the historian of ideas, and lies outside the purpose of this paper.

The Concept of Scientific History

HISTORY, according to Aristotle, is an account of what individual human beings have done and suffered. In a still wider sense, history is what historians do. Is history then a natural science, as, let us say, physics or biology or psychology are sciences? And if not, should it seek to be one? And if it fails to be one, what prevents it? Is this due to human error or impotence, or to the nature of the subject, or does the very problem rest on a confusion between the concept of history and that of natural science? These have been questions that have occupied the minds of both philosophers and philosophically minded historians at least since the beginning of the nineteenth century, when men became self-conscious about the purpose and logic of their intellectual activities. But two centuries before that, Descartes had already denied to history any claim to be a serious study. Those who accepted the validity of the Cartesian criterion of what constitutes rational method could (and did) ask how they could find the clear and simple elements of which historical judgements were composed, and into which they could be analysed: where were the definitions, the logical transformation rules, the rules of inference, the rigorously deduced conclusions? While the accumulation of this confused amalgam of memories and travellers' tales, fables and chroniclers' stories, moral reflections and gossip, might be a harmless pastime, it was beneath the dignity of serious men seeking what alone is worth seeking – the discovery of the truth in accordance with principles and rules which alone guarantee scientific validity.

Ever since this doctrine of what was and what was not a science was enunciated, those who have thought about the nature of historical studies have laboured under the stigma of the Cartesian condemnation. Some have tried to show that history could be made respectable by being assimilated to one of the natural sciences, whose overwhelming success and prestige in the seventeenth and eighteenth centuries held out promise of rich fruit wherever their methods were applicable; others declared that history was indeed a science, but a science in some different sense, with its own methods and canons, no less exacting, perhaps, than those of the sciences of nature, but resting on foundations different from them; there were those who defiantly declared that history was indeed subjective, impressionistic, incapable of being made rigorous, a branch of literature, or an embodiment of a personal vision – or that of a class, a church, a nation – a form of self-expression which was, indeed, its pride and justification: it laid no claim to universal and eternal objectivity and preferred to be judged as an interpretation of the past in terms of the demands of the present, or a philosophy of life, not as a science. Still others have tried to draw distinctions between sociology, which was a true science, and history, which was an art or, perhaps, something altogether *sui generis*, neither a science nor an art, but a discipline with its own structure and purposes, misunderstood by those who tried to draw false analogies between it and other intellectual activities.

In any case, the logic of historical thought and the validity of its credentials are issues that do not preoccupy the minds of the leading logicians of our day. The reasons for this are not far to seek. Nevertheless it remains surprising that philosophers pay more attention to the logic of such natural sciences as mathematics and physics, which comparatively few of them know well at first hand, and neglect that of history and the other humane studies, with which in the course of their normal education they tend to be more familiar.

Be that as it may, it is not difficult to see why there has been a strong desire to regard history as a natural science. History purports to deal with facts. The most successful method of identifying, discovering and inferring facts is that of the natural sciences. This is the only region of human experience, at any rate in modern times, in which progress has indubitably been made. It is natural to wish to apply methods successful and authoritative in one sphere to another, where there is far less agreement among specialists. The whole trend of modern empiricism has tended towards such a view. History is an account of what men have done and of what has happened to them. Man is largely, some would say wholly, a three-dimensional object in space and time, subject to natural laws: his bodily wants can be studied empirically as those of other animals. Basic human needs for, say, food or shelter or procreation, and his other biological or physiological requirements, do not seem to have altered greatly through the millennia, and the laws of the interplay of these needs with one another and with the human environment can all in principle be studied by the methods of the biological and, perhaps, psychological sciences. This applies particularly to the results of man's collective activities, unintended by the agent, which, as the Historical

School has emphasised since the days of Bossuet and Vico, play a decisive part in influencing his life, and which can surely be explained in purely mechanistic terms as fields of force or causal or functional correlations of human action and other natural processes. If only we could find a series of natural laws connecting at one end the biological and physiological states and processes of human beings with, at the other, the equally observable patterns of their conduct – their social activities in the wider sense – and so establish a coherent system of regularities, deducible from a comparatively small number of general laws (as Newton, it is held, had so triumphantly done in physics), we should have in our hands a science of human behaviour. Then we could perhaps afford to ignore, or at least treat as secondary, such intermediate phenomena as feelings, thoughts, volitions, of which men's lives seem to themselves to be largely composed, but which do not lend themselves easily to exact measurement. If these data could be regarded as by-products of other, scientifically observable and measurable, processes, then we could predict the publicly observable behaviour of men (what more can a science ask for?) without taking the vaguer and more elusive data of introspection much into account. This would constitute the natural sciences of psychology and sociology, predicted by the materialists of the French Enlightenment, particularly Condillac and Condorcet and their nineteenth-century followers – Comte, Buckle, Spencer, Taine, and many a modern behaviourist, positivist and 'physicalist' since their day.

What kind of science would history constitute? The traditional division of the sciences is into the inductive and the deductive. Unless one claimed acquaintance with *a priori* propositions or rules, derived not from observation but from knowledge, based on intuition or revelation, of the laws governing the behaviour of men and of their goals, or of the specific purposes of their creator – and few historians since the Middle Ages have openly professed to possess such knowledge – this science could not be wholly deductive. But is it then inductive? It is difficult or impossible to conduct large-scale experiments on human beings, and knowledge must therefore largely rest on observation. However, this disability has not prevented astronomy or geology from becoming flourishing sciences, and the mechanists of the eighteenth century confidently looked forward to a time when the application of the methods of the mathematical sciences to human affairs would explode such myths as those of revealed truths, the inner light, a personal deity, an immaterial soul, freedom of the will, and so forth; and so solve all social problems by means of a scientific sociology as clear, exact, and capable of predicting future behaviour as, to use Condorcet's phrase, the sciences that study the societies of bees or beavers. In the nineteenth century this claim came to be regarded as too sweeping and too extravagant. It became clear that the methods and concepts of the mechanists were not adequate for dealing with growth and change; the adoption of more complex vitalistic or evolutionary categories and models served to demarcate the procedures of the biological from those of the purely physical sciences; the former seemed clearly more appropriate to the behaviour and development of human beings. In the twentieth century psychology has begun to assume the role that biology had played in the previous century, and its methods and discoveries with regard both to individuals and to groups have in their turn transformed our approach to history.

Why should history have had so long to wait to become a science? Buckle, who believed in the science of history more passionately, perhaps, than any man who ever lived, explained this very simply by the fact that historians were 'inferior in mental power' to the mathematicians and physicists and chemists. He declared that those sciences advanced fastest which in the first instance attracted the attention of the cleverest men, and their successes naturally in their turn attracted other able heads into their services. In other words, if men as gifted as Galileo or Newton, or even Laplace or Faraday, had devoted themselves to dealing with the disordered mass of truth and falsehood that went by the name of history, they could soon have set it to rights and made a firmly built, clear, and fertile natural science of it.[1] This was a promise held out by those who were, very understandably, hypnotised

[1] 'In regard to nature, events apparently the most irregular and capricious have been explained, and have been shown to be in accordance with certain fixed and universal laws. This has been done because men of ability, and, above all, men of patient, untiring thought, have studied natural events with the view of discovering their regularity: and if human events were subjected to a similar treatment, we have every right to expect similar results . . . Whoever is at all acquainted with what has been done during the last two centuries, must be aware that every generation demonstrates some events to be regular and predictable, which the preceding generation had declared to be irregular and unpredictable: so that the marked tendency of advancing civilisation is to strengthen our belief in the universality of order, of method, and of law. This being the case, it follows that if any facts, or class of facts, have not yet been reduced to order, we, so far from pronouncing them to be irreducible, should

by the magnificent progress of the natural sciences of their day. Intelligent and sceptical thinkers like Taine and Renan in France, not to speak of really passionate positivists like Comte, and, in some of their writings, Engels and Plekhanov, profoundly believed in this prospect. Their hopes have scarcely been fulfilled. It may be profitable to ask why this is so.

Before an answer to this question is attempted, two further sources of the belief that history can, at least in principle, be transformed into a natural science may be noted. The first is perhaps conveyed best by the metaphors that, at any rate since the nineteenth century, all educated men have tended to use. When we speak of rational as opposed to Utopian policies, we tend to say of the latter that they ignore, or are defeated by, the 'inexorable logic of the (historical) facts' or the 'wheels of history', which it is idle to try to stay. We speak of the futility of defying the 'forces of history', or the absurdity of efforts to 'put the clock back' or to 'restore the past'. We speak of the youth, the maturity, the decay of peoples or cultures, of the ebb and flow of social movements, of the rise and fall of nations. Such language serves to convey the idea of an inexorably fixed time order – the 'river of time' on which we float, and which we must willy-nilly accept; a moving stair which we have not created, but on which we are borne, obeying, as it were, some natural law governing the order and shape of events – in this case, events consisting of, or at any rate affecting, human lives, activities,

---

rather be guided by our experience of the past, and should admit the probability that what we now call inexplicable will at some future time be explained. This expectation of discovering regularity in the midst of confusion is so familiar to scientific men, that among the most eminent of them it becomes an article of faith: and if the same expectation is not generally found among historians, it must be ascribed partly to their being of inferior ability to the investigators of nature, and partly to the greater complexity of those social phenomena with which their studies are concerned.

'. . . The most celebrated historians are manifestly inferior to the most successful cultivators of physical science: no one having devoted himself to history who in point of intellect is at all to be compared with Kepler, Newton, or many others . . .

'[Nevertheless] I entertain little doubt that before another century has elapsed, the chain of evidence will be complete, and it will be as rare to find an historian who denies the undeviating regularity of the moral world, as it now is to find a philosopher who denies the regularity of the material world.' Henry Thomas Buckle, *History of Civilization in England* (London, 1857), vol. 1, pp. 6–7 and 31.

and experiences. Metaphorical and misleading though such uses of words can be, they are pointers to categories and concepts in terms of which we conceive the 'stream of history', namely, as something possessing a certain objective pattern that we ignore at our peril. It is a short step from this to conclude that whatever has a pattern exhibits regularities capable of being expressed in laws; and the systematic interconnection of laws is the content of a natural science.

The second source of this belief lies deeper still. Patterns of growth, or of the march of events, can plausibly be represented as a succession of causes and effects, capable of being systematised by natural science. But sometimes we speak as if something more fundamental than empirical connections (which idealist philosophers call 'mechanical' or 'external' or 'mere brute conjunctions') give their unity to the aspects, or the successive phases, of the existence of the human race on earth. When we say, for instance, that it is absurd to blame Richelieu for not acting like Bismarck because it is obvious that Richelieu could not have acted like a man living in Germany in the nineteenth century; and that conversely Bismarck could not have done what Richelieu accomplished, because the seventeenth century had its own character, very different from the deeds, events, characteristics of the eighteenth century which it uniquely determined, and which in their turn uniquely determined those of the nineteenth; what we are then affirming is that this order is an objective order; that those who do not understand that what is possible in one age and situation may be wholly inconceivable in another fail to understand something universal and fundamental about the only way in which social life, or the human mind, or economic growth, or some other sequence, not merely does, but can, or perhaps must, develop. Similarly, when we say that the proposition that *Hamlet* was written at the court of Genghis Khan in Outer Mongolia is not merely false but absurd; that if someone acquainted with the relevant facts seriously supposes that it could have been written at that time and in that place he is not merely unusually ignorant or mistaken, but out of his mind; that *Hamlet* not merely was not, but could not have been, written there or then – that we can dismiss this hypothesis without discussion – what is it that entitles us to feel so certain? What kind of 'could not' is this 'could not'? Do we rule out propositions asserting possibilities of this kind as being false on scientific, that is, empirical-inductive grounds? It seems to me that we call them grotesque (and not merely implausible or false) because they conflict, not just with this or that fact or generalisation which we accept, but with presuppositions which are entailed by our whole thinking about the world – the basic categories that govern such central concepts of our thought as man, society, history, development, growth, barbarism, maturity, civilisation, and the like. These presuppositions may turn out to be false or misleading (as, for example, teleology or deism are considered to have been by positivists or atheists), but they are not refuted by experiment or empirical observation. They are destroyed or transformed by those changes in the total outlook of a man or a milieu or a culture which it is the hardest (and the most important) test of the history of ideas (and, in the end, of history as such) to be able to explain. What is here involved is a deeply ingrained, widespread, long-lived *Weltanschauung* – the unquestioning (and not necessarily valid) assumption of one particular objective order of events or facts. Sometimes it is a vertical order – succession in time – which makes us realise that the events or institutions of, say, the fourteenth century, because they were what they were, of necessity (however we analyse this sort of necessity), and not just as a matter of fact – contingently – occurred earlier than those of the sixteenth, which were 'shaped', that is in some sense determined (some would say caused), by them; so that anyone who tries to date the works of Shakespeare before those of Dante, or to omit the fifteenth century altogether, fitting the end of the fourteenth into the beginning of the sixteenth century without a break, can be convicted of suffering from a defect different in kind, not degree, from (and less easily remediable than) ignorance or lack of scientific method. At other times we conceive of the order as 'horizontal'; that is, it underlies the perception of the interconnections between different aspects of the same stage of culture – the kinds of assumptions and categories that the anti-mechanistic German philosophers of culture, Herder and his disciples (and before them Vico), brought to light. It is this kind of awareness (the historical sense) that is said to enable us to perceive that a certain type of legal structure is 'intimately connected' with, or is part of the same complex as, an economic activity, a moral outlook, a style of writing or of dancing or of worship; it is by means of this gift (whatever may be its nature) that we recognise various manifestations of the human spirit as 'belonging to' this or that culture or nation or historical period, although these manifestations may be as different from one another as the way in which men form letters on paper from their system of land tenure. Without this faculty we should attach no sense to such social-historical notions as 'the typical', or 'the normal', or 'the discordant', or 'the anachronistic', and consequently we should be unable to conceive the history of an institution as an intelligible pattern, or to attribute a work of art to its time and civilisation and milieu, or indeed to understand or explain how one phase of a civilisation 'generates' or 'determines' another. This sense of what remains identical or unitary in differences and in change (of which idealist philosophers have made altogether too much) is also a dominant factor in giving us our sense of unalterable trends, of the 'one-directional' flow of history. From this it is easy to pass to the far more questionable belief that whatever is unalterable is so only because it obeys laws, and that whatever obeys laws can always be systematised into a science.

These are among the many factors that have made men crave for a natural science of history. All seemed ready, particularly in the nineteenth century, for the formulation of this new, powerful, and illuminating discipline, which would do away with the chaotic accumulation of facts, conjectures, and rules of thumb that had been treated with such disdain by Descartes and his scientifically-minded successors. The stage was set, but virtually nothing materialised. No general laws were formulated – nor even moderately reliable maxims – from which historians could deduce (together with knowledge of the initial conditions) either what would happen next, or what had happened in the past. The great machine which was to rescue them from the tedious labours of adding fact to fact and of attempting to construct a coherent account out of their hand-picked material, seemed like a plan in the head of a cracked inventor. The immense labour-saving instrument which, when fed with information, would itself order it, deduce the right conclusions, and offer the proper explanations, removing the need for the uncertain, old-fashioned, hand-operated tools with which historians had fumbled their way in the unregenerate past, remained a bogus prospectus, the child of an extravagant imagination, like designs for a perpetual motion machine. Neither psychologists nor sociologists, neither the ambitious Comte nor the more modest Wundt, had been able to create the new mechanism: the 'nomothetic' sciences – the system of laws and rules under which the factual material could be ordered so as to yield new knowledge – remained stillborn.

One of the criteria of a natural science is rightly regarded as being its capacity for prediction; or, in the case of a historical study, retrodiction – filling in gaps in the past for which no direct testimony exists with the aid of extrapolation performed according to relevant rules or laws. A method of this conjectural sort is employed in archaeology or palaeontology where vast gaps in knowledge exist and there is no better

– more dependable – avenue to factual truth in the absence of concrete factual evidence. In archaeology we make efforts to link our knowledge of one remote period to our knowledge of another by trying to reconstruct what must, or at least may have, occurred to account for the transition from one stage to the other through many unknown intermediate phases. But this way of filling gaps is commonly regarded as a none too reliable method of discovery of the past, and one to which no one would wish to resort if he could find the more concrete kind of evidence (however the quality and extent of such concreteness is assessed) on which we base knowledge of the historical, as opposed to prehistoric, period of human life; still less as a 'scientific' substitute for it.

What would the structure of such a science be like, supposing that one were able to formulate it? It would, presumably, consist of causal or functional correlations – a system of interrelated general propositions of the type 'Whenever or wherever ϕ then or there ψ' – variables into which precise dates and places could be fitted; and it would possess two forms: the 'pure' and the 'applied'. The 'pure' sciences of social statics or social dynamics, of which Herbert Spencer perhaps a little too optimistically proclaimed the existence, would then be related to the 'applied' science of history, somewhat as physics is to mechanics, or at least as anatomy applies to the diagnosis of specific cases by a physician. If it existed, such a science would have revolutionised the old empirical, hand-woven history by mechanising it, as astronomy abolished the rules of thumb accumulated by Babylonian star-gazers, or as Newtonian physics transformed older cosmologies. No such science exists. Before we ask why this is so, it would perhaps be profitable to consider some of the more obvious ways in which history, as it has been written until our day, differs from a natural science conceived in this fashion.

Let me begin by noting one conspicuous difference between history and the natural sciences. Whereas in a developed natural science we consider it more rational to put our confidence in general propositions or laws than in specific phenomena (indeed this is part of the definition of rationality), this rule does not seem to operate successfully in history. Let me give the simplest possible kind of example. One of the common-sense generalisations that we regard as most firmly established is that the normal inhabitants of this planet can see the sun rise every morning. Suppose a man were to say that on a given morning he had not, despite repeated attempts, seen the sun rise; and that since one negative instance is, by the rules of our ordinary logic, sufficient to kill a general proposition, he regarded his carefully carried out observation as fatal not merely to the hitherto accepted generalisation about the succession of night and day, but to the entire system of celestial mechanics, and indeed of physics, which purports to reveal the causes of this phenomenon. This startling claim would not normally be regarded as a conclusion to be unhesitatingly accepted. Our first reaction would be to try to construct an *ad hoc* hypothesis to save our system of physics, supported as it is by the most systematic accumulation of controlled observation and deductive reasoning made by men. We should suggest to the objector that perhaps he was not looking at the right portion of the sky; that clouds intervened; that he was distracted; that his eyes were closed; that he was asleep; that he was suffering from a hallucination; that he was using words in unfamiliar senses; that he was lying or joking or insane; we should advance other explanations, any one of which would be compatible with his statement, and yet preserve physical science intact. It would not be rational to jump to the immediate conclusion that if the man, in our considered judgement, had told the truth, the whole of our hard-won physics must be rejected, or even modified. No doubt, if the phenomenon repeated itself, and other men failed to perceive the sun rising under normal conditions, some physical hypotheses, or indeed laws, might have to be drastically altered, or even rejected; perhaps the foundations of our physical sciences would have to be built anew. But we should only embark on this in the last resort. Yet if *per contra* a historian were to attempt to cast doubt on – or explain away – some piece of individual observation of a type not otherwise suspect, say, that Napoleon had been seen in a three-cornered hat at a given moment during the battle of Austerlitz; and if the historian did so solely because he put his faith, for whatever reason, in a theory or law according to which French generals or heads of state never wore three-cornered hats during battles, his method, one can safely assert, would not meet with universal or immediate recognition from his profession. Any procedure designed to discredit the testimony of normally reliable witnesses or documents as, let us say, lies or forgeries, or as being defective at the very point at which the report about Napoleon's hat occurred, would be liable to be regarded as itself suspect, as an attempt to alter the facts to fit a theory. I have chosen a crude and trivial instance; it would not be difficult to think of more sophisticated examples, where a historian lays himself open to the charge of trying to press the facts into the service of a particular theory. Such historians are accused of being prisoners of their theories; they are accused of being fanatical or cranky or doctrinaire, of misrepresenting or misreading reality to fit in with their obsessions, and the like. Addiction to theory – being doctrinaire – is a term of abuse when applied to historians; it is not an insult if applied to a natural scientist. We are saying nothing derogatory if we say of a natural scientist that he is in the grip of a theory. We may complain if we think that his theory is false, or that he is ignoring relevant evidence, but we do not deplore the fact that he is trying to fit the facts into the pattern of a theory; for that is his business. It is the business of a natural scientist to be a theorist; that is, to formulate doctrines – true rather than false, but, above all, doctrines; for natural science is nothing if it is not a systematic interlacing of theories and doctrines, built up inductively, or by hypothetical-deductive methods, or whatever other method is considered best (logically reputable, rational, publicly testable, fruitful) by the most competent practitioners in the field. It seems clear that whereas in history we tend, more often than not, to attach greater credence to the existence of particular facts than to general hypotheses, however well supported, from which these facts could in theory be deduced, in a natural science the opposite seems more often to be the case: there it is (in cases of conflict) often more rational to rely upon a properly supported general theory – say that of gravitation – than on particular observations. This difference alone, whatever its root, must cast prima facie doubt upon any attempt to draw too close an analogy between the methods of history and those of natural science.

It may be objected at this point that the only logical justification for belief in particular facts must involve general propositions, and therefore always in the end rests on some form of induction. For what other way of justifying beliefs about facts have we? The first of these assertions is true, but the second is not, and their conflation leads to confusion. It needs no deep reflection to realise that all our thought is shot through with general propositions. All thinking involves classification; all classification involves general terms. My very notion of Napoleon or hats or battles involves some general beliefs about the entities which these words denote. Moreover, my reasons for trusting an eye-witness account or a document entail judgements about the reliability of different kinds of testimony, or the range within which the behaviour of individuals is or is not variable and the like – judgements which are certainly general. But in the first place, it is a far cry from the scattered generalisations implicit in the everyday use of words (or ideas) to the systematic structure of even the most rudimentary science;[1] and in the second place, I am certain, for example, that I am not at this moment the Emperor of Mars dreaming a dream in which I am a university teacher on the earth; but I should find it exceedingly hard to justify my certainty by inductive methods that avoid circularity. Most of the certainties on which our lives are founded would scarcely pass this test. The vast majority of the types of reasoning on which our beliefs rest, or by which we should seek to justify them if they were challenged, are not reducible to formal deductive or inductive schemata, or combinations of them. If I am asked what rational grounds I have for supposing that I am not on Mars, or that the Emperor Napoleon existed and was not merely a sun myth, and if in answer to this I try to make explicit the general propositions which entail this conclusion, together with the specific evidence for them, and the evidence for the reliability of this evidence, and the evidence for that evidence in its turn, and so on, I shall not get very far. The web is too complex, the elements too many and not, to say the least, easily isolated and tested one by one; anyone can satisfy himself of this by trying to analyse and state them explicitly. The true reason for accepting the propositions that I live on earth, and that an Emperor Napoleon I existed, is that to assert their contradictories is to destroy too much of what we take for granted about the present and the past. Any given generalisation may be capable of being tested or refined by inductive or other scientific tests; but we accept the total texture, compounded as it is out of literally countless strands – including both general and particular beliefs – without the possibility, even in principle, of any test for it in its totality. For the total texture is what we begin and end with. There is no Archimedean point outside it whence we can survey the whole of it and pronounce upon it. We can test one part in terms of another, but not the whole, as it were, at one go. When the proposition that the earth was flat was abandoned, this wrought great havoc in the assumptions of common sense; but it could not in principle destroy them all. For in that case nothing would have remained that could be called thinking or criticism. It is the sense of the general texture of experience – the most rudimentary awareness of such patterns – that constitutes the foundation of knowledge, that is

[1] This can be put in another way by saying that the generalisations of history, like those of ordinary thought, are sometimes unconnected; so that a change in the degree of belief in any one of these does not, as in a natural science, *automatically* affect the status of all the others. This is a crucial difference.

itself not open to inductive or deductive reasoning: for both these methods rest upon it. Any one proposition or set of propositions can be shaken in terms of those that remain fixed; and then these latter in their turn; but not all simultaneously. All my beliefs cannot be overthrown. Even if the ground beneath one of my feet is crumbling, my other foot must rest securely planted, at least for the time being; otherwise there is no possibility of thought or communication. It is this network of our most general assumptions, called commonsense knowledge, that historians to a greater degree than scientists are bound, at least initially, to take for granted: and they must take a good deal of it for granted, since their subject-matter can be detached from it to a far smaller degree than that of natural science.

Let us look at this from another angle. The natural sciences largely consist of logically linked laws about the behaviour of objects in the world. In certain cases these generalisations can be represented in the form of an ideal model – an imaginary entity whose characteristics are by definition what they must be if the entity in question obeys the general laws in question, and can be exhaustively described solely in terms of obeying these laws; that is, it consists of nothing but what instantiates such laws. Such models (or deductive schemata) exhibit most vividly and clearly the laws which we attempt to apply to reality; the objects of the natural world can then be described in terms of the degree of deviation that they exhibit from the ideal model. The degree to which these differences can be systematically described, the simplicity of the models, and the range of their application largely determine the success or failure of a given science to perform its task. The electron, the chromosome, the state of perfect competition, the Oedipus complex, the ideal democracy, are all such models; they are useful to the degree to which the actual behaviour of real entities in the world can be represented with lesser or greater precision in terms of their deviation from the frictionless behaviour of the perfect model. This is the purpose for which the model is constructed; its usefulness corresponds to the degree to which it fulfils it.

Such a model or deductive schema is not much in evidence in normal historical writing; if only because the general propositions out of which it must be constructed, and which, if they existed, would require to be precisely formulated, turn out to be virtually impossible to specify. The general concepts that necessarily are employed by historians – notions like state or development or revolution or trend of opinion or economic decline or political power – enter into general propositions of far lesser range or dependability (or specifiability) than those that occur in even the least developed natural science worthy of its title. Such historical generalisations turn out too often to be tautological, or vague or inaccurate; 'All power tends to corrupt', 'Every revolution is followed by a reaction', 'Change in the economic structure leads to novel forms of music and painting', will yield, taken with some specified initial conditions, e.g. 'Cromwell had a great deal of power' or 'A revolution broke out in Russia in 1917' or 'The United States went through a period of radical industrialisation', scarcely any reliable historical or sociological deductions. What is lacking here is an interconnected tissue of generalisations which an electronic brain could mechanically apply to a situation mechanically specifiable as relevant. What occurs in historical thinking seems much more like the operation of common sense, where we weave together various prima facie logically independent concepts and general propositions, and bring them to bear on a given situation as best we can. The capacity to do this successfully – the ability to 'weave together', 'bring to bear' various concepts – is a skill, an empirical knack (sometimes called judgement) which electronic brains cannot be given by their manufacturers.

At this point we may be told that the mysterious capacity of weighing or assessing a concrete situation, the arts of diagnosis and prognosis (the so-called faculty of judgement) is not unique to history and the other humane studies, or to thinking and decision-making in ordinary life; for in the natural sciences too the capacity for perceiving the relevance of one rather than another theory or concept to the solution of a given problem, and the 'bringing to bear' (sometimes with the most dramatic effect) upon a given body of data of notions sometimes derived from very remote fields, is nothing if not the peculiar skill of a gifted investigator, sometimes amounting to the insight of genius, which techniques or machines cannot in principle be made to replace. This is, of course, true; yet there exists one striking difference between the canons of explanation and logical justification used by the sciences and the humanities that will serve to indicate the difference between them. In a developed work of natural science – say a textbook of physics or biology (I do not refer to speculative or impressionistic discourses which are to be found in scientific treatises) – the links between the propositions are, or should be, logically obvious; the propositions follow from each other; that is to say, the conclusions are seen logically to follow from premises, either with demonstrative certainty, or else with varying degrees of probability which, in the sciences which use statistical methods, should be capable of being estimated with a fair degree of precision. Even if such symbols of inference as 'because', or 'therefore', or 'hence' were omitted, a piece of reasoning in mathematics or physics or any other developed natural science (if it were clearly set out) should be able to exhibit its inner logical structure by the sheer meaning and order of its component propositions. As for the propositions that are stated without argument, these are, or should be, such that, if challenged, their truth or probability could be demonstrated by recognised logical steps from truths established experimentally and accepted by virtually all the relevant specialists. This is very far from being the case in even the best, most convincing, most rigorously argued works of history. No student of the subject can, I think, fail to note the abundance in works of history of such phrases as 'small wonder if', 'it was therefore hardly surprising when', 'the inevitable consequences swiftly followed', 'events took their inexorable course', 'in the circumstances', 'from this it was but a short step to', and most often of all the indispensable, scarcely noticeable, and deeply treacherous 'thus', 'whereupon', 'finally', and the like. If these bridges from one set of facts or statements to another were suddenly withdrawn from our textbooks, it is, I think, not too much to say that the transition from one set of statements to the other would become a great deal less smooth: the bald juxtaposition of events or facts would at times be seen to carry no great logical force in itself, and the best constructed cases of some of our best historians (and lawyers) would begin – to minds conditioned by the logical criteria of natural science – to seem less irresistible.

I do not mean to imply that the humanities, and particularly history, take their readers in by a species of confidence trick – by simulating the outer shell, the logical structure, of scientific method without its substance; only that the force of such convenient, and perhaps indispensable, links as 'because' and 'therefore' is not identical in the two spheres; each performing their own legitimate – and parallel – functions, and leading to difficulties only if they are regarded as performing logically identical tasks in both spheres. This point will, I hope, become clearer still if it is further developed.

Let us assume that an historian who is attempting to discover and explain the course of a large historical phenomenon, such as a war or a revolution, is pressed to state those laws and general propositions which alone (at least in theory) could justify his constant use of such logical links as 'hence', 'therefore', 'the unavoidable result was', 'from this there was no turning back', and the rest of his stock-in-trade, what could his answer be? He might hesitantly trot out some general maxims about the influence of environment or a particular state of affairs – a bad harvest, or an inflationary spiral, or a wound to national pride – as it affects men in general or a specific group of human beings in particular; or he might speak about the influence of the interests of this or that class or nation, or the effect of religious convictions or social habits or political traditions. But if he is then pressed about the evidence for these generalisations, and upon marshalling what he can, is then told that no self-respecting natural science would tolerate so vague, unsifted, and above all exiguous a body of factual evidence, nor such impressionistic methods of surveying it or deriving conclusions from it, he would not (if he were honest or wise) insist on claiming the authority of the methods of a fully-fledged natural science for his activity. At this point someone might quite correctly point out to him that not all social sciences are in so deplorable a condition; that, for example, there exist disciplines – economics is perhaps the best known – where something resembling scientific procedure does appear to take place. In economics concepts can, we are assured, be defined with a fair measure of precision: there is here to be found distinct awareness of the differences between definitions, hypotheses, and inductive generalisations; or between the empirical evidence and the conclusions drawn from it; or between the model and the reality to which it is applied; or between the fruit of observation and that of extrapolation; and so forth. This is then held up as a model to the unfortunate historian, wandering helplessly in his dark and pathless wood. Yet if he tries to follow such advice, and to apply to his own subject apparatus recommended by either metaphysical or positivist discoverers of historical patterns, his progress is soon arrested. Attempts to provide history with laws have taken two main directions: all-embracing schemata, and division into specialised disciplines. The first has given us the systems of historiosophers, culminating in the vast edifices of Hegel, Spengler, Toynbee and the like, which turn out to be either too general, vague, and occasionally tautological to cast new light on anything in particular, or, when the specific findings of the formulas are tested by exact scholars in the relevant fields, to yield implausible results. The second path leads to monographs about selected aspects of human activity – for example, the history of technology, or of a given science or art or craft or social activity. These do indeed, at their best, satisfy some of the criteria of natural scientists, but only at the expense of leaving out the greater part of what is known of the lives of the human beings whose histories are in this way recorded. In the case of a limited field – say the history of coinage in ancient Syracuse – this is, of course, deliberate and desirable as well as unavoidable; my point is that it is only the deliberate limitation of the field that renders it so.

Any attempt to 'integrate' these isolated strands, treated by the special disciplines, into something approaching (as near as we can make it so) a 'total' description of human experience – of what, in Aristotle's words, 'Alcibiades did and suffered' – comes up against an insurmountable obstacle: that the facts to be fitted into the scientific grid and subsumed under the adopted laws or model (even if public criteria for selecting what is important, relevant, etc. from what is trivial, peripheral, etc. can be found and employed) are too many, too minute, too fleeting, too blurred at the edges. They criss-cross and penetrate each other at many levels simultaneously, and the attempt to prise them apart, as it were, and pin them down, and classify them, and fit them into their specific compartments turns out to be impracticable. Wherever efforts to pursue this policy have been pressed with real vehemence – by those who were obsessed with the dominant role of some one factor, as Buckle was by that of climate, or Taine by his trinity of the milieu, the moment, and the race, or Marxists by that of base and superstructure and the class struggle – they lead to distortions, and the accounts that result, even when they contain illuminating ideas and *aperçus*, are liable to be rejected as being over-schematised, that is as exaggerating and omitting too much, as too unfaithful to human life as we know it.

The fact that this is so seems to me of cardinal importance and to carry a crucial implication. For one of the central differences between such genuine attempts to apply scientific method to human affairs as are embodied in, say, economics or social psychology, and the analogous attempt to apply it in history proper, is this: scientific procedure is directed in the first place to the construction of an ideal model, with which the portion of the real world to be analysed must, as it were, be matched, so that it can be described and analysed in terms of its deviation from the model. But to construct a useful model will only be feasible when it is possible to abstract a sufficient number of sufficiently stable similarities from the things, facts, events, of which the real world – the flow of experience – is composed. Only where such recurrences in the real world are frequent enough, and similar enough to be classifiable as so many deviations from the selfsame model, will the idealised model that is compounded of them – the electron, the gene, the economic man – do its job of making it possible for us to extrapolate from the known to the unknown. It follows from this that the greater the number of similarities[1] that we are able to collect (and the more dissimilarities we are able to ignore) – that is to say the more successfully we abstract – the simpler our model will be, the narrower will be the range of characteristics to which it will apply, and the more precisely it will apply to it; and, conversely, the greater the variety of objects to which we want our model to apply, the less we shall be able to exclude, and consequently the more complex the model will become, and the less precisely it will fit the rich diversity of objects which it is meant to summarise, and so the less of a model, of a master key, it will necessarily be. A theory festooned with *ad hoc* hypotheses to account for each specific deviation from the norm will, like Ptolemy's epicycles, in the end cease to be useful. Exclusion – neglect of what is beyond the defined frontiers – is entailed in model-building as such. Hence it begins to look as if, given the world as it is,[2] the utility of a theory or a model tends to vary directly as the number of cases, and inversely as the number of characteristics, which it succeeds in covering. Consequently one may, at times, be compelled to choose between the rival rewards of increased extension or intension – between the range of a theory and the richness of its content. The most rigorous and universal of all models is that of mathematics, because it operates at the level of the highest possible abstraction from natural characteristics. Physics, similarly, ignores deliberately all but the very narrow group of characteristics which material objects possess in common, and its power and scope (and its great triumphs) are directly attributable to its rejection of all but certain selected ubiquitous and recurrent similarities. As we go down the scale, sciences become richer in content and correspondingly less rigorous, less susceptible to quantitative techniques. Economics is a science precisely to the degree to which it can successfully eliminate from consideration those aspects of human activity which are not concerned with production, consumption, exchange, distribution, etc. The attempt to eliminate from the

[1] Or at best significant similarities, that is, those in which we are interested.

[2] This is an empirical fact. The world might have been different; if, for example, it possessed fewer characteristics and these coexisted or recurred with much greater uniformity and regularity, the facts of history could more easily be reduced to a natural science or sciences. But human experience would then be altogether different, and not describable in terms of our familiar categories and concepts. The tidier and more uniform such a universe, the less like our own, the less able are we to imagine it or conceive what our experience would be like.

consideration of economists psychological factors, such as, for instance, the springs of human action, or the variety of purposes or states of mind connected with or expressed by them; or to exclude moral or political considerations such as, for example, the respective values of motives and consequences, or of individual versus group satisfaction – such procedure is wholly justified so long as its sole aim is to render economics as much of a science as possible: that is to say, an instrument capable of analysis and prediction. If anyone then complains that economics, so conceived, leaves out too much, or fails to solve some of the most fundamental problems of individual and social welfare – among them questions which had originally stimulated this science into existence – one is entitled to reply that the omitted sides of life can be accommodated, and moral, psychological, political, aesthetic, metaphysical questions can perhaps be answered, but only at the price of departing from the rigour and the symmetry – and predictive power – of the models with which economic science operates; that versatility, richness of content, capacity to deal with many categories of problems, adaptability to the complexities of widely varying situations – all this may be purchasable only at the expense of logical simplicity, coherence, economy, width of scope, and, above all, capacity to move from the known to the unknown. These latter characteristics, with which Newtonian physics had, understandably enough, hypnotised the entire intellectual world, can only be obtained by drawing precise frontiers for a given activity and ruthlessly casting out (so far as possible) whatever has not been provided for in this specification. It is for this reason that even in the case of the more descriptive and time-bound (biological and genetic) disciplines, the more general and rigorous the concepts involved and the more 'technical' the approach, the better able they are to use methods similar to those of the physical sciences; the more elastic their concepts and the richer their content, the remoter from a natural science they will be.

If this is true, then there is a good deal in the Comtean classification of the sciences: mathematics, physics, biology, psychology, sociology, are indeed rungs in a descending order of comprehensiveness and precision, and in an ascending order of concreteness and detail. General history – the richest of all human studies – shows this very plainly. If I am purely an economic historian, I can probably establish certain generalisations about the behaviour of some commodity – say wool – in some portion of the Middle Ages, for which enough documentary evidence exists to enable me to establish correlations between the production, sale, distribution of wool etc., and certain other related social and economic facts and events. But I am able to do this only by averting my gaze from questions – sometimes very important and fascinating ones – about other characteristics of the wool producers or wool merchants; at least I do not attempt to establish measurable correlations between the sources and movements of the bales of wool and the religious, and moral, and aesthetic attitudes of wool growers or wool users, and their political ideals, and their conduct as husbands or citizens and churchmen, all at once. For the model which attempted to deal with all these aspects of life would (as things are) lose in predictive power and the precision of its results, even if the story gained in comprehensiveness, richness, depth and interest. For this reason, I find it useful to employ technical terms (always symptomatic of the fact that a model is at work) in an artificially delimited field – namely that of economic history. The same considerations apply, for example, to the history of technology, or of mathematics, or of clothing, and the like. I construct the model by abstracting; by noting only what, say, industrial techniques, or mathematical methods, or methods of composing music, have in common, and constructing my model out of these common characteristics, however much of general interest I may be leaving out. The more I wish to put in, the more over-weighted and, in due course, cluttered up and shapeless, my model is bound to become, until it is scarcely a model at all, for it no longer covers a sufficient number of actual and possible cases in a sufficient variety of places and times. Its utility as a model will steadily diminish.

The proposition that sciences deal with the type, not the individual, was accepted and indeed insisted upon by those philosophical historians, particularly in France, who desired to assimilate their activities to those of scientists. When Renan, or Taine, or Monod preached the necessity of scientific history, they did not merely mean (as I suspect that, for example, Bury did) that historians should seek to be precise, or exercise rigour in observation or reasoning, or apply the findings of the natural sciences to the explanation of human action or experience wherever possible, or that they should grind no axe but that of objective truth, and state it without qualification whatever the moral or social or political consequences. They claimed much more. Taine states this point of view clearly, when he declares that historians work with samples:[1]

[1] *Discours de M. Taine prononcé à l'Académie française* (Paris, 1880), pp. 24–7.

What was there in France in the eighteenth century? Twenty million men ... twenty million threads the criss-crossing of which makes a web. This immense web, with innumerable knots, cannot be grasped clearly in its entirety by anyone's memory or imagination. Indeed all we have is mere fragments ... the historian's sole task is to restore them – he reconstructs the wisps of the threads that he can see so as to connect them with the myriad threads that have vanished ... Fortunately, in the past as now, society included groups, each group consisting of men who were like one another, born in the same condition, moulded by the same education, moved by the same interests, with the same needs, same tastes, same *moeurs*, same culture, same basis to their lives. In seeing one, you have seen all. In every science we study each class of facts by means of chosen samples.

He goes on to say that one must enter into the private life of a man, his beliefs, sentiments, habits, behaviour. Such a sample will give us

insight into the force and direction of the current that carries forward the whole of his society. The monograph, then, is the historian's best tool: he plunges it into the past like a lancet and draws it out charged with complete and authentic specimens. One understands a period after twenty or thirty such soundings: only they must be carried out and interpreted correctly.

This is characteristic of the high tide of positivist optimism in which truth is mixed with error. No doubt it is true that our only key to understanding a culture or an age is the detailed study of the lives of representative individuals or families or groups. We cannot examine all the acts and thoughts of all (or even a large number) of the human beings alive during the age in question (or any other age): we generalise from samples. We integrate the results of such generalisations into what Taine calls the total 'web'. In 'reconstructing' the 'vanished threads', we make use of chemistry, astronomy, geology, palaeontology, epigraphy, psychology, every scientific method known to us. But the objective of all this is to understand the relation of parts to wholes, not, as Taine believed, of instance to general law. In a natural science – physics and zoology, economics and sociology – our aim is to construct a model ('the meson', 'the mammal', 'the monopolistic firm', 'the alienated proletarian') which we can apply, with which we can reach out into the unknown past or future with a fair degree of confidence in the result; for the central criterion of whether or not a study is a true science is its capacity to infer the unknown from the known. The process that Taine describes is not this at all; it is reconstruction in terms of a pattern, an interrelated social whole, obtained from 'entering into' individual human lives, provided that they turn out to be 'typical' – that is, significant or characteristic beyond themselves. The recognition of what is characteristic and representative, of what is a 'good' sample suitable for being generalised, and, above all, of how the generalisations fit in with each other – that is the exercise of judgement, a form of thinking dependent on wide experience, memory, imagination, on the sense of 'reality', of what goes with what, which may need constant control by, but is not at all identical with, the capacity for logical reasoning and the construction of laws and scientific models – the capacity for perceiving the relations of particular case to law, instance to general rule, theorems to axioms, not of parts to wholes or fragments to completed patterns. I do not mean that these are incompatible 'faculties' capable of functioning in isolation from each other. Only that the gifts are dissimilar, that the qualitative distinctions and similarities are not reducible without residue to quantitative ones, that the capacity for perceiving the former is not translatable into models, and that Buckle and Comte and Taine and Engels and their cruder or more extremist modern disciples, when they bandy the word 'scientific', are sometimes blind to this, and so lead men astray.

Let me put this in yet another way. Every student of historiography knows that many of the major achievements of modern historians come from their practice of certain rules, which the more reflective among them sometimes express in advice to practitioners of this craft. Historical students are told not to pay too much attention to personal factors or heroic and unusual figures in human history. They are told to attend to the lives of ordinary men, or to economic considerations or social factors or irrational impulses or traditional, collective and unconscious springs of action; or not to forget such impersonal, inconspicuous, dull, slowly or imperceptibly altering factors of change as erosion of the soil, or systems of irrigation and drainage, which may be more influential than spectacular victories, or catastrophic events, or acts of genius; they are told not to allow themselves to be carried away by the desire to be entertaining or paradoxical, or over-rationalistic, or to point a moral or demonstrate a theory; and much else of this kind. What justifies such maxims? They do not follow automatically from the rules of the deductive or inductive disciplines; they are not even rules of specialised techniques (like, say, the *a fortiori* principle in rhetoric, or that of *difficilior lectio* in textual criticism). What logical or technical rules can be laid down for determining precisely what, in a given situation, is due to rational or purposive, and what to 'senseless' or irrational, factors, how much to personal action, how much to impersonal forces? If anyone supposes that such rules can be drawn up, let him attempt to do so. It seems plain that such maxims are simply distillations of generalised sagacity – of practical judgement founded on observation, intelligence, imagination, on empirical insight, knowledge of what can and what cannot be, something that resembles a skill or gift more than it does factual knowledge[1] but is not identical with either; a capability of the highest value to action (in this case to mental labour) which scientific techniques can direct, aid, sharpen, criticise, radically correct, but never replace.

All this may be no more than another way of saying something trite but true – that the business of a science is to concentrate on similarities, not differences, to be general, to omit whatever is not relevant to answering the severely delimited questions that it sets itself to ask; while those historians who are concerned with a field wider than the specialised activities of men are interested at least as much in the opposite – in that which differentiates one thing, person, situation, age, pattern of experience, individual or collective, from another. When such historians attempt to account for and explain, say, the French Revolution, the last thing that they seek to do is to concentrate only on those characteristics which the French Revolution has in common with other revolutions, to abstract only common recurrent characteristics, to formulate a law on the basis of them, or at any rate a hypothesis, from which something about the pattern of all revolutions as such (or, more modestly, all European revolutions), and therefore of this revolution in particular, could in principle be reliably inferred. This, if it were feasible, would be the task of sociology, which would then stand to history as a 'pure' science to its application. The validity of the claim of this type of sociology to the status of a natural science is another story, and not directly related to history, whose tasks are different. The immediate purpose of narrative historians (as has often been repeated), whatever else it may be besides this, is to paint a portrait of a situation or a process, which, like all portraits, seeks to capture the unique pattern and peculiar characteristics of its particular subject; not to be an X-ray which eliminates all but what a great many subjects have in common. This is, by now, a truism, but its bearing on the possibility of transforming history into a natural science has not always been clearly perceived. Two great thinkers understood this, and

[1] See pp. 127–8 and p. 136 below.

grappled with the problem: Leibniz and Hegel. Both made heroic efforts to bridge the gulf by such doctrines as those of 'individual essences' and 'concrete universals' – a desperate dialectical attempt to fuse together individuality and universality. The imaginative brilliance of the metaphysical constructions in which the passage of the Rubicon is deducible from the essence of Julius Caesar, or the even more ambitious inevitabilities of the *Phenomenology*, and their failure, serves to indicate the central character of the problem.

One way of appreciating this contrast is by contrasting two uses of the humble word 'because'. Max Weber, whose discussion of this problem is extraordinarily illuminating, asked himself under what conditions I accept an explanation of a given individual action or attitude as adequate, and whether these conditions are the same as those that are required in the natural sciences – that is to say, he tried to analyse what is meant by rational explanation in these contrasted fields. If I understand him correctly, the type of argument he uses goes somewhat as follows: Supposing that a doctor informs me that his patient recovered from pneumonia because he was injected with penicillin, what rational grounds have I for accepting this 'because'? My belief is rational only if I have rational grounds for believing the general proposition 'Penicillin is effective against pneumonia', a causal proposition established by experiment and observation, which there is no reason to accept unless, in fact, it has been arrived at by valid methods of scientific inference. No amount of general reflection would justify my accepting this general proposition (or its application in a given case) unless I know that it has been or could be experimentally verified. The 'because' in this case indicates a claim that a *de facto* correlation between penicillin and pneumonia has, in fact, been established. I may find this correlation surprising or I may not; this does not affect its reality; scientific investigation – the logic of which, we now think, is hypo- thetical-deductive – establishes its truth or probability; and this is the end of the matter. If, on the other hand, I am told, in the course of a historical narrative (or in a work of fiction, or ordinary life) that *x* resented the behaviour of *y*, because *x* was weak and *y* was arrogant and strong; or that *x* forgave the insult he had received from *y*, because he was too fond of *y* to feel aggrieved; and if, having accepted these 'because' statements as adequate explanations of the behaviour of *x* and *y*, I am then challenged to produce the general law which I am leaning on, consciously or not, to 'cover' these cases, what would it be reasonable for me to reply? I may well produce something like 'The weak often resent the arrogant and strong', or 'Human beings forgive insults from those they love.' But supposing I am then asked what concrete evidence I have for the truth of these general propositions, what scientific experiments I or anyone else have performed to establish these generalisations, how many observed and tested cases they rest on – I may well be at a loss to answer. Even if I am able to cite examples from my own or others' experience of the attitude of the weak to the strong, or of the behaviour of persons capable of love and friendship, I may be scornfully told by a psychologist – or any other devotee of strict scientific method – that the number of instances I have produced is ludicrously insufficient to be adequate evidence for a generalisation of such scope; that no respectable science would accept these few positive or negative instances, which, moreover, have not been observed under scientific conditions, as a basis for serious claims to formulate laws; that such procedures are impressionistic, vague, pre-scientific, unworthy to be reckoned as ground for a scientific hypothesis. And I may further be told that what cannot enter a natural science cannot be called fully rational but only an approximation to it (an 'explanation sketch'). Implicit in this approach is Descartes' criterion, the setting up of the methods of mathematics (or physics) as the standard for all rational thought. Nevertheless, the explanation that I have given in terms of the normal attitude of the weak to the strong, or of friends to one another, would, of course, be accepted by most rational beings (writers and readers of history among them) as an adequate explanation of the behaviour of a given individual in the relevant situation. This kind of explanation may not be admissible in a treatise on natural science, but in dealing with others, or describing their actions, we accept it as being both normal and reasonable; neither as inescapably shallow, or shamefully unexamined, or doubtful, nor as necessarily needing support from the laboratory. We may, of course, in any given case, be mistaken – mistaken about particular facts to be accounted for, about the attitudes of the relevant individuals to one another, or in taking for granted the generalisations implicit in our judgement; these may well be in need of correction from psychologists or sociologists. But because we may be in error in a given instance, it does not follow that this type of explanation is always systematically at fault, and should or could always be replaced by something more searching, more inductive, more like the type of evidence that is alone admitted in, say, biology. If we probe further and ask why it is that such explanations – such uses of 'because' – are accepted in history, and what is meant by saying that it is rational to accept them, the answer must surely be that what in ordinary life we call adequate explanations often rest not on specific pieces of scientific reasoning, but on our experience in general, on our capacity for understanding the habits of thought and action that are embodied in human attitudes and behaviour, on what is called knowledge of life, sense of reality. If someone tells us '*x* forgave *y* because he loved him' or '*x* killed *y* because he hated him', we accept these propositions easily, because they, and the propositions into which they can be generalised, fit in with our experience, because we claim to know what men are like, not, as a rule, by careful observation of them as psychological specimens (as Taine recommends), or as members of some strange tribe whose behaviour is obscure to us and can only be inferred from (preferably controlled) observation, but because we claim to know (not always justifiably) what – in essentials – a human being is, in particular a human being who belongs to a civilisation not too unlike our own, and consequently one who thinks, wills, feels, acts in a manner which (rightly or wrongly) we assume to be intelligible to us because it sufficiently resembles our own or those of other human beings whose lives are intertwined with our own. This sort of 'because' is the 'because' neither of induction nor of deduction, but the 'because' of understanding – *Verstehen* – of recognition of a given piece of behaviour as being part and parcel of a pattern of activity which we can follow, which we can remember or imagine, and which we describe in terms of the general laws which cannot possibly all be rendered explicit (still less organised into a system), but without which the texture of normal human life – social or personal – is not conceivable. We make mistakes; we may be shallow, unobservant, naïve, unimaginative, not allow enough for unconscious motives, or unintended consequences, or the play of chance or some other factor; we may project the present into the past or assume uncritically that the basic categories and concepts of our civilisation apply to remote or dissimilar cultures which they do not fit. But although any one explanation or use of 'because' and 'therefore' may be rejected or shaken for any of these or a hundred other reasons (which scientific discoveries in, say, physics or psychology, running against the complacent assumptions of common sense, may well provide), *all* such explanations cannot be rejected *in toto* in favour of inductive procedures derived from the natural sciences, because that would cut the ground from beneath our feet: the context in which we think, act, expect to be understood or responded to, would be destroyed. When I understand a sentence which someone utters, my claim to know what he means is not, as a rule, based on an inductively reached conclusion that the statistical probability is that the noises he emits are, in fact, related and expressive in the way that I take them to be – a conclusion derived from a comparison of the sounds he utters with a great many other sounds that a great many other beings have uttered in corresponding situations in the past. This must not be confused with the fact that, if pressed to justify my claim, I could conduct an experiment which would do something to support my belief. Nevertheless, my belief is usually a good deal stronger than that which any process of reasoning that I may perform with a view to bolstering it up would, in a natural science, be held to justify. Yet we do not for this reason regard such claims to understanding as being less rational than scientific convictions, still less as being arbitrary. When I say that I realise that x forgave y because he loved him or was too good-natured to bear a grudge, what I am ultimately appealing to is my own (or my society's) experience and imagination, my (or my associates') knowledge of what such relationships have been and can be. This knowledge, whether it is my own, or taken by me on trust – accepted uncritically – may often be inadequate, and may lead me to commit blunders – a Freudian or a Marxist may open my eyes to much that I had not yet understood – but if *all* such knowledge were rejected unless it could pass scientific tests, I could not think or act at all.

The world of natural science is the world of the external observer noting as carefully and dispassionately as he can the compresence or succession (or lack of it), or the extent of correlation, of empirical characteristics. In formulating a scientific hypothesis I must, at least in theory, start from the initial assumption that, for all I know, anything might occur next door to, or before or after, or simultaneously with, anything else; nature is full of surprises; I must take as little as possible for granted; it is the business of natural science to establish general laws recording what most often or invariably does occur. But in human affairs, in the interplay of men with one another, of their feelings, thoughts, choices, ideas about the world or each other or themselves, it would be absurd (and if pushed to extremes, impossible) to start in this manner. I do not start from an ignorance which leaves all doors – or as many of them as possible – open, for here I am not primarily an external observer, but myself an actor; I understand other human beings, and what it is to have motives, feelings, or follow rules, because I am human myself, and because to be active – that is, to want, intend, make plans, speculate, do, react to others self-consciously, be aware of

129

my situation *vis-à-vis* other conscious beings and the non-human environment – is *eo ipso* to be engaged in a constant fitting of fragments of reality into the single all-embracing pattern that I assume to hold for others besides myself, and which I call reality. When, in fact, I am successful in this – when the fragments seem to me to fit – we call this an explanation; when in fact they do fit, I am called rational; if they fit badly, if my sense of harmony is largely a delusion, I am called irrational, fanciful, distraught, silly; if they do not fit at all, I am called mad.

So much for differences in method. But there is also a profound difference of aim between scientific and historical studies. What they seek for is not the same. Let me illustrate this with a simple example. Supposing that we look at an average, unsophisticated European or American school text of modern European history that offers a sample of the kind of elementary historical writing upon which most of us have been brought up. Let us consider the kind of account that one finds (or used to find) in routine works of this type, of, say, the causes of the French Revolution. It is not unusual to be told that among them were – to give the headings – (i) the oppression of French peasants by the aristocracy, the Church, the King etc.; (ii) the disordered state of French finances; (iii) the weak character or the stupidity of Louis XVI; (iv) the subversive influence of the writings of Voltaire, the Encyclopedists, Rousseau, and other writers; (v) the mounting frustration of the ambitions of the economically rising French *bourgeoisie,* barred from its proper share of political power; and so on. One may reasonably protest against the crudity and *naïveté* of such treatments of history: Tolstoy has provided some very savage and entertaining parodies of it and its practitioners. But if one's main anxiety is to convert history into a science, one's indignation should take a different and much more specific form. One should declare that what is here manifested is a grotesque confusion of categories, an outrage to scientific method. For the analysis of the condition of the peasants belongs to the science of economics, or perhaps of social history; that of French fiscal policy to the science of public finance, which is not primarily a historical study, but one founded (according to some) on timeless principles; the weakness of the King's character or intellect is a matter for individual psychology (or biography); the influence of Voltaire and Rousseau belongs to the history of ideas; the pressure of the middle classes is a sociological topic, and so forth. Each of these disciplines must surely possess its own factual content, methods, canons, concepts, categories, logical structure. To

130

heap them into one, and reel off a list of causes, as if they all belonged to the same level and type, is intellectually scandalous: the rope composed of these wholly heterogeneous strands must at once be unwound; each of the strands must then be treated separately in its proper logical box. Such should be the reaction of someone who takes seriously the proposition that history is, or at any rate should be, a natural science or a combination of such sciences. Yet the truth about history – perhaps the most important truth of all – is that general history is precisely this amalgam, a rich brew composed of apparently disparate ingredients, that we do in fact think of these different causes as factors in a single unitary sequence – the history of the French nation or French society during a particular segment of time – and that although there may be great profit to be gained from detaching this or that element of a single process for analysis in a specialised laboratory, yet to treat them as if they were genuinely separate, insulated streams which do not compose a single river, is a far wilder departure from what we think history to be than the indiscriminate compounding of them into one string of causes, as is done in the simple-minded schoolbooks. 'History is what historians do', and what at any rate some historians aim at is to answer those who wish to be told what important changes occurred in French public life between 1789 and 1794, and why they took place. We wish, ideally at least, to be presented, if not with a total experience – which is a logical as well as practical impossibility – at least with something full enough and concrete enough to meet our conception of public life (itself an abstraction, but not a deductive schema, not an artificially constructed model), seen from as many points of view and at as many levels as possible, including as many components, factors, aspects, as the widest and deepest knowledge, the greatest analytical power, insight, imagination, can present. If we are told that this cannot be achieved by a natural science – that is, by the application of models to reality, because models can only function if their subject-matter is relatively 'thin', consisting as it does of deliberately isolated strands of experience, and not 'thick', that is, not with the texture constituted by the interwoven strands – then history, if it is set on dealing with the compound and not some meticulously selected ingredient of it, as it must be, will, in this sense, not be a science after all. A scientific cast of mind is seldom found together with historical curiosity or historical talent. We can make use of the techniques of the natural sciences to establish dates, order events in time and space, exclude untenable hypotheses and suggest new explanatory factors (as sociology, psychology, economics, medicine have so notably done), but the function of all these techniques, indispensable as they are today, can be no more than ancillary, for they are determined by their specific models, and are consequently 'thin', whereas what the great historians sought to describe and analyse and explain is necessarily 'thick'; that is the essence of history, its purpose, its pride, and its reason for existence.

History, and other accounts of human life, are at times spoken of as being akin to art. What is usually meant is that writing about human life depends to a large extent on descriptive skill, style, lucidity, choice of examples, distribution of emphasis, vividness of characterisation, and the like. But there is a profounder sense in which the historian's activity is an artistic one. Historical explanation is to a large degree arrangement of the discovered facts in patterns which satisfy us because they accord with life – the variety of human experience and activity – as we know it and can imagine it. That is the difference that distinguishes the humane studies – *Geisteswissenschaften* – from those of nature. When these patterns contain central concepts or categories that are ephemeral, or confined to trivial or unfamiliar aspects of human experience, we speak of such explanations as shallow, or inadequate, or eccentric, and find them unsatisfactory on those grounds. When these concepts are of wide scope, permanent, familiar, common to many men and many civilisations, we experience a sense of reality and dependability that derives from this very fact, and regard the explanation as well-founded, serious, satisfactory. On some occasions (seldom enough) the explanation not only involves, but reveals, basic categories of universal import, which, once they are forced upon consciousness, we recognise as underlying all our experience; yet so closely interwoven are they with all that we are and feel, and therefore so totally taken for granted, that to touch them at all is to communicate a shock to the entire system; the shock is one of recognition and one that may upset us, as is liable to happen when something deep-set and fundamental that has lain unquestioned and in darkness is suddenly illuminated or prised out of its frame for closer inspection. When this occurs, and especially when the categories thus uncovered seem applicable to field after field of human activity, without apparent limits – so that we cannot tell how far they may yet extend – we call such explanations profound, fundamental, revolutionary, and those who proffer them – Vico, Kant, Marx, Freud – men of depth of insight and genius.

This kind of historical explanation is related to moral and aesthetic analysis, in so far as it presupposes conceiving of human beings not merely as organisms in space, the regularities of whose behaviour can be described and locked in labour-saving formulas, but as active beings, pursuing ends, shaping their own and others' lives, feeling, reflecting, imagining, creating, in constant interaction and intercommunication with other human beings; in short, engaged in all the forms of experience that we understand because we share in them, and do not view them purely as external observers. This is what is called the inside view: and it renders possible and indeed inescapable explanation whose primary function is not to predict or extrapolate, or even control, but fit the loose and fleeting objects of sense, imagination, intellect, into the central succession of patterns that we call normal, and which is the ultimate criterion of reality as against illusion, incoherence, fiction. History is merely the mental projection into the past of this activity of selection and adjustment, the search for coherence and unity, together with the attempt to refine it with all the self-consciousness of which we are capable, by bringing to its aid everything that we conceive to be useful – all the sciences, all the knowledge and skills, and all the theories that we have acquired, from whatever quarter. This, indeed, is why we speak of the importance of allowing for imponderables in forming historical judgement, or of the faculty of judgement that seems mysterious only to those who start from the preconception that their induction, deduction and sense perception are the only legitimate sources of, or at least certified methods justifying claims to, knowledge. Those who, without mystical undertones, insist on the importance of common sense, or knowledge of life, or width of experience, or breadth of sympathy or imagination, or natural wisdom, or 'depth' of insight – all normal and empirical attributes – are suspected of seeming to smuggle in some kind of illicit, metaphysical faculty only because the exercise of these gifts has relatively little value for those who deal with inanimate matter, for physicists or geologists. Capacity for understanding people's characters, knowledge of ways in which they are likely to react to one another, ability to 'enter into' their motives, their principles, the movement of their thoughts and feelings (and this applies no less to the behaviour of masses or to the growth of cultures) – these are the talents that are indispensable to historians, but not (or not to such a degree) to natural scientists. The capacity for knowing which is like knowing someone's character or face, is as essential to historians as knowledge of facts. Without sufficient knowledge of facts a historical construction may be no more than a coherent fiction, a work of the romantic imagination; it goes without saying that if its claim to be true is to

133

be sustained, it must be, as the generalisations which it incorporates must in their turn be, tethered to reality by verification of the facts, as in any natural science. Nevertheless, even though in this ultimate sense what is meant by real and true is identical in science, in history and in ordinary life, yet the differences remain as great as the similarities.

This notion of what historians are doing when they are explaining may cast light also upon something that was mentioned earlier; namely, the idea of the inexorable succession of the stages of development, which made it not merely erroneous but absurd to suppose that *Hamlet* could have been written at the court of Genghis Khan, or that Richelieu could have pursued the policies realised by Bismarck. For this kind of certainty is not something that we derive from a careful inductive investigation of conditions in Outer Mongolia, as opposed to those of Elizabethan England, or of the political relations between the great powers in the nineteenth century as opposed to those in the seventeenth, but from a more fundamental sense of what goes with what. We conceive of historical succession as being akin to that of the growth of the individual personality; to suggest that a child thinks or wills or acts like an old man, or vice versa, is something that we reject on the basis of our own direct experience (I mean by this not introspection, but knowledge of life – something that springs from interaction with others and with the surrounding environment and constitutes the sense of reality). Our conception of a civilisation is analogous to this. We do not feel it necessary to enumerate all the specific ways in which a wild nomad differs from a European of the Renaissance, or ask ourselves why it is that – what inductive evidence we have for the contingent proposition that – the culture of the Renaissance is not merely different from, but represents a more mature phase of human growth than, that of Outer Mongolia two thousand years ago. The proposition that the culture of the Renaissance not merely did not precede, but cannot have preceded, the nomadic stage in the continuous development that we call a single culture, is something bound up so closely with our conception of how men live, of what societies are, of how they develop, indeed of the very meaning of the concepts of man, growth, society, that it is logically prior to our investigations and not their goal or product. It is not so much that it stands in no need of justification by their methods or results, as that it is logically absurd to bolster it up in this way. For this reason one might hesitate to call such knowledge empirical, for it is not confirmable or corrigible by the normal empirical methods, in relation to which it functions as base – as a frame of reference. But neither, of course, is it *a priori* (as Vico and Hegel, who showed original insight into this matter, sometimes imply) if by that is meant that it is obtainable in some special, non-naturalistic way. Recognition of the fundamental categories of human experience differs from both the acquisition of empirical information and deductive reasoning; such categories are logically prior to either, and are least subject to change among the elements that constitute our knowledge. Yet they are not unalterable; and we can ask ourselves to what degree this or that change in them would affect our experience. It is possible, although *ex hypothesi* not easy, to conceive of beings whose fundamental categories of thought or perception radically differ from ours; the greater such differences, the harder it will be for us to communicate with them, or, if the process goes further, to regard them as being human or sentient; or, if the process goes far enough, to conceive of them at all.

It is a corollary of this that one of the difficulties that beset historians and do not plague natural scientists is that of reconstructing what occurred in the past in terms not merely of our own concepts and categories, but also of how such events must have looked to those who participated in or were affected by them – psychological facts that in their turn themselves influenced events. It is difficult enough to develop an adequate consciousness of what we are and what we are at, and how we have arrived where we have done, without also being called upon to make clear to ourselves what such consciousness and self-consciousness must have been like for persons in situations different from our own; yet no less is expected of the true historian. Chemists and physicists are not obliged to investigate the states of mind of Lavoisier or Boyle; still less of the unenlightened mass of men. Mathematicians need not worry themselves with the general outlook of Euclid or Newton. Economists *qua* economists need not grasp the inner vision of Adam Smith or Keynes, still less of their less gifted contemporaries. But it is the inescapable business of the historian who is more than a compiler or the slave of a doctrine or a party to ask himself not merely what occurred (in the sense of publicly observable events), but also how the situation looked to various representative Greeks or Romans, or to Alexander or Julius Caesar, and above all to Thucydides, Tacitus or anonymous medieval chroniclers, or to Englishmen or Germans in the sixteenth century, or Frenchmen in 1789 or Russians in 1917, or to Luther, or Cromwell, or Robespierre or Lenin. This kind of imaginative projection of ourselves into the past, the attempt to capture concepts and categories that differ from those of the investigator by means of concepts and categories

135

that cannot but be his own, is a task that he can never be sure that he is even beginning to achieve, yet is not permitted to abjure. He seeks to apply scientific tests to his conclusions, but this will take him but a little way. For it is a commonplace by now that the frontiers between fact and interpretation are blurred and shifting, and that what is fact from one perspective is interpretation from another. Even if chemical and palaeographic and archaeological methods yield some hard pebbles of indubitable fact, we cannot evade the task of interpretation, for nothing counts as a historical interpretation unless it attempts to answer the question of how the world must have looked to other individuals or societies if their acts and words are to be taken as the acts and words of human beings neither wholly like ourselves nor so different as not to fit into our common past. Without a capacity for sympathy and imagination beyond any required by a physicist, there is no vision of either past or present, neither of others nor of ourselves; but where it is wholly lacking, ordinary thinking – as well as historical thinking – cannot function at all.

The contrast which I am trying to draw is not that between the two permanently opposed but complementary human demands: one for unity and homogeneity, the other for diversity and heterogeneity, which Kant has made so clear.[1] The contrast I mean is one between different types of knowledge. When the Jews are enjoined in the Bible to protect strangers, ' for ye know the heart of a stranger, seeing ye were strangers in the land of Egypt',[2] this knowledge is neither deductive, nor inductive, nor founded on direct inspection, but akin to the 'I know' of 'I know what it is to be hungry and poor', or 'I know how political bodies function', or 'I know what it is to be a Brahmin.' This is neither (to make use of Gilbert Ryle's useful classification) the 'knowing that' which the sciences provide, nor the 'knowing how' which is the possession of a disposition or skill, nor the knowledge of direct perception, acquaintance, memory, but the type of knowledge that an administrator or politician must possess of the men with whom he deals. If the historian (or, for that matter, the contemporary commentator on events) is endowed with this too poorly, if he can fall back only on inductive techniques, then, however accurate his discoveries of fact, they remain those of an antiquarian, a chronicler, at best an

[1] *Critique of Pure Reason*, trans. Norman Kemp Smith (London, 1933), p. 540.
[2] Exodus, chapter 23, verse 9.

archaeologist, but not those of an historian. It is not only erudition or belief in theories of human behaviour that enabled Marx or Namier to write history of the first order.

Perhaps some light may be cast on this issue by comparing historical method with that of linguistic or literary scholarship. No scholar could emend a text without a capacity (for which no technique exists) for 'entering into the mind of' another society and age. Electronic brains cannot perform this: they can offer alternative combinations of letters but not choose between them successfully, since the infallible rules for 'programming' have not been formulated. How do gifted scholars in fact arrive at their emendations? They do all that the most exacting natural science would demand; they steep themselves in the material of their authors; they compare, contrast, manipulate combinations like the most accomplished cypher breakers; they may find it useful to apply statistical and quantitative methods; they formulate hypotheses and test them; all this may well be indispensable but it is not enough. In the end what guides them is a sense (which comes from study of the evidence) of what a given author could, and what he could not, have said; of what fits and what does not fit into the general pattern of his thought. This, let me say again, is not the way in which we demonstrate that penicillin cures pneumonia.

It might be that the deepest chasm which divides historical from scientific studies lies between the outlook of the external observer and of the actor. It is this that was brought out by the contrast between 'inner' and 'outer' which Vico initiated, and after him the Germans, and is so suspect to modern positivists; between the questions 'How?' or 'What?' or 'When?' on one side, and the questions 'Why?', 'Following what rule?', 'Towards what goal?', 'Springing from what motive?' on the other. It lies in the difference between the category of mere together-ness or succession (the correlations to which all sciences can in the end be reduced), and that of coherence and interpretation; between factual knowledge and understanding. The latter alone makes intelligible that celebrated identity in difference (which the idealist philosophers exaggerated and abused) in virtue of which we conceive of one and the same outlook as being expressed in diverse manifestations, and perceive affinities (that are often difficult and at times impossible to formulate) between the dress of a society and its morals, its system of justice and the character of its poetry, its architecture and its domestic habits, its sciences and its religious symbols. This is Montesquieu's notorious 'spirit' of the laws (or institutions) that belong to a society. Indeed, this alone gives its sense to the very notion of belonging;[1] without it we should not understand what is meant when something is described as belonging to, or as characteristic or typical of, an age or a style or an outlook, nor, conversely, should we know what it is for some interpretation to be anachronistic, what is meant by an incompatibility between a given phenomenon and its alleged context in time; this type of misattribution is different in kind from formal inconsistency, a logical collision of theories or propositions. A concentrated interest in particular events or persons or situations as such,[2] and not as instances of a generalisation, is a prerequisite of that historical sense which, like a sense of occasion in agents intent on achieving some specific purpose, is sharpened by love or hate or danger; it is this that guides us in understanding, discovering and explaining. When historians assert particular propositions like 'Lenin played a crucial role in making the Russian Revolution', or 'Without Churchill Britain would have been defeated in 1940', the rational grounds for such assertions, whatever their degree of plausibility, are not identical with generalisations of the type 'Such men, in such conditions, usually affect events in this fashion' for which the evidence may be exceedingly feeble; for we do not test the propositions solely – or indeed generally – by their logical links with such general propositions (or explanation sketches), but rather in terms of their coherence with our picture of a specific situation. To analyse this type of knowledge into a finite collection of general and particular, categorical and hypothetical, propositions, is not practicable. Every judgement that we formulate, whether in historical thought or ordinary life, involves general ideas and propositions without which there can be no thought or language. At times some among these generalisations can be clearly stated, and combined into models; where this occurs, natural sciences

---

[1] Cf. p. 109 above.

[2] 'There are really only two ways of acquiring knowledge of human affairs' says Ranke: 'through the perception of the particular, or through abstraction . . . the former [is the method] of history. There is no other way . . .

'Two qualities, I think, are required for the making of the true historian: first he must feel a participation and pleasure in the particular for itself . . . Just as one takes delight in flowers without thinking to what genus of Linnaeus . . . they belong . . . without thinking how the whole manifests itself in the particular.

'Still, this does not suffice; . . . while [the historian] reflects on the particular, the development of the world in general will become apparent to him.' In *The Varieties of History*, ed. Fritz Stern (New York, 1956), pp. 58–9.

arise. But the descriptive and explanatory language of historians, because they seek to record or analyse or account for specific or even unique phenomena as such[1] – as often as not for their own sakes – cannot, for that reason, be reduced without residue to such general formulas, still less to models and their applications. Any attempt to do so will be halted at the outset by the discovery that the subject-matter involves a 'thick' texture of criss-crossing, constantly changing and melting conscious and unconscious beliefs and assumptions some of which it is impossible and all of which it is difficult to formulate, on which, nevertheless, our rational views and rational acts are founded, and, indeed, which they exhibit or articulate. This is the 'web' of which Taine speaks, and it is possible to go only some way (it is impossible to say in advance how far) towards isolating and describing its ingredients if our rationality is challenged. And even if we succeed in making explicit all (which is absurd) or many (which is not practicable) of our general propositions or beliefs, this achievement will not take us much nearer the scientific ideal; for between a collection of generalisations – or unanalysed knots of them – and the construction of a model there still lies difficult or impassable country: the generalisations must exhibit an exceptional degree of constancy and logical connection if this passage is to be negotiated.

What are we to call the faculty which an artist displays in choosing his material for his particular purpose; or which a politician or a publicist needs when he adopts a policy or presents a thesis, the success of which may depend on the degree of his sensitiveness to circumstances and to human characters, and to the specific interplay between them, with which, and upon which, he is working? The *Wirkungszusammenhang*, the general structure or pattern of experience – understanding of this may be uniquely valuable for scientists, but it is absolutely indispensable to the historian. Without it, he remains at best a chronicler or technical specialist; at worst a distorter and writer of inferior fiction. He may achieve accuracy, objectivity, lucidity, literary quality, breadth of knowledge, but unless he conveys a recognisable vision of life, and exhibits that sense of what fits into a given situation and what does not which is the ultimate test of sanity, a perception of a social *Gestalt*, not, as a rule, capable of being formalised in terms, let us say, of a field theory – unless he possesses a minimal capacity for this, the result is not recognised by us as an account of reality, that is, of what human

[1] All facts are, of course, unique, those dealt with by natural scientists no less than any others; but it is not their uniqueness that interests scientists.

beings, as we understand the term, could have felt or thought or done.

It was, I think, L. B. Namier who once remarked about historical sense that there was no *a priori* short-cut to knowledge of the past; what actually happened can only be established by scrupulous empirical investigation, by research in its normal sense. What is meant by historical sense is the knowledge not of what happened, but of what did not happen. When a historian, in attempting to decide what occurred and why, rejects all the infinity of logically open possibilities, the vast majority of which are obviously absurd, and, like a detective, investigates only those possibilities which have at least some initial plausibility, it is this sense of what is plausible – what men, being men, could have done or been – that constitutes the sense of coherence with the patterns of life that I have tried to indicate. Such words as plausibility, likelihood, sense of reality, historical sense, denote typical qualitative categories which distinguish historical studies as opposed to the natural sciences that seek to operate on a quantitative basis. This distinction, which orginated in Vico and Herder, and was developed by Hegel and (*malgré soi*) Marx, Dilthey and Weber, is of fundamental importance.

The gifts that historians need are different from those of the natural scientists. The latter must abstract, generalise, idealise, qualify, dissociate normally associated ideas (for nature is full of strange surprises, and as little as possible must be taken for granted), deduce, establish with certainty, reduce everything to the maximum degree of regularity, uniformity, and, so far as possible, to timeless repetitive patterns. Historians cannot ply their trade without a considerable capacity for thinking in general terms; but they need, in addition, peculiar attributes of their own: a capacity for integration, for perceiving qualitative similarities and differences, a sense of the unique fashion in which various factors combine in the particular concrete situation, which must at once be neither so unlike any other situation as to constitute a total break with the continuous flow of human experience, nor yet so stylised and uniform as to be the obvious creature of theory and not of flesh and blood. The capacities needed are rather those of association than of dissociation, of perceiving the relation of parts to wholes, of particular sounds or colours to the many possible tunes or pictures into which they might enter, of the links that connect individuals viewed and savoured as individuals, and not primarily as instances of types or laws. It is this that Hegel tried to put under the head of the synthesising 'Reason' as opposed to the analytic 'Understanding'; and to provide it with a logic of its own. It is the 'logic' that proved incapable of clear formulation or utility: it is this that cannot be incorporated in electronic brains. Such gifts relate as much to practice as to theory; perhaps to practice more directly. A man who lacks common intelligence can be a physicist of genius, but not even a mediocre historian. Some of the characteristics indispensable to (although not, by themselves, sufficient to move) historians are more akin to those needed in active human intercourse, than in the study or the laboratory or the cloister. The capacity for associating the fruits of experience in a manner that enables its possessors to distinguish, without the benefit of rules, what is central, permanent, or universal from what is local, or peripheral, or transient – that is what gives concreteness and plausibility, the breath of life, to historical accounts. Skill in establishing hypotheses by means of obser-vation or memory or inductive procedures, while ultimately indispens-able to the discovery of all forms of truth about the world, is not the rarest of the qualities required by historians, nor is the desire to find recurrences and laws itself a symptom of historical talent.

If we ask ourselves which historians have commanded the most lasting admiration, we shall, I think, find that they are neither the most ingenious, nor the most precise, nor even the discoverers of new facts or unsuspected causal connections, but those who (like imaginative writers) present men or societies or situations in many dimensions, at many intersecting levels simultaneously, writers in whose accounts human lives, and their relations both to each other and to the external world, are what (at our most lucid and imaginative) we know that they can be. The gifts that scientists most need are not these: they must be ready to call everything into question, to construct bold hypotheses unrelated to customary empirical procedures, and drive their logical implications as far as they will go, free from control by common sense or too great a fear of departing from what is normal or possible in the world. Only in this way will new truths and relations between them be found – truths which, in psychology or anthropology as well as physics or mathematics, do not depend upon preserving contact with common human experience. In this sense, to say of history that it should approxi-mate to the condition of a science is to ask it to contradict its essence.

It would be generally agreed that the reverse of a grasp of reality is the tendency to fantasy or Utopia. But perhaps there exist more ways than one to defy reality. May it not be that to be unscientific is to defy, for no good logical or empirical reason, established hypotheses and laws; while to be unhistorical is the opposite – to ignore or twist one's view of particular events, persons, predicaments, in the name of laws, theories, principles derived from other fields, logical, ethical, metaphysical, scientific, which the nature of the medium renders inapplicable? For what else is it that is done by those theorists who are called fanatical because their faith in a given pattern is not overcome by their sense of reality? For this reason the attempt to construct a discipline which would stand to concrete history as pure to applied, no matter how successful the human sciences may grow to be – even if, as all but obscurantists must hope, they discover genuine, empirically confirmed, laws of individual and collective behaviour – seems an attempt to square the circle. It is not a vain hope for an ideal goal beyond human powers, but a chimera, born of lack of understanding of the nature of natural science, or of history, or of both.

Does Political Theory Still Exist?

I

Is there still such a subject as political theory? This query, put with suspicious frequency in English-speaking countries, questions the very credentials of the subject: it suggests that political philosophy, whatever it may have been in the past, is today dead or dying. The principal symptom which seems to support this belief is that no commanding work of political philosophy has appeared in the twentieth century. By a commanding work in the field of general ideas I mean at the very least one that has in a large area converted paradoxes into platitudes or vice versa. This seems to me no more (but also no less) than an adequate criterion of the characteristic in question.

But this is scarcely conclusive evidence. There exist only two good reasons for certifying the demise of a discipline: one is that its central presuppositions, empirical, or metaphysical, or logical, are no longer accepted because they have (with the world of which they were a part) withered away, or because they have been discredited or refuted. The other is that new disciplines have come to perform the work originally undertaken by the older study. These disciplines may have their own limitations, but they exist, they function, and have either inherited or usurped the functions of their predecessors: there is no room left for the ancestor from whom they spring. This is the fate that overtook astrology, alchemy, phrenology (positivists, both old and new, would include theology and metaphysics). The postulates on which these disciplines were based either were destroyed by argument or collapsed for other reasons; consequently they are today regarded merely as instances of systematic delusion.

The original version of this article appeared in French as 'La théorie politique existe-t-elle?', *Revue française de science politique* 11 (1961), 309–37. It was then revised by the author for publication in English, and he is grateful to S. N. Hampshire, H. L. A. Hart, F. Rossi Landi, P. L. Gardiner, G. J. Warnock, and most of all to M. W. Dick, for reading and commenting on it in its earlier form.

F
143

This type of systematic parricide is, in effect, the history of the natural sciences in their relation to philosophy, and so has a direct bearing upon the question before us. The relevant consideration is this: there exist at least two classes of problems to which men have succeeded in obtaining clear answers. The first have been so formulated that they can (at least in principle, if not always in practice) be answered by observation and by inference from observed data. These determine the domains of natural science and of everyday common sense. Whether I ask simple questions about whether there is any food in the cupboard, or what kind of birds are to be found in Patagonia, or the intentions of an individual; or more complicated ones about the structure of matter, or the behaviour of social classes or international markets; I know that the answer, to have any genuine claim to truth, must rest on someone's observation of what exists or happens in the spatio-temporal world. Some would say 'organised observation'. I should be inclined to agree. But differences on this issue, while they are crucial for the philosophy of science and the theory of knowledge, do not affect my argument. All the generalisations and hypotheses and models with which the most sophisticated sciences work can be established and discredited ultimately only by the data of inspection or introspection.

The second type of question to which we can hope to obtain clear answers is formal. Given certain propositions called axioms, together with rules for deducing other propositions from them, I can proceed by mere calculation. The answers to my questions will be valid or invalid according to whether the rules that I accept without question as part of a given discipline have been correctly used. Such disciplines contain no statements based on observation of fact, and therefore are not nowadays expected to provide information about the universe, whether or not they are used in providing it. Mathematics and formal logic are, of course, the best-known examples of formal sciences of this type, but heraldry, chess, and theories of games in general, are similar applications of the formal methods which govern such disciplines.

These two methods of answering questions may be, very generally, denominated empirical and formal. Among the characteristics of both are at least these:

1 That even if we do not know the answer to a given question, we know what kinds of methods are appropriate in looking for the answer; we know what kinds of answers are relevant to these questions, even if they are not true. If I am asked how the Soviet system of

criminal law functions or why Mr Kennedy was elected President of the United States, I may not be able to answer the question, but I know within what region the relevant evidence must lie, and how an expert would use such evidence to obtain the answer; I must be able to state this in very general terms, if only to show that I have understood the question. Similarly, if I am asked for the proof of Fermat's theorem, I may not be able to give it, indeed I may know that no one has yet been able to provide it, but I also know what kinds of demonstration would count as answers to this problem, even though they may be incorrect or inconclusive, and can discriminate these from assertions which are irrelevant to the topic. In other words, in all these cases, even if I do not know the answer, I know where to look for it, or how to identify an authority or expert who knows how to set about looking for it.

2 This means, in effect, that where the concepts are firm, clear and generally accepted, and the methods of reasoning, arriving at conclusions etc. are agreed between men (at least the majority of those who have anything to do with these matters), there and only there is it possible to construct a science, formal or empirical. Wherever this is not the case – where the concepts are vague or too much in dispute, and methods of argument and the minimum qualifications that constitute an expert are not generally agreed, where we find frequent recriminations about what can or what cannot claim to be a law, an established hypothesis, an undisputed truth, and so on – we are at best in the realm of quasi-science. The principal candidates for inclusion into the charmed circle, who have not succeeded in passing the required tests, are the occupants of the large, rich and central, but unstable, volcanic and misty region of 'ideologies'. One of the rough and ready tests for finding out which region we are in, is whether a set of rules, accepted by the great majority of experts in the subject, and capable of being incorporated in a textbook, can be applied in the field in question. To the degree to which such rules are applicable, a discipline approaches the coveted condition of an accepted science. Psychology, sociology, semantics, logic, perhaps certain branches of economics, are in a no-man's-land, some nearer to, some further from, the frontier which demarcates, less or more clearly, the territory of the established sciences.

3 But besides these two major categories, there arise questions which fall outside either group. It is not only that we may not know the answers to certain questions, but that we are not clear how to set about trying to answer them – where to look – what would constitute

evidence for an answer and what would not. When I am asked 'Where is the image in the mirror?' or 'Can time stand still?' I am not sure what kind of question it is that is being asked, or whether indeed it makes any sense at all. I am in not much better plight with some traditional questions which have probably been asked since the dawn of thought, such as 'How did the world begin?' and, following that, 'What happened before the beginning?' Some say that these are not legitimate questions; but then what makes them illegitimate? There is something that I am trying to ask; for I am certainly puzzled by something. When I ask 'Why can I not be in two places at once?', 'Why can I not get back into the past?' or, to move to another region, 'What is justice?' or 'Is justice objective, absolute etc.?' or again 'How can we ever be sure that an action is just?' – no obvious method of settling these questions lies to hand. One of the surest hallmarks of a philosophical question – for this is what all these questions are – is that we are puzzled from the very outset, that there is no automatic technique, no universally recognised expertise, for dealing with such questions. We discover that we do not feel sure how to set about clearing our minds, finding out the truth, accepting or rejecting earlier answers to these questions. Neither induction (in its widest sense of scientific reasoning), nor direct observation (appropriate to empirical inquiries), nor deduction (demanded by formal problems) seem to be of help. Once we do feel quite clear about how we should proceed, the questions no longer seem philosophical.

The history – and indeed the advance – of human thought (this is perhaps a truism) have, in fact, largely consisted in the gradual shuffling of all the basic questions that men ask into one or the other of two well-organised compartments – the empirical and the formal. Wherever concepts grow firm and clear and acquire universal acceptance, a new science, natural or formal, comes into being. To use a simile that I cannot claim to have invented, philosophy is like a radiant sun that, from time to time, throws off portions of itself; these masses, when they cool down, acquire a firm and recognisable structure of their own and acquire independent careers as tidy and regular planets; but the central sun continues on its path, and does not seem to diminish in mass or radiance. The 'status' and vitality of philosophy is another matter, and seems to be directly connected with the extent to which it deals with issues that are of concern to the common man. The relation of philosophy to opinion and conduct is a central question of both history and sociology, too large to be considered here. What concerns us is that philosophy in one state of development may turn into a science in the next.

It is no confusion of thought that caused astronomy, for example, to be regarded as a philosophical discipline in, say, the time of Scotus Erigena, when its concepts and methods were not what we should today regard as firm or clear, and the part played by observation in relation to *a priori* teleological notions (e.g. the yearning of each body to realise the full perfection of its nature) made it impossible to determine whether the amalgam that went under the name of the knowledge of celestial bodies was empirical or formal. As soon as clear concepts and specific techniques developed, the science of astronomy emerged. In other words, astronomy in its beginning could not be relegated to either compartment, even if such compartments as the empirical and the formal had been clearly distinguished; and it was, of course, part of the 'philosophical' status of early medieval astronomy that the civilisation of that time (Marxists would say 'the superstructure') did not permit the distinction between the two compartments to be clearly demarcated.

What, therefore, is characteristic of specifically philosophical questions is that they do not (and some of them perhaps never will) satisfy conditions required by an independent science, the principal among which is that the path to their solution must be implicit in their very formulation. Nevertheless, there are some subjects which clearly are near the point of taking flight and divorcing themselves from the main body in which they were born, much as physics and mathematics and chemistry and biology have done in their day. One of these is semantics; another is psychology; with one foot, however reluctantly, they are still sunk in philosophical soil; but they show signs of a tendency to tear themselves loose and emancipate themselves, with only historical memories to tell them of their earlier, more confused, if in some respects richer, years.

II

Among the topics that remain obstinately philosophical, and have, despite repeated efforts, failed to transform themselves into sciences, are some that in their very essence involve value judgements. Ethics, aesthetics, criticism explicitly concerned with general ideas, all but the most technical types of history and scholarship, still live at various points of this limbo, unable or unwilling to emerge by either the empirical or the formal door. The mere fact that value judgements are relevant to an intellectual pursuit is clearly not sufficient to disqualify it from being a recognised science. The concept of normal health certainly embodies a valuation, and although there is sufficient universal consensus about what constitutes good health, a normal state, disease and so on, this concept, nevertheless, does not enter as an intrinsic element into the sciences of anatomy, physiology, pathology, etc. Pursuit of health may be the strongest sociological and psychological (and moral) factor in creating and promoting these sciences; it may determine which problems and aspects of the subject have been most ardently attended to; but it is not referred to in the science itself, any more than the uses of history or logic need be mentioned in historical or logical works. If so clear, universally accepted, 'objective' a value as that of desirable state of health is extruded from the structure of the natural sciences, this fact is even more conspicuous in more controversial fields. The attempts, from Plato to our own day (particularly persistent and numerous in the eighteenth century), to found objective sciences of ethics and aesthetics on the basis of universally accepted values, or of methods of discovering them, have met with little success; relativism, subjectivism, romanticism, scepticism with regard to values, keep breaking in.

What, we may ask at this point, is the position of political theory? What are its most typical problems? Are they empirical, or formal, or neither? Do they necessarily entail questions of value? Are they on the way to independent status, or are they by their very nature compelled to remain only an element in some wider body of thought?

Among the problems which form the core of traditional political theory are those, for instance, of the nature of equality, of rights, law, authority, rules. We demand the analysis of these concepts, or ask how these expressions function in our language, or what forms of behaviour they prescribe or forbid and why, or into what system of value or outlook they fit, and in what way. When we ask, what is perhaps the most fundamental of all political questions, 'Why should anyone obey anyone else?', we ask not 'Why do men obey?' – something that empirical psychology, anthropology and sociology might be able to answer – nor yet 'Who obeys whom, when and where, and determined by what causes?', which could perhaps be answered on the basis of evidence drawn from these and similar fields. When we ask why a man should obey, we are asking for the explanation of what is normative in such notions as authority, sovereignty, liberty, and the justification of their validity in political arguments. These are words in the name of which orders are issued, men are coerced, wars are fought, new societies are created and old ones destroyed – expressions which play as great a part as any in our lives today. What makes such questions prima facie philosophical is the fact that no wide agreement exists on the meaning of some of the concepts involved. There are sharp differences on what constitute valid reasons for actions in these fields; on how the relevant propositions are to be established or even rendered plausible; on who or what constitutes recognised authority for deciding these questions; and there is consequently no consensus on the frontier between valid public criticism and subversion, or freedom and oppression and the like. So long as conflicting replies to such questions continue to be given by different schools and thinkers, the prospects of establishing a science in this field, whether empirical or formal, seem remote. Indeed, it seems clear that disagreements about the analysis of value concepts, as often as not, spring from profounder differences, since the notions of, say, rights or justice or liberty will be radically dissimilar for theists and atheists, mechanistic determinists and Christians, Hegelians and empiricists, romantic irrationalists and Marxists, and so forth. It seems no less clear that these differences are not, at least prima facie, either logical or empirical, and have usually and rightly been classified as irreducibly philosophical.

This carries at least one important implication. If we ask the Kantian question 'In what kind of world is political philosophy – the kind of discussion and argument in which it consists – in principle possible?' the answer must be 'Only in a world where ends collide.' In a society dominated by a single goal there could in principle only be arguments about the best means to attain this end – and arguments about means are technical, that is, scientific and empirical in character: they can be settled by experience and observation or whatever other methods are used to discover causes and correlations; they can, at least in principle, be reduced to positive sciences. In such a society no serious questions about political ends or values could arise, only empirical ones about the most effective paths to the goal. And indeed, something amounting to this was, in effect, asserted by Saint-Simon and Comte; and, on some interpretations of his thought, by Marx also, at any rate after 'prehistory', i.e. the class war, is over, and man's true 'history' – the united attack on nature to obtain goods upon whose desirability the whole of society is agreed – has begun. It follows that the only society in which political philosophy in its traditional sense, that is, an inquiry concerned not solely with elucidation of concepts, but with the critical examination of presuppositions and assumptions, and the questioning of the order of priorities and ultimate ends, is possible, is a society in which there is no total acceptance of any single end. There may be a variety of reasons for this: because no single end has been accepted by a sufficient number of persons; because no one end can be regarded as ultimate, since there can, in principle, exist no guarantee that other values may not at some time engage men's reason or their passions; because no unique, final end can be found – inasmuch as men can pursue many distinct ends, none of them means to, or parts of, one another; and so on. Some among these ends may be public or political; nor is there any reason to suppose that all of them must, even in principle, be compatible with one another. Unless political philosophy is confined to the analysis of concepts or expressions, it can be pursued consistently only in a pluralist, or potentially pluralist, society. But since all analysis, however abstract, itself involves a critical approach to the assumptions under analysis, this distinction remains purely academic. Rigid monism is compatible with philosophical analysis only in theory. The plight of philosophy under despotism in our own times provides conclusive concrete evidence for this thesis.

III

Let me try to make this clearer. If we could construct a society in which it was believed universally (or at least by as many people as believe that the purpose of medicine is to promote or maintain health and are agreed about what constitutes health) that there was only one overriding human purpose: for example, a technocratic society dedicated to the single end of the richest realisation of all human faculties; or a utilitarian society dedicated to the greatest happiness of men; or a Thomist or communist or Platonic or anarchist, or any other society which is monistic in this sense – then plainly all that would matter would be to find the right roads to the attainment of the universally accepted end.

This statement needs to be qualified in at least two respects. The schema is in the first place artificially over-simplified. In practice, the kind of goal that can command the allegiance of a society – happiness, power, obedience to the divine will, national glory, individual self-realisation, or some other ultimate pattern of life, is so general that it leaves open the question of what kind of lives or conduct incarnate it. No society can be so 'monolithic' that there is no gap between its culminating purpose and the means towards it – a gap filled with secondary ends, penultimate values, which are not means to the final end, but elements in it or expressions of it; and these in their turn incarnate themselves in still more specific purposes at still lower levels, and so on downwards to the particular problem of everyday conduct. 'What is to be done?' is a question which can occur at any level – from the highest to the lowest: doubts and disputes concerning the values involved at any of these levels, and the relationships of these values to one another, can arise at any point.

These questions are not purely technical and empirical, not merely problems about the best means to a given end, nor are they mere questions of logical consistency, that is, formal and deductive; but properly philosophical. To take contemporary examples: what is claimed for integration of Negroes and whites in the Southern states of the United States is not that it is a means towards achieving a goal external to itself – social justice or equality – but that it is itself a form of it, a value in the hierarchy of values. Or again 'One man one vote', or the rights of minorities or of colonial territories, are likewise not simply questions of machinery – a particular means of promoting equality which could, in theory, be equally well realised by other means, say by more ingenious voting devices – but, for those who believe in these principles, intrinsic ingredients in the ideal of social equality, and consequently to be pursued as such, and not solely for the sake of their results. It follows that even in a society dominated by a single supreme purpose, questions of what is to be done, especially when the subordinate ends come into conflict, cannot be automatically answered by deductive reasoning from accepted premises, aided by adequate knowledge of facts, as certain thinkers, Aristotle at times, or Bertrand Russell in his middle phase, or a good many Catholic casuists, seem to have assumed.

Moreover, and this is our second qualification, it might well be the case that although the formulas accepted by a society were sacred and immutable, they might carry different – and perhaps incompatible – meanings for different persons and in different situations; philosophical analysis of the relevant concepts might well bring out sharp disagreements. This has been the case conspicuously where the purpose or ideal of a society is expressed in such vague and general terms as the common good, or the fulfilment of the law of God, or rights to life, liberty and the pursuit of happiness and the like.

Nevertheless, and in spite of these qualifications, the stylised model of a society whose ends are given once and for all, and which is merely concerned with discovery of means, is a useful abstraction. It is useful because it demonstrates that to acknowledge the reality of political questions presupposes a pluralism of values – whether ultimate ones, or on the lower slopes of the hierarchy of values – recognition of which is incompatible with a technocratic or authoritarian everything-is-either-an-indisputable-end-or-a-means, monistic structure of values. Nor is the monistic situation entirely a figment of theory. In critical situations where deviation from the norm may involve disastrous consequences – in battles, surgical operating rooms, revolutions, the end is wholly concrete, varying interpretations of it are out of place, and all action is conceived as a means towards it alone. It is one of the stratagems of totalitarian regimes to represent all situations as critical emergencies, demanding ruthless elimination of all goals, interpretations, forms of behaviour save for one absolutely specific, concrete, immediate end, binding on everyone, which calls for ends and means so narrow and clearly definable that it is easy to impose sanctions for failing to pursue them.

To find roads is the business of experts. It is therefore reasonable for such a society to put itself into the hands of specialists of tested experience, knowledge, gifts and probity, whose business it is, to use Saint-Simon's simile, to conduct the human caravan to the oasis the reality and desirability of which are recognised by all. In such a society, whatever its other characteristics, we should expect to find intensive study of social causation, especially of what types of political organisation yield the best results, that is, are best at advancing society towards the overriding goal. Political thought in such a society would be fed by all the evidence that can be supplied by the empirical sciences of history, psychology, anthropology, sociology, comparative law, penology, biology, physiology and so forth. The goal (and the best ways of avoiding obstacles to it) may become clearer as the result of careful studies of human thought and behaviour; and its general character must not at any stage be obscure or doubtful; otherwise differences of value judgement will creep into the political sciences as well, and inject what can only be called philosophical issues (or issues of principle) incapable of being resolved by either empirical or formal means. Differences of interpretation of fact – provided these are uncontaminated by disagreements about the ends of life – can be permitted; but if political theory is to be converted into an applied science, what is needed is a single dominant model – like the doctor's model of a healthy body – accepted by the whole, or the greater part, of the society in question. The model will be its 'ideological foundation'. Although such a model is a necessary condition for such a science, it may not, even then, begin to be a sufficient one.

It is at this point that the deep division between the monists and pluralists becomes crucial and conspicuous. On one side stand Platonists and Aristotelians, Stoics and Thomists, positivists and Marxists, and all those who seek to translate political problems into scientific terms. For them human ends are objective: men are what they are, or change in accordance with discoverable laws; and their needs or interests or duties can be established by the correct (naturalistic, or transcendental, or theological) methods. Given that we can penetrate past error and confusion by true and reliable modes of investigation – metaphysical insight or the social sciences, or some other dependable instrument – and thereby establish what is good for men and how to effect this, the only unsolved problems will be more or less technical: how to obtain the means for securing these ends, and how to distribute what the technical means provide in the socially and psychologically best manner. This, in the most general terms, is the ideal both of the enlightened atheists of the eighteenth century and the positivists of the nineteenth; of some Marxists of the twentieth, and of those Churches which know the end for which man is made, and know that it is in principle attainable – or at least is such that the road towards it can be discerned – here, below.

On the other side are those who believe in some form of original sin or the impossibility of human perfection, and therefore tend to be sceptical of the empirical attainability of any final solution to the deepest human problems. With them are to be found the sceptics and relativists and also those who believe that the very efforts to solve the problems of one age or culture alter both the men who strive to do so and those for whose benefit the solutions are applied, and thereby create new men and new problems, the character of which cannot today be anticipated, let alone analysed or solved, by men bounded by their own historical horizons. Here too belong the many sects of subjectivists and irrationalists; and in particular those romantic thinkers who hold that ends of action are not discovered, but are created by individuals or cultures or nations as works of art are, so that the answer to the question 'What should we do?' is undiscoverable not because it is beyond our powers to find the answer, but because the question is not one of fact at all, the solution lies not in discovering something which is what it is, whether it is discovered or not – a proposition or formula, an objective good, a principle, a system of values objective or subjective, a relationship between a mind and something non-mental – but resides in action: something which cannot be found, only invented – an act of will or faith or creation obedient to no pre-existent rules or laws or facts.

Here too stand those twentieth-century heirs of romanticism, the existentialists, with their belief in the free self-commitment by individuals to actions or forms of life determined by the agent choosing freely; such choice does not take account of objective standards, since these are held to be a form of illusion or 'false consciousness', and the belief in such figments is psychologically traced to fear of freedom – of being abandoned, left to one's own resources – a terror which leads to uncritical acceptance of systems claiming objective authority, spurious theological or metaphysical cosmologies which undertake to guarantee the eternal validity of moral or intellectual rules and principles. Not far from here, too, are fatalists and mystics, as well as those who believe that accident dominates history, and other irrationalists; but also those indeterminists and those troubled rationalists who doubt the possibility of discovering a fixed human nature obedient to invariant laws; especially those for whom the proposition that the future needs of men and their satisfaction are predictable does not fit into an idea of human nature which entails such concepts as will, choice, effort, purpose, with their presupposition of the perpetual opening of new paths of action – a presupposition which enters into the very definition of what we mean by man. This last is the position adopted by those modern Marxists who, in the face of the cruder and more popular versions of the doctrine, have understood the implications of their own premises and principles.

IV

Men's beliefs in the sphere of conduct are part of their conception of themselves and others as human beings; and this conception in its turn, whether conscious or not, is intrinsic to their picture of the world. This picture may be complete and coherent, or shadowy or confused, but almost always, and especially in the case of those who have attempted to articulate what they conceive to be the structure of thought or reality, it can be shown to be dominated by one or more models or paradigms: mechanistic, organic, aesthetic, logical, mystical, shaped by the strongest influence of the day – religious, scientific, metaphysical or artistic. This model or paradigm determines the content as well as the form of beliefs and behaviour. A man who, like Aristotle or Thomas Aquinas, believes that all things are definable in terms of their purpose, and that nature is a hierarchy or an ascending pyramid of such purposive entities, is committed to the view that the end of human life consists in self-fulfilment, the character of which must depend on the kind of nature that a man has, and on the place that he occupies in the harmonious activity of the entire universal, self-realising enterprise. It follows that the political philosophy and, more particularly, the diagnosis of political possibilities and purposes of an Aristotelian or a Thomist will *ipso facto* be radically different from that of, let us say, someone who has learned from Hobbes or Spinoza or any modern positivist that there are no purposes in nature, that there are only causal (or functional or statistical) laws, only repetitive cycles of events, which may, however, within limits, be harnessed to fulfil the purposes of men; with the corollary that the pursuit of purposes is itself nothing but a product in the human consciousness of natural processes the laws of which men can neither significantly alter nor account for, if by accounting is meant giving an explanation in terms of the goals of a creator who does not exist, or of a nature of which it is meaningless to say that it pursues purposes — for what is that but to attempt to apply to it a subjective human category, to fall into the fallacy of animism or anthropomorphism?

The case is similar with regard to the issue of freedom and authority. The question 'Why should I obey (rather than do as I like)?' will be (and has been) answered in one way by those who, like Luther, or Bodin, or the Russian Slavophils and many others whose thoughts have been deeply coloured by biblical imagery, conceive of life (although in very different fashions) in terms of the relations of children to their father, and of laws as his commands, where loyalty, obedience, love, and the presence of immediate authority are all unquestioned, and surround life from birth to death as real and palpable relationships or agencies. This question will be answered very differently by the followers of, say, Plato, or Kant (divided by a whole heaven as these thinkers are), who believe in permanent, impersonal, universal, objective truths, conceived on the model of logical or mathematical or physical laws, by analogy with which their political concepts will be formed. Yet other, and wholly dissimilar, sets of answers will be determined by the great vitalistic conceptions, the model for which is drawn from the facts of growth as conceived in early biology, and for which reality is an organic, qualitative process, not analysable into quantitative units. Others again will originate in minds dominated by the image of some central force, thrusting forward in many guises, like some gnostic or Brahmin notion of perpetual self-creation; or be traceable to a concept drawn from artistic activity, in which the universe is seen not as an unconscious quasi-biological process of the spirit or the flesh, but as the endless creation of a demiurge, in which freedom and self-fulfilment lie in the recognition by men of themselves as involved in the purposive process of cosmic creation – a vision fully revealed only to those beings to whom the nature of the world is disclosed, at least fragmentarily, through their own experience as creators (something of this kind emanated from the doctrines of Fichte, Schelling, Carlyle, Nietzsche and other romantic thinkers, as well as Bergson and in places Hegel, and, in his youth, Marx, who were obsessed by aesthetico-biological models); some among these, anarchists and irrationalists, conceive of reality as freedom from all rules and set ideals – fetters, even when they are self-imposed, upon the free creative spirit – a doctrine of which we have heard, if anything, too much. The model itself may be regarded as the product of historical factors: the social (and psychological) consequences of the development of productive forces, as Marx taught, or the effects in the minds of individuals of purely psychological processes which Freud and his disciples have investigated. The study of myths, rationalisations, ideologies and obsessive patterns of many kinds, has become a great and fertile preoccupation of our time. The fundamental assumption underlying this approach is that the 'ideological' model has not been arrived at by rational methods, but is the product of causal factors; it may disguise itself in rational dress, but, given the historical, or economic, or geographical, or psychological situation, must, in any case, have emerged in one form or another.

For political thinkers, however, the primary question is not that of genesis and conditions of growth, but that of validity and truth: does the model distort reality? Does it blind us to real differences and similarities and generate other, fictitious ones? Does it suppress, violate, invent, deceive? In the case of scientific (or commonsense) explanations or hypotheses, the tests of validity include increase in the power of accurate (or more refined) prediction or control of the behaviour of the subject-matter. Is political thought practical and empirical in this sense? Machiavelli, and in differing degrees Hobbes, Spinoza, Helvétius, Marx, at times speak as if this were so. This is one of the interpretations of the famous doctrine of the unity of theory and practice. But is it an adequate account of the purpose or achievements of – to take only the moderns – Locke or Kant or Rousseau or Mill or the liberals, the existentialists, the logical positivists and linguistic analysts and natural law theorists of our own day? And if not, why not?

To return to the notion of models. It is by now a commonplace that the data of observation can be accommodated to almost any theoretical model. Those who are obsessed by one model can accept facts, general propositions, hypotheses and even methods of argument, adopted and perfected by those who were dominated by quite a different model. For this reason, political theory, if by theories we mean no more than causal or functional hypotheses and explanations designed to account only for what happens – in this case for what men have thought or done or will think or do – can perfectly well be a progressive empirical inquiry, capable of detaching itself from its original metaphysical or ethical foundations, and sufficiently adaptable to preserve through many changes of intellectual climate its own character and development as an independent science. After all, even mathematics, although bound up with – and obstructed by – metaphysics and theology, has nevertheless progressed from the days of the Greeks to our own; so too have the natural sciences, at any rate since the seventeenth century, despite vast upheavals in the general *Weltanschauungen* of the societies in which they were created.

But I should like to say once again that unless political theory is conceived in narrowly sociological terms, it differs from political science or any other empirical inquiry in being concerned with somewhat different fields; namely with such questions as what is specifically human and what is not, and why; whether specific categories, say those of purpose or of belonging to a group or of law, are indispensable to understanding what men are; and so, inevitably, with the source, scope and validity of certain human goals. If this is its task, it cannot, from the very nature of its interests, avoid evaluation; it is thoroughly committed not only to the analysis of, but to conclusions about the validity of, ideas of the good and the bad, the permitted and the forbidden, the harmonious and the discordant problems which any discussion of liberty or justice or authority or political morality is sooner or later bound to encounter. These central conceptions, moral, political, aesthetic, have altered as the all-inclusive metaphysical models in which they are an essential element have themselves altered. Any change in the central model is a change in the ways in which the data of experience are perceived and interpreted. The degree to which such categories are shot through with evaluation will doubtless depend on their direct connection with human desires and interests. Statements about physical nature can achieve neutrality in this respect; this is more difficult when the data are those of history, and nearly impossible in the case of moral and social life, where the words themselves are inescapably charged with ethical or aesthetic or political content.

To suppose, then, that there have been or could be ages without political philosophy, is like supposing that as there are ages of faith, so there are or could be ages of total disbelief. But this is an absurd notion: there is no human activity without some kind of general outlook: scepticism, cynicism, refusal to dabble in abstract issues or to question values, hard boiled opportunism, contempt for theorising, all the varieties of nihilism, are, of course, themselves metaphysical and ethical positions, committal attitudes. Whatever else the existentialists have taught us, they have made this fact plain. The idea of a completely *wertfrei* theory (or model) of human action (as contrasted, say, with animal behaviour) rests on a naïve misconception of what objectivity or neutrality in the social studies must be.

v

The notion that a simile or model, drawn from one sphere, is necessarily misleading when applied to another, and that it is possible to think without such analogies in some direct fashion – 'face-to-face' with the facts – will not bear criticism. To think is to generalise, to generalise is to compare. To think of one phenomenon or cluster of phenomena is to think in terms of its resemblances and differences with others. This is by now a hoary platitude. It follows that without parallels and analogies between one sphere and another of thought and action, whether conscious or not, the unity of our experience – our experience itself – would not be possible. All language and thought is, in this sense, necessarily 'metaphorical'. The models, once they are made conscious and explicit, may turn out to be obsolete or misleading. Yet even the most discredited among these models in politics – the social contract, patriarchalism, the organic society and so forth, must have started with some initial validity to have had the influence on thought that they have had.

No analogy powerful enough to govern the concepts of generations of men can have been wholly specious. When Jean Bodin or Herder or the Russian Slavophils or the German sociologist Tönnies transfer the notion of family nexus to political life, they remind us of aspects of relationships between men united by traditional bonds or bound by common habits and loyalties, which had been misrepresented by the Stoics or Machiavelli or Bentham or Nietzsche or Herbert Spencer. So too, assimilation of law to a command issued by some constituted authority in any one of the three types of social order distinguished by Max Weber throws some light on the concept of law. Similarly, the

158

social contract is a model which to this day helps to explain something of what it is that men feel to be wrong when a politician pronounces an entire class of the population (say capitalists or Negroes) to be outside the community – not entitled to the benefits conferred by the state and its laws. So too, Lenin's image of the factory which needs no supervision by coercive policemen after the state has withered away; Maistre's image of the executioner and his victims as the cornerstone of all authority, or of life as a perpetual battlefield in which only terror of supernatural power keeps men from mutual extermination; the state's role as traffic policeman and night-watchman (Lassalle's contemptuous description of the liberal ideal); Locke's analogy of government with trusteeship; the constant use by Burke and the entire romantic movement of metaphors drawn from organic growth and decay; the Soviet model of an army on the march, with its accompanying attributes and values, such as uncritical loyalty, faith in leadership, and military goals such as the need to overtake, destroy, conquer some specified enemy – all these illuminate some types of social experience.

The great distortions, the errors and crimes that have sought their inspiration and justification in such images, are evidence of mechanical extrapolation, or over-enthusiastic application of what, at most, explains a sector of life, to the whole. It is a form of the ancient fallacy of the Ionian philosophers, who wanted a single answer to the question 'What are all things made of?' Everything is not made of water, nor fire, nor is explained by the irresistible march towards the world state or the classless society. The history of thought and culture is, as Hegel showed with great brilliance, a changing pattern of great liberating ideas which inevitably turn into suffocating straitjackets, and so stimulate their own destruction by new, emancipating, and at the same time enslaving, conceptions. The first step to the understanding of men is the bringing to consciousness of the model or models that dominate and penetrate their thought and action. Like all attempts to make men aware of the categories in which they think, it is a difficult and sometimes painful activity, likely to produce deeply disquieting results. The second task is to analyse the model itself, and this commits the analyst to accepting or modifying or rejecting it, and, in the last case, to providing a more adequate one in its stead.

It is seldom, moreover, that there is only one model that determines our thought; men (or cultures) obsessed by single models are rare, and while they may be more coherent at their strongest, they tend to collapse more violently when, in the end, their concepts are blown up by reality

– experienced events, 'inner' or 'outer', that get in the way. Most men wander hither and thither, guided and, at times, hypnotised by more than one model, which they seldom trouble to make consistent, or even fragments of models which themselves form a part of some none too coherent or firm pattern or patterns. To drag them into the light makes it possible to explain them and sometimes to explain them away. The purpose of such analysis is to clarify; but clarification may expose shortcomings and subvert what it describes. That has often and quite justly been charged against political thought, which, at its best, does not disclaim this dangerous power. The ultimate test of the adequacy of the basic patterns by which we think and act is the only test that common sense or the sciences afford, namely, whether it fits in with the general lines on which we think and communicate; and if some among these in turn are called into question, then the final measure is, as it always must be, direct confrontation with the concrete data of observation and introspection which these concepts and categories and habits order and render intelligible. In this sense, political theory, like any other form of thought that deals with the real world, rests on empirical experience, though in what sense of 'empirical' still remains to be discussed.

VI

When one protests (as we ourselves did above) that the application of such (social or political) models or combinations of overlapping models which at most hold a part of our experience, causes distortion when applied beyond it, how do we set about justifying this charge? How do we know that the result is distortion? We usually think this because the universal application of a simile or a pattern – say that of the general will, or the organic society, or basic structure and superstructure, or the liberating myth – seems to those who reject it to ignore something that they know directly of human nature and thereby to do violence to what we are, or what we know, by forcing it into the Procrustean bed of some rigid dogma; that is to say, we protest in the name of our own view of what men are, have been, could be.

How do we know these things? How do we know what is and what is not an adequate programme for human beings in given historical circumstances? Is this knowledge sociological, or psychological? Is it empirical at all, or metaphysical and even theological? How do we argue with those whose notions are different from ours? Hume, Helvétius, Condorcet, Comte, are clear that such knowledge must be based on empirical data and the methods of the natural sciences; all else is imaginary and worthless.

The temptation to accept this simple solution was (and is) very great. The conflict of the rival explanations (or models) of social and individual life had, by the late eighteenth century, grown to be a scandal. If one examines what answers were offered, let us say, between the death of Newton and the birth of Darwin, to a central political question – why anyone should obey anyone else – the babel of voices is appalling, perhaps the most confused in recorded history. Some said that I should obey those rules or institutions submission to which alone would fulfil my nature, with the rider that my needs and the correct path to their satisfaction were clear only to those privileged observers who grasped at least some part of the great hierarchy of being. Others said that I should obey this or that authority or law because only in that way could I (without aid of experts) fulfil my 'true' nature, or be able to fit into a harmonious whole. Some supposed this whole to be static; others taught that it was dynamic, but could not agree on whether it moved in recurrent cycles, or a straight, or spiral, or irregular evolutionary line, or by a series of oscillations leading to 'dialectical' explosions; or again, whether it was teleological or functional or causally determined.

Some conceived the ultimate universal pattern in mechanistic, others in organic, others still in aesthetic terms. There were those who said that men must obey because they had promised to do so, or others had promised on their behalf; or that they were behaving as if they had promised and this was tantamount to having promised, whether they admitted this or no; or, if this seemed unconvincing, that it were best that they should behave as if they had so promised, since otherwise no one would know where he was and chaos would ensue. Some told men to obey because they would be happier if they did, or because the majority, or all men, would be happier; or because it was God's will that they should obey, or the will of the sovereign, or of the majority, or of the best or wisest, or of history, or of their state, or their race, or their culture, or their church.

They were told also that they must obey because the natural law laid down that they must do so, but there were differences about how the precepts of natural law were to be discovered, whether by rational or by empirical means, or by intuition, and again, by common men or only by the experts; the experts in their turn were identified by some with natural scientists, by others with specialists in metaphysics or theology, or perhaps in some other discipline – mass psychology, mystical revelation, the laws of history, of economics, of natural evolution, of a new synthesis of all or some of these. Some people supposed that truth in these matters could be discovered by a faculty which they called moral sense, or common sense, or the perception of the fitness of things, or that it consisted in what they had been told by their parents or nurses or was to be found in accepted views which it was mere perversity to question, or came from one or other of many sources of this sort which Bentham mocks at so gaily and effectively. Some (and perhaps these have always been the majority) felt it to be in some degree subversive to raise such questions at all.

This situation caused justified indignation in a country dominated by free inquiry and its greatest triumph, Newtonian science. Surely this monstrous muddle could be cleared away by the strong new broom of scientific method – a similar chaos had, after all, not so long ago prevailed in the natural sciences too. Galileo and Newton – and the light of reason and experiment – had silenced for ever the idle chatter of the ignoramus, the dark muttering of the metaphysician, the thunder of the preacher, the hysterical shrieks of the obscurantist. All genuine questions were questions of discoverable fact – *calculemus*, Condorcet declared, was to be the motto of the new method; all problems must be so reformulated that inspection of the facts – aided by mathematical techniques – would answer them decisively, with a clear, universally valid, empirical statement of verifiable fact.

VII

Nevertheless, attempts by the *philosophes* of the eighteenth century to turn philosophy, and particularly moral and political philosophy, into an empirical science, into individual and social psychology, did not succeed. They failed over politics because our political notions are part of our conception of what it is to be human, and this is not solely a question of fact, as facts are conceived by the natural sciences; nor the product of conscious reflection upon the specific discoveries of anthropology or sociology or psychology, although all these are relevant and indeed indispensable to an adequate notion of the nature of man in general, or of particular groups of men in particular circumstances. Our conscious idea of man – of how men differ from other entities, of what is human and what is not human or inhuman – involves the use of some among the basic categories in terms of which we perceive and order and interpret data. To analyse the concept of man is to recognise these categories for what they are. To do this is to realise that they are categories, that is, that they are not themselves subjects for scientific hypotheses about the data which they order.

The analogy with the sciences which dominates the pre-Kantian thinkers of the eighteenth century – Locke, Hume and Condillac, for example, is a typical misapplication of a model that works in one sphere to a region where it will obscure at least as much as it illuminates.

Let me try to make this more specific. When the theological and metaphysical models of the Middle Ages were swept away by the sciences of the seventeenth and eighteenth centuries, they disappeared largely because they could not compete in describing, predicting, controlling the contents of the external world with new disciplines. To the extent to which man was regarded as an object in material nature the sciences of man – psychology, anthropology, economics, sociology and so on – began to supplant their theologico-metaphysical predecessors. The questions of the philosophers were affected by this; some were answered or rendered obsolete: but some remained unanswered. The new human sciences studied men's actual habits; they promised, and in some cases provided, analyses of what men said, wanted, admired, abhorred; they were prepared to supply empirical evidence for this, or experimental demonstration; but their efforts to solve normative problems were less successful. They tried to reduce questions of value to questions of fact – of what caused what kind of men to feel or behave as they did in various circumstances. But when Kant or Herder or Dostoevsky or Marx duly rejected the Encyclopedists' answers, the charge against them was not solely that of faulty observation or invalid inference; it was that of a failure to recognise what it is to be a man, that is, failure to take into account the nature of the framework – the basic categories – in terms of which we think and act and assume others to think and act, if communication between us is to work.

In other words, the problem the solutions of which were found insufficient is not in the usual sense empirical, and certainly not formal, but something that is not adequately described by either term. When Rousseau (whether he understood him correctly or not) rejected Hobbes's account of political obligation on the ground that Hobbes seemed to him to explain it by mere fear of superior force, Rousseau claimed not that Hobbes had not seen certain relevant empirical, psychologically discoverable, facts, nor that he had argued incorrectly from what he had seen – but that his account was in conflict with what, in thinking of human beings as human, and distinguishing them, even the most degraded among them, not only in explicit thought, but in our feelings and in our action, from beings that we regard as inhuman or non-human, we all know men to be. His argument is not that the facts used to construct Hobbes's model had gaps in them, but that the model was inadequate in principle; it was inadequate not because this or that psychological or sociological correlation had been missed out, but because it was based on a failure to understand what we mean by motive, purpose, value, personality and the like.

When Kant breaks with the naturalistic tradition, or Marx rejects the political morality of Bentham, or Tolstoy expresses a low opinion of the doctrines of Karl Marx, they are not complaining merely of empirical ignorance or poor logic or insufficient experimental evidence, or internal incoherence. They denounce their adversaries mainly for not understanding what men are and what relationships between them – or between them and outside forces – make them men; they complain of blindness not to the transient aspects of such relations, but to those constant characteristics (such as discrimination of right from good for Kant, or, for Marx, systematic self-transmutation by their own labour) that they regard as fundamental to the notion of man as such. Their criticisms relate to the adequacy of the categories in terms of which we discuss men's ends or duties or interests, the permanent framework in terms of which, not about which, ordinary empirical disagreements can arise.

What are these categories? How do we discover them? If not empirically, then by what means? How universal and unchanging are they? How do they enter into and shape the models and paradigms in terms of which we think and respond? Do we discover what they are by attention to thought, or action, or unconscious processes, and how do we reconcile these various sources of knowledge? These are characteristically philosophical questions, since they are questions about the all but permanent ways in which we think, decide, perceive, judge, and not about the data of experience – the items themselves. The test of the adequate working of the methods, analogies, models which operate in discovering and classifying the behaviour of these empirical data (as natural science and common sense do) is ultimately empirical: it is the degree of their success in forming a coherent and enduring conceptual system.

To apply these models and methods to the framework itself by means of which we perceive and think about them is a major fallacy, by the analysis of which Kant transformed philosophy. In politics it was committed (by Hume and Russell, for example) when enquiry into the empirical characteristics of men was confounded with the analysis of the notion of man (or 'self' or 'observer' or 'moral agent' or 'individual' or 'soul' etc.) in terms of which the empirical characteristics were themselves collected and described. Kant supposed these categories to be discoverable *a priori*. We need not accept this; this was an unwarranted conclusion from the valid perception that there exist central features of our experience that are invariant and omnipresent, or at least much less variable than the vast variety of its empirical characteristics, and for that reason deserve to be distinguished by the name of categories. This is evident enough in the case of the external world: the three-dimensionality of (psychological, commonsense) space, for example, or the solidity of things in it, or the 'irreversibility' of the time order, are among the most familiar and inalienable kinds of characteristics in terms of which we think and act. Empirical sciences of these properties do not exist, not because they exhibit no regularities – on the contrary they are the very paradigm of the concept of regularity itself – but because they are presupposed in the very language in which we formulate empirical experience. That is why it seems absurd to ask for evidence for their existence, and imaginary examples are enough to exhibit their structure; for they are presupposed in our commonest acts of thought or decision; and where imaginary examples are, for the purpose of an inquiry, as good as, or even better than, empirical data drawn from actual experience, we may be sure that the inquiry is not, in the normal sense, an empirical one. Such permanent features are to be found in the moral and political and social worlds too: less stable and universal, perhaps, than in the physical one, but just as indispensable for any kind of intersubjective communication, and therefore for thought and action. An inquiry that proceeds by examples, and is therefore not scientific, but not formal, that is deductive, either, is most likely to be philosophical.

There is an ultimate sense, of course, in which such facts as that space has three dimensions, or that men are beings who demand reasons or make choices, are simply given: brute facts and not *a priori* truths; it is not absurd to suppose that things could have been otherwise. But if they had been (or will one day be) other than they are now, our entire conceptual apparatus – thought, volition, feeling, language – and therefore our very nature, would have been (or will be) different in ways that it is impossible or difficult to describe with the concepts and words available to us as we are today. Political categories (and values) are a part of this all but inescapable web of ways of living, acting and thinking, a network liable to change only as a result of radical changes in reality, or through dissociation from reality on the part of individuals, that is to say, madness.

VIII

The basic categories (with their corresponding concepts) in terms of which we define men – such notions as society, freedom, sense of time and change, suffering, happiness, productivity, good and bad, right and wrong, choice, effort, truth, illusion (to take them wholly at random) – are not matters of induction and hypothesis. To think of someone as a human being is *ipso facto* to bring all these notions into play: so that to say of someone that he is a man, but that choice, or the notion of truth, mean nothing to him, would be eccentric: it would clash with what we mean by 'man' not as a matter of verbal definition (which is alterable at will), but as intrinsic to the way in which we think, and (as a matter of 'brute' fact) evidently cannot but think.

This will hold of values too (among them political ones) in terms of which men are defined. Thus, if I say of someone that he is kind or cruel, loves truth or is indifferent to it, he remains human in either case. But if I find a man to whom it literally makes no difference whether he kicks a pebble or kills his family, since either would be an antidote to *ennui* or inactivity, I shall not be disposed, like consistent relativists, to attribute to him merely a different code of morality from my own or that of most men, or declare that we disagree on essentials, but shall begin to speak of insanity and inhumanity; I shall be inclined to consider him mad, as a man who thinks he is Napoleon is mad; which is a way of saying that I do not regard such a being as being fully a man at all. It is cases of this kind, which seem to make it clear that ability to recognise universal – or almost universal – values enters into our analysis of such fundamental concepts as 'man', 'rational', 'sane', 'natural' etc. – which are usually thought of as descriptive and not evaluative – that lie at the basis of modern translations into empirical terms of the kernel of truth in the old *a priori* natural law doctrines. It is considerations such as these, urged by neo-Aristotelians and the followers of the later doctrines of Wittgenstein, that have shaken the faith of some devoted empiricists in the complete logical gulf between descriptive statements and statements of value, and have cast doubt on the celebrated distinction derived from Hume.

166

Extreme cases of this sort are of philosophical importance because they make it clear that such questions are not answered by either empirical observation or formal deduction. Hence those who confine themselves to observation of human behaviour and empirical hypotheses about it, psychologists, sociologists, historians, however profound and original they may be, are not, as such, political theorists, even though they may have much to say that is crucial in the field of political philosophy. That is why we do not consider such dedicated empiricists as the students, say, of the formation and behaviour of parties or élites or classes, or of the methods and consequences of various types of democratic procedure, to be political philosophers or social theorists in the larger sense.

Such men are in the first place students of facts, and aspire to formulate hypotheses and laws like the natural scientists. Yet as a rule these thinkers cannot go any further: they tend to analyse men's social and political ideas in the light of some overriding belief of their own – for example, that the purpose of all life is or should be the service of God, however interpreted; or on the contrary that it is the pursuit of experimentally discoverable individual or collective satisfaction; or that it lies in the self-realision of a historical (or psychological or aesthetic) pattern, grasp of which alone can explain men to themselves and give meaning to their thoughts and action; or, on the contrary, that there exists no human purpose; or that men cannot but seek conflicting ends; or cannot (without ceasing to be human) avoid activities that must end in self-frustration, so that the very notion of a final solution is an absurdity. In so far as it is such fundamental conceptions of man that determine political doctrines (and who will deny that political problems, e.g. about what men and groups can or should be or do, depend logically and directly on what man's nature is taken to be?), it is clear that those who are governed by these great integrating syntheses bring to their study something other than empirical data.

If we examine the models, paradigms, conceptual structures that govern various outlooks whether consciously or not, and compare the various concepts and categories involved with respect, for example, to their internal consistency or their explanatory force, then what we are engaged upon is not psychology or sociology or logic or epistemology, but moral or social or political theory, or all these at once, depending on whether we confine ourselves to individuals, or to groups, or to the particular types of human arrangements that are classified as political, or deal with them all in one. No amount of careful empirical observation and bold and fruitful hypothesis will explain to us what those men see who see the state as a divine institution, or what their words mean and how they relate to reality; nor what those believe who tell us that the state was sent upon us only for our sins; or those who say that it is a school through which we must go before we are adult and free and can dispense with it; or that it is a work of art; or a utilitarian device; or the incarnation of natural law; or a committee of the ruling class; or the highest stage of the self-developing human spirit; or a piece of criminal folly. But unless we understand (by an effort of imaginative insight such as novelists usually possess in a higher degree than logicians) what notions of man's nature (or absence of them) are incorporated in these political outlooks, what in each case is the dominant model, we shall not understand our own or any human society: neither the conceptions of reason and nature which governed Stoics or Thomists or govern the European Christian Democrats today; nor the very different image which is at the heart of the holy war in which the national-Marxist movements in Africa or in Asia are or may soon be marching; nor the very different notions that animate the liberal and democratic compromises of the west.

It is by now a platitude to say that understanding human thought and action is in large measure understanding what problems and perplexities they strive with. When these problems, whether empirical or formal, have been conceived in terms of models of reality so ancient, widely accepted and stable that we use them to this day, we understand the problems and difficulties and the attempted solutions without explicit reference to the governing categories; for these, being common to us and to cultures remote from us, do not obtrude themselves on us; stay, as it were, out of sight. In other cases (and this is conspicuously true of politics) the models have not stood still: some of the notions of which they were compounded are no longer familiar. Yet unless we have the knowledge and imagination to transpose ourselves into states of mind dominated by the now discarded or obsolescent model, the thoughts and actions that had them at their centre will remain opaque to us. It is failure to perform this difficult operation that marks much of the history of ideas, and turns it into either a superficial literary exercise, or a dead catalogue of strange, at times almost incomprehensible, errors and confusions.

This may not matter too much in the empirical and formal disciplines, where the test of a belief is, or should be, verification or logical coherence; and where one can accept the latest solutions, and reject the falsified or incoherent solutions of the past without bothering (if one is incurious) to understand why they were ever held. But philosophical doctrines are not established or discredited in this final fashion; for they are concerned with – indeed they owe their existence to – problems that cannot be settled in these ways. They are not concerned with specific facts, but with ways of looking at them; they do not consist of first-order propositions concerning the world. They are second- or higher-order statements about whole classes of descriptions of, or responses to, the world and man's activities in it; and these are in turn determined by models, networks of categories, descriptive, evaluative, and hybrids compounded of the two, in which the two functions cannot be disentangled even in thought – categories which, if not eternal and universal, are far more stable and widespread than those of the sciences; sufficiently continuous, indeed, to constitute a common world which we share with medieval and classical thinkers.

Ionian cosmology, the biology of Aristotle, Stoic logic, Arab algebra, Cartesian physics, may be of interest to historical specialists, but need not occupy the minds of physicists or biologists or mathematicians who are solely interested in the discovery of new truth. In these studies there is genuine progress: what is past is largely obsolete. But the political philosophy of Plato or Aristotle or Machiavelli, the moral views of the Hebrew prophets or of the Gospels or of the Roman jurists or of the medieval church – these, whether in the original or in the works of their modern expositors, are incomparably more intelligible and more relevant to our own preoccupations than the sciences of antiquity. The subject-matter of these disciplines – the most general characteristics of men as such, that is as beings engaged in moral or social or spiritual activities – seems to present problems which preserve a considerable degree of continuity and similarity from one age and culture to another. Methods of dealing with them vary greatly; but none have as yet achieved so decisive a victory as to sweep all their rivals into oblivion. The inadequate models of political thought evidently have, by and large, perished and been forgotten; the great illuminating models are still controversial today, stir us still to adherence or criticism or violent indignation.

We might take as examples Karl Popper's denunciation of Plato's political theory or Irving Babbitt's philippics against Rousseau, Simone Weil's violent distaste for the morality of the Old Testament, or the frequent attacks made today on eighteenth-century positivism or 'scientism' in political ethics.[1] Some of the classical constructions are in conflict with one another, but, inasmuch as each rests on a vivid vision of permanent human attributes and is capable of satisfying some inquiring minds in each generation, no matter how different the circumstances of time and place, the models of Plato, or of Aristotle, or of Judaism, Christianity, Kantian liberalism, romanticism, historicism, all survive and contend with each other today in a variety of guises. If men or circumstances alter radically, or new empirical knowledge is gained which will revolutionise our conception of man, then certainly some of these edifices will cease to be relevant and will be forgotten like the ethics and metaphysics of the Egyptians or the Incas. But so long as men are as they are, the debate will continue in terms set by these visions and others like them: each will gain or lose in influence as events force this or that aspect of men into prominence. One thing alone is certain, that save to those who understand and even feel what a philosophical question is, how it differs from an empirical or formal question (although this difference need not be explicitly present to the mind, and overlapping or borderline questions are frequent enough), the answers – in this case the main political doctrines of the west – may well seem intellectual fancies, detached philosophical speculations and constructions without much relation to acts or events.

Only those who can to some degree re-enact within themselves the states of mind of men tormented by questions to which these theories claim to be solutions, or at any rate the states of mind of those who may accept the solutions uncritically but would, without them, fall into a state of insecurity and anxiety – only these are capable of grasping what part philosophical views, and especially political doctrines, have played in history, at any rate in the west. The work of the logicians or physicists of the past has receded because it has been superseded. But there is something absurd in the suggestion that we reject Plato's political doctrines or Kant's aesthetics or ethics because they have been 'superseded'. This consideration alone should prevent facile assimilation of the two cases. It may be objected to this line of argument that we look upon old ethical or political doctrines as still worth discussion because they are part of our cultural tradition – that if Greek philosophy, biblical ethics, etc. had not been an intrinsic element in western education, they would by now have been as remote from us as early Chinese

[1] What thinker today entertains violent emotions towards the errors of Cartesian physicists or medieval mapmakers?

speculation. But this merely takes the argument a step backwards: it is true that if the general characteristics of our normal experience had altered radically enough – through a revolution in our knowledge or some natural upheaval which altered our reactions – these ancient categories would probably by now have been felt to be as obsolete as those of Hammurabi or the epic of Gilgamesh. That this is not so is doubtless due partly to the fact that our experience is itself organised and 'coloured' by ethical or political categories that we have inherited from our ancestors, ancient spectacles through which we are still look- ing. But the spectacles would long ago have caused us to blunder and stumble and would have given way to others, or been modified out of recognition as our physical and biological and mathematical spectacles have been, if they had not still performed their task more or less ade- quately: which argues a certain degree of continuity in at least two millennia of moral and political consciousness.

IX

We may be told that whatever we may maintain about the sources, motives or justification of our beliefs, the content of what adherents of divers philosophies believe tends to be similar if they belong to the same social or economic or cultural milieu or have other – psychological or physiological – characteristics in common. The English philosophers, T. H. Green and J. S. Mill, preached philosophically contradictory doctrines: Green was a quasi-Hegelian metaphysician, Mill a Humean empiricist, yet their political conclusions were close to one another's; both were humane Victorian liberals with a good deal of sympathy for socialism. This, we shall further be told, was because men are conditioned to believe what they believe by objective historical factors – their social position, or the class structure of their society and their position in it, although their own (erroneous) rationalisation of their beliefs may be as widely different as those of Mill and Green.

So, too, it has been said, the outlook – the 'operational ideas' – of Fascists and Communists display a surprising degree of similarity, given the extreme opposition and incompatibility of the official axioms from which these movements logically start. Hence the plausibility of some of the methods of the 'sociology of knowledge', whether Marxist or Paretian or psychoanalytic, and of the various eclectic forms which, in the hands of Weber, Mannheim and others, this instrument has acquired. Certainly such theorists have cast light on the obscure roots

171

of our beliefs. We may be conditioned to believe what we believe irrationally, by circumstances mainly beyond our control, and perhaps beyond our knowledge too. But whatever may in fact causally determine our beliefs, it would be a gratuitous abdication of our powers of reasoning – based on a confusion of natural science with philosophical enquiry – not to want to know what we believe, and for what reason, what the metaphysical implications of such beliefs are, what their relation is to other types of belief, what criteria of value and truth they involve, and so what reason we have to think them true or valid. Rationality rests on the belief that one can think and act for reasons that one can understand, and not merely as the product of occult causal factors which breed 'ideologies', and cannot, in any case, be altered by their victims. So long as rational curiosity exists – a desire for justification and explanation in terms of motives and reasons, and not only of causes or functional correlations or statistical probabilities – political theory will not wholly perish from the earth, however many of its rivals, such as sociology, philosophical analysis, social psychology, political science, economics, jurisprudence, semantics, may claim to have dispelled its imaginary realm.

It is a strange paradox that political theory should seem to lead so shadowy an existence at a time when, for the first time in history, literally the whole of mankind is violently divided by issues the reality of which is, and has always been, the sole *raison d'être* of this branch of study. But this, we may be sure, is not the end of the story. Neo-Marxism, neo-Thomism, nationalism, historicism, existentialism, anti-essentialist liberalism and socialism, transpositions of doctrines of natural rights and natural law into empirical terms, discoveries made by skilful application of models derived from economic and related techniques to political behaviour, and the collisions, combinations, and consequences in action of these ideas, indicate not the death of a great tradition, but, if anything, new and unpredictable developments.

'From Hope and Fear Set Free'

I

DOES knowledge always liberate? The view of the classical Greek philosophers, shared by much, though perhaps not all Christian theology, is that it does. 'And ye shall know the truth, and the truth shall make you free.'[1] Ancient Stoics and most modern rationalists are at one with Christian teaching on this issue. According to this view freedom[2] is the unimpeded fulfilment of my true nature – unimpeded by obstacles whether external or internal. In the case of the passage from which I have quoted, the freedom in question (I follow Festugière's interpretation on this point) is freedom from sin, that is, from false beliefs about God, nature and myself, which obstruct my understanding. The freedom is that of self-realisation or self-direction – the realisation by the individual's own activity of the true purposes of his nature (however such purposes or such natures are defined) which is frustrated by his misconceptions about the world and man's place in it. If to this I add the corollary that I am rational – that is, that I can understand or know (or at least form a correct belief about) why I do what I do, that is, distinguish between acting (which entails making choices, forming intentions, pursuing goals) and merely behaving (that is, being acted upon by causes the operations of which may be unknown to me or unlikely to be affected by my wishes or attitudes) – then it will follow that knowledge of the relevant facts – about the external world, other persons and my own nature – will remove impediments to my policies that are due to ignorance and delusion. Philosophers (and theologians, dramatists, poets) have differed widely about the character of man's nature and its ends; what kind and degree of control of the external world is needed in order to achieve fulfilment, complete or partial, of this nature and its ends; whether such a general nature or objective ends exist at all; and

[1] Gospel according to St John, chapter 8, verse 32.
[2] I propose to use the words 'freedom' and 'liberty' interchangeably throughout.

where the frontier dividing the external world of matter and non-rational creatures from active agents is to be found. Some thinkers have supposed that such fulfilment was (or had once been, or would one day be) possible on earth, others have denied this; some maintained that the ends of men were objective and capable of being discovered by special methods of inquiry, but disagreed on what these were: empirical or *a priori*; intuitive or discursive; scientific or purely reflective; public or private; confined to specially gifted or fortunate inquirers, or in principle open to any man. Others believed that such ends were subjective, or determined by physical or psychological or social factors, which differed widely. Again, Aristotle, for example, supposed that if external conditions were too unfavourable – if a man suffered Priam's misfortunes – this made self-fulfilment, the proper realisation of one's nature, impossible. On the other hand the Stoics and Epicureans held that complete rational self-control could be achieved by a man whatever his external circumstances, since all that he needed was a sufficient degree of detachment from human society and the external world; to this they added the optimistic belief that the degree sufficient for self-fulfilment was in principle perfectly attainable by anyone who consciously sought independence and autonomy, that is, escape from being the plaything of external forces which he could not control.

Among the assumptions that are common to all these views are

(i) that things and persons possess natures – definite structures independent of whether or not they are known;

(ii) that these natures or structures are governed by universal and unalterable laws;

(iii) that these structures and laws are, at least in principle, all knowable; and that knowledge of them will automatically keep men from stumbling in the dark and dissipating effort on policies which, given the facts – the nature of things and persons and the laws that govern them – are doomed to failure.

According to this doctrine men are not self-directed and therefore not free when their behaviour is caused by misdirected emotions – for example, fears of non-existent entities, or hatreds due not to a rational perception of the true state of affairs but to illusions, fantasies, results of unconscious memories and forgotten wounds. Rationalisations and ideologies, on this view, are false explanations of behaviour the true roots of which are unknown or ignored or misunderstood; and these in their turn breed further illusions, fantasies and forms of irrational and compulsive behaviour. True liberty consists, therefore, in self-direction: a man is free to the degree that the true explanation of his activity lies in the intentions and motives of which he is conscious, and not in some hidden psychological or physiological condition that would have produced the same effect, i.e. the same behaviour (posing as choice), whatever explanation or justification the agent attempted to produce. A rational man is free if his behaviour is not mechanical, and springs from motives and is intended to fulfil purposes of which he is, or can at will be, aware; so that it is true to say that having these intentions and purposes is a necessary, if not sufficient, condition for his behaviour. The unfree man is like someone who is drugged or hypnotised – whatever explanations he may himself advance for his behaviour, it remains unaltered by any change in his ostensible, overt motives and policies; we consider him to be in the grip of forces over which he has no control, not free, when it is plain that his behaviour will be predictably the same whatever reasons he advances for it.

To put matters in this way is to identify rationality and freedom, or at least to go a long way towards it. Rational thought is thought the content or, at least, the conclusions of which obey rules and principles and are not merely items in a causal or random sequence; rational behaviour is behaviour which (at least in principle) can be explained by the actor or observer in terms of motives, intentions, choices, reasons, rules, and not solely of natural laws – causal or statistical, or 'organic' or others of the same logical type (whether explanations in terms of motives, reasons and the like, and those in terms of causes, probabilities etc. are 'categorially' different and cannot in principle clash or indeed be relevant to one another, is of course a crucial question; but I do not wish to raise it here). To call a man a thief is *pro tanto* to attribute rationality to him: to call him a kleptomaniac is to deny it of him. If degrees of a man's freedom directly depend on (or are identical with) the extent of his knowledge of the roots of his behaviour, then a kleptomaniac who knows himself to be one is, to that extent, free; he may be unable to stop stealing or even to try to do so; but his recognition of this, because he is now – so it is maintained – in a position to choose whether to try to resist this compulsion (even if he is bound to fail) or to let it take its course, renders him not merely more rational (which seems indisputable), but more free. But is this always so? Is awareness of a disposition or causal characteristic on my part identical with – or does it necessarily provide me with – the power to manipulate or alter it? There is, of course, a clear but platitudinous sense in which all knowledge increases freedom in some respect: if I know that I am liable to epileptic fits, or feelings of class consciousness, or the spell-binding effect of certain kinds of music, I can – in some sense of 'can' – plan my life accordingly; whereas if I do not know this, I cannot do so; I gain some increase in power and, to that extent, in freedom. But this knowledge may also decrease my power in some other respect: if I anticipate an epileptic fit or the onset of some painful, or even agreeable, emotion, I may be inhibited from some other free exercise of my power, or be precluded from some other experience – I may be unable to continue to write poetry, or understand the Greek text which I am reading, or think about philosophy, or get up from my chair: I may, in other words, pay for an increase of power and freedom in one region by a loss of them in another. (I propose to return to this point later, in a slightly different context.)[1] Nor am I necessarily rendered able to control my fits of epilepsy or of class consciousness or addiction to Indian music by recognising their incidence. If by knowledge is meant what the classical authors meant by it – knowledge of facts – not knowledge of 'what to do' – which may be a disguised way of stating not that something is the case, but a commitment to certain ends or values, or of expressing, not describing, a decision to act in a certain fashion; if, in other words, I claim to have the kind of knowledge about myself that I might have about others, then even though my sources may be better or my certainty greater, such self-knowledge, it seems to me, may or may not add to the sum total of my freedom. The question is empirical: and the answer depends on specific circumstances. From the fact that every gain in knowledge liberates me in some respect, it does not follow, for the reasons given above, that it will necessarily add to the total sum of freedom that I enjoy: it may, by taking with one hand more than it gives with the other, decrease it.

But there is a more radical criticism of this view to be considered. To say that one is free only if one understands oneself (even if this is not a sufficient condition of freedom) presupposes that we have a self to be understood – that there is a structure correctly described as human nature which is what it is, obeys the laws that it does, and is an object of natural study. This has itself been questioned, notably by certain existentialist philosophers. By these it is maintained that far more is a matter of human choice than has usually and complacently been supposed. Since choice involves responsibility, and some human beings at most times, and most human beings at some times, wish to

[1] See p. 194.

avoid this burden, there is a tendency to look for excuses and alibis. For this reason men tend to attribute too much to the unavoidable operations of natural or social laws – for instance, to the workings of the unconscious mind, or unalterable psychological reflexes, or the laws of social evolution. Critics who belong to this school (which owes much both to Hegel and Marx and to Kierkegaard) say that some notorious impediments to liberty – say, the social pressures of which J. S. Mill made so much – are not objective forces the existence and effects of which are independent of human wishes or activities or alterable only by means not open to isolated individuals – by revolutions or radical reforms that cannot be engineered at the individual's will. What is maintained is the contrary: that I need not be bullied by others or pressed into conformity by schoolmasters or friends or parents; need never be affected in some way that I cannot help by what priests or colleagues or critics or social groups or classes think or do. If I am so affected, it is because I choose it. I am insulted when I am mocked as a hunchback, a Jew, a Negro, or unnerved by the feeling that I am suspected of being a traitor, only if I choose to accept the opinion – the valuation – of hunchbacks or race or treason of those by whose views and attitudes I am dominated. But I can always choose to ignore or resist this – to snap my fingers at such views and codes and outlooks; and then I am free. This is the very doctrine, though built on different premises, of those who drew the portrait of the Stoic sage. If I choose to knuckle under to public sentiment or the values of this or that group or person, the responsibility is mine and not that of outside forces – forces, personal or impersonal, to whose allegedly irresistible influence I attribute my behaviour, attribute it only too eagerly in order to escape blame or self-blame. My behaviour, my character, my personality, according to these critics, is not a mysterious substance or the referent of a pattern of hypothetical general (causal) propositions, but a pattern of choices or of failures to choose which themselves represent a kind of choice to let events take their course, not to assert myself as an active agent. If I am self-critical and face the facts, I may find that I shuffle off my responsibilities too easily. This applies both in the realms of theory and in those of practical affairs. Thus, if I am a historian, my view of the factors significant in history may well be profoundly affected by my desire to glorify or detract from the reputation of individuals or classes – an act, so it is argued, of free valuation on my part. Once I am aware of this, I can select and judge as I will: 'the facts' never speak – only I, the chooser, the evaluator, the judge, can do so, and do so according to my own sweet will, in accordance with principles, rules, ideals, prejudices, feelings which I can freely view, examine, accept, reject. If I minimise the human cost of a given political or economic policy, in the past or present or future, I shall upon examination often find that I do so because I disapprove of or bear a grudge against the critics or opponents of those who conduct the policy. If I seek to explain away, whether to others or to myself, some unworthy act on my part, on the ground that something – the political or military situation, or my emotion or inner state – was 'too much for me', then I am cheating myself, or others, or both. Action is choice; choice is free commitment to this or that way of behaving, living, and so on; the possibilities are never fewer than two: to do or not to do; be or not be. Hence, to attribute conduct to the unalterable laws of nature is to misdescribe reality: it is not true to experience, verifiably false; and to perpetrate such falsification – as most philosophers and ordinary men have done and are constantly doing – is to choose to evade responsibility for making choices or failing to make them, to choose to deny that to drift down a current of accepted opinion and behave semi-mechanically is itself a kind of choice – a free act of surrender; this is so because it is always possible, though sometimes painful, to ask myself what it is that I really believe, want, value, what it is that I am doing, living for; and having answered as well as I am able, to continue to act in a given fashion or alter my behaviour.

I do not wish to deny that all this needs saying: that to look on the future as already structured, solid with future facts, is conceptually fallacious; that the tendency to account both for the whole of our own behaviour and that of others in terms of forces regarded as being too powerful to resist is empirically mistaken, in that it goes beyond what is warranted by the facts. In its extreme form this doctrine does away with determination at one blow: I am determined by my own choices; to believe otherwise – say, in determinism or fatalism or chance – is itself a choice, and a particularly craven one at that. Yet it is surely arguable that this very tendency itself is a symptom of man's specific nature. Such tendencies as looking on the future as unalterable – a symmetrical analogue of the past – or the quest for excuses, escapist fantasies, flights from responsibility, are themselves psychological data. To be self-deceived is *ex hypothesi* something that I cannot have chosen consciously, although I may have consciously chosen to act in a manner likely to produce this result, without shrinking from this consequence. There is a difference between choices and compulsive behaviour, even if the compulsion is itself the result of an earlier uncompelled choice. The illusions from which I suffer determine the field of my choice; self-knowledge – destruction of the illusions – will alter this field, make it more possible for me to choose genuinely rather than suppose that I have chosen something when, in fact, it has (as it were) chosen me. But in the course of distinguishing between true and counterfeit acts of choice (however this is done – however I discover that I have seen through illusions), I nevertheless discover that I have an ineluctable nature. There are certain things that I cannot do. I cannot (logically) remain rational or sane and believe no general propositions, or remain sane and use no general terms; I cannot retain a body and cease to gravitate. I can perhaps in some sense try to do these things, but to be rational entails knowing that I shall fail. My knowledge of my own nature and that of other things and persons, and of the laws that govern them and me, saves my energies from dissipation or misapplication; it exposes bogus claims and excuses; it fixes responsibilities where they belong and dismisses false pleas of impotence as well as false charges against the truly innocent; but it cannot widen the scope of my liberty beyond frontiers determined by factors genuinely and permanently outside my control. To explain these factors is not to explain them away. Increase of knowledge will increase my rationality, and infinite knowledge would make me infinitely rational; it might increase my powers and my freedom: but it cannot make me infinitely free.

To return to the main theme: how does knowledge liberate me? Let me state the traditional position once again. On the view that I am trying to examine, the classical view which descends to us from Aristotle, from the Stoics, from a great part of Christian theology, and finds its rationalist formulation in the doctrines of Spinoza and his followers both among the German idealists and modern psychologists, knowledge, by uncovering little-recognised and therefore uncontrolled forces that affect my conduct, emancipates me from their despotic force, the greater when they have been concealed and therefore misinterpreted. Why is this so? Because once I have uncovered them, I can seek to direct them, or resist them, or create conditions in which they will be canalised into harmless channels, or turned to use – that is, for the fulfilment of my purposes. Freedom is self-government – whether in politics or in individual life – and anything that increases the control of the self over forces external to it contributes to liberty. Although the frontiers that divide self and personality from 'external' forces, whether in the individual-moral or in the public-social field, are still exceedingly vague –

perhaps necessarily so – this Baconian thesis seems valid enough so far as it goes. But its claims are too great. In its classical form it is called the doctrine of self-determination. According to this, freedom consists in playing a part in determining one's own conduct; the greater this part, the greater the freedom. Servitude, or lack of freedom, is being determined by 'external' forces – whether these be physical or psychological; the greater the part played by these forces, the smaller the freedom of the individual. So far, so good. But if it be asked whether the part that I play – my choices, purposes, intentions – might not themselves be determined – caused – to be as they are by 'external' causes, the classical reply seems to be that this does not greatly matter; I am free if and only if I can do as I intended: whether my state of mind is itself the causal product of something else – physical or psychological, of climate, or blood pressure, or my character – is neither here nor there; it may or may not be so: this, if it is so, may be known or unknown; all that matters, all that those worried about whether a man's acts are free or not wish to know, is whether my behaviour has as a necessary condition my own conscious choice. If it has, I am free in the only sense that any rational being can ask for: whether the choice itself – like the rest of me – is caused or uncaused, is not what is at stake; even if it is wholly caused by natural factors, I am no less free.

Anti-determinists have naturally retorted that this merely pushed the problem a step backwards: the 'self' played its part, indeed, but was itself hopelessly 'determined'. It may be worth going back to the origins of this controversy, for, as often happens, its earliest form is also the clearest. It came up so far as I can tell as a consequence of the interest taken by the early Greek Stoics in two, at first unconnected, ideas: that of causation, i.e. the conception, new in the fourth century B.C., of unbreakable chains of events in which each earlier event acts as a necessary and sufficient cause of the later; and the much older notion of individual moral responsibility. It was perceived as early as the beginning of the next century that there was something paradoxical, and indeed incoherent, in maintaining that men's states of mind, feeling and will as well as their actions were links in unbreakable causal chains, and at the same time that men were responsible, that is, that they could have acted otherwise than in fact they did.

Chrysippus was the first thinker to face this dilemma, which did not seem to trouble Plato or Aristotle, and he invented the solution known as self-determination – the view that so long as men were conceived of as being acted upon by outside forces without being able to resist them, they were as stocks and stones, unfree, and the concept of responsibility was plainly inapplicable to them; if, however, among the factors that determined behaviour was the bending of the will to certain purposes, and if, moreover, such a bending of the will was a necessary (whether or not it was a sufficient) condition of a given action, then they were free: for the act depended on the occurrence of a volition and could not happen without it. Men's acts of will and the characters and dispositions from which, whether or not they were fully aware of it, such acts issued, were intrinsic to action: this is what being free meant. Critics of this position, Epicureans and sceptics, were not slow to point out that this was but a half-solution. We are told that they maintained that although it might be that the operations of the will were a necessary condition of what could properly be called acts, yet if these operations were themselves links in causal chains, themselves effects of causes 'external' to the choices, decisions and so on, then the notion of responsibility remained as inapplicable as before. One critic[1] called such modified determination *hemidoulia* – 'half-slavery'. I am only half free if I can correctly maintain that I should not have done *x* if I had not chosen it, but add that I could not have chosen differently. Given that I have decided on *x*, my action has a motive and not merely a cause; my 'volition' is itself among the causes – indeed, one of the necessary conditions – of my behaviour, and it is this that is meant by calling me or it free. But if the choice or decision is itself determined, and cannot, causally, be other than what it is, then the chain of causality remains unbroken, and, the critics asserted, I should be no more truly free than I am on the most rigidly determinist assumptions. It is over this issue that the immense discussion about free will that has preoccupied philosophers ever since originally arose. Chrysippus' answer, that all that I can reasonably ask for is that my own character should be among the factors influencing behaviour, is the central core of the classical doctrine of freedom as self-determination. Its proponents stretch in unbroken line from Chrysippus and Cicero to Aquinas, Spinoza, Locke and Leibniz, Hume, Mill, Schopenhauer, Russell, Schlick, Ayer, Nowell-Smith, and the majority of the contributors to the subject in our own day. Thus when a recent writer in this chronological order, Richard Hare, in one of his books[2] distinguishes free acts from mere behaviour by saying that a pointer to whether I am free to do *x* is provided by asking

[1] The Cynic Oenamaus.
[2] R. M. Hare, *Freedom and Reason* (Oxford, 1963).

oneself whether it makes sense to ask 'Shall I do x?' or 'Ought I to do x?', he is restating the classical thesis. Hare correctly says that one can ask 'Will I make a mistake?' or 'Will I be wrecked on the sea-shore?' but not 'Shall I make a mistake?' or 'Ought I to be wrecked?; for to be wrecked or make a mistake cannot be part of a conscious choice or pur- pose – cannot, in the logical or conceptual sense of the word. And from this he concludes that we distinguish free from unfree behaviour by the presence or absence of whatever it is that makes it intelligible to ask 'Shall I climb the mountain?' but not 'Shall I misunderstand you?' But if, following Carneades, I were to say 'I can indeed ask "Shall I climb the mountain?", but if the answer – and the action – are determined by factors beyond my control, then how does the fact that I pursue pur- poses, make decisions, etc. liberate me from the causal chain?', this would be regarded as a misconceived inquiry by the Stoics and the entire classical tradition. For if my choice is indispensable to the production of a given effect, then I am not causally determined as, say, a stone or a tree that has no purposes and makes no choices is determined, and that is all that any libertarian can wish to establish. But no libertarian can in fact accept this. No one genuinely concerned by the problem constituted by the prima facie incompatibility between determinism and freedom to choose between alternatives will settle for saying 'I can do what I choose, but I cannot choose otherwise than as I do.' Self-determination is clearly not the same as mechanical determination. If the determinists are right (and it may well be that they are) then the sort of determina- tion in terms of which human behaviour should be described is not behaviouristic, but precisely Chrysippus' *hemidoulia*. But half a loaf is not the bread that libertarians crave. For if my decisions are wholly determined by antecedent causes, then the mere fact that they are decisions, and the fact that my acts have motives and not only antecedents, do not of themselves provide that line of demarcation between freedom and necessitation, or freedom and its absence, which the ordinary notion of responsibility seems, at least for libertarians, so clearly to entail. It is in this sense that Bacon's followers claim too much.

This may be seen from another angle which will bring us back to the relations of knowledge and liberty. The growth of knowledge increases the range of predictable events, and predictability – inductive or intuitive – despite all that has been said against this position, does not seem compatible with liberty of choice. I may be told that if I say to someone 'I always knew that you would behave with wonderful courage in this situation' the person so complimented will not suppose that his capacity for freedom of choice is being impugned. But that seems to be so only because the word 'knew' is being used, as it were, in a conventionally exaggerated way. When one man says to another 'I know you well: you simply cannot help behaving generously; you could not help it if you tried', the man so addressed may be thought susceptible to flattery, because of the element of complimentary hyperbole in the words 'cannot help' and 'could not . . . if you tried'. If the words were intended to be taken literally – if the flatterer meant to be understood as saying 'You can no more help being generous than being old, or ugly, or thinking in English and not in Chinese' – the notion of merit or desert would evaporate, and the compliment would be transformed from a moral into a quasi-aesthetic one. This may be made clearer if we take a pejorative example: if I were to say of x 'x can no more help being cruel and malicious than a volcano can help erupting – one should not blame him, only deplore his existence or seek to tame him or restrain him as one would a dangerous animal', x might well feel more deeply insulted than if we lectured him on his habits on the assumption that he was free to choose between acting and refraining from acting as he did, free to choose to listen to our homily or pay no attention to it. The mere fact that it is my character that determines my choices and actions does not, if my character itself and its effects are due to ineluctable causes, render me free in the sense that appears to be required by the notions of responsibility or of moral praise and blame. Knowledge of the causes and conditions that determine my choice – knowledge, indeed, that there are such conditions and causes, knowledge that choice is not free (without analysis of this proposition), knowledge that shows that the notion of moral responsibility is wholly compatible with rigorous determinism, and exposes libertarianism as a confusion due to ignorance or error – that kind of knowledge would assimilate our moral views to aesthetic ones, and would lead us to look on heroism or honesty or justice as we now do on beauty or kindness or strength or genius: we praise or congratulate the possessors of the latter qualities with no implication that they could have chosen to own a different set of characteristics. This world view, if it became generally accepted, would mark a radical shift of categories. If this ever occurs, it will tend to make us think of much of our present moral and our legal outlook, and of a great deal of our penal legislation, as so much barbarism founded on ignorance; it will enlarge the scope and depth of our sympathy; it will substitute knowledge and understanding for attribution of responsibility; it will render indignation, and the kind of admiration that is its opposite, irrational and obsolete; it will expose such notions as desert, merit, responsibility, remorse, and perhaps right and wrong too, as incoherent or, at the very least, inapplicable; it will turn praise and blame into purely corrective or educational instruments, or confine them to aesthetic approval or disapproval. All this it will do, and if truth is on its side, it will benefit mankind thereby. But it will not increase the range of our freedom. Knowledge will only render us freer, if in fact there is freedom of choice – if on the basis of our knowledge we can behave differently from the way in which we would have behaved without it – can, not must or do – if, that is to say, we can and do behave differently on the basis of our new knowledge, but need not. Where there is no antecedent freedom – and no possibility of it – it cannot be increased. Our new knowledge will increase our rationality, our grasp of truth will deepen our understanding, add to our power, inner harmony, wisdom, effectiveness, but not, necessarily, to our liberty. If we are free to choose, then an increase in our knowledge may tell us what are the limits of this freedom and what expands or contracts it. But only to know that there are facts and laws that I cannot alter does not itself render me able to alter anything: if I have no freedom to begin with, knowledge will not increase it. If everything is governed by natural laws, then it is difficult to see what could be meant by saying that I can 'use' them better on the basis of my knowledge, unless 'can' is not the 'can' of choice – not the 'can' which applies only to situations in which I am correctly described as being able to choose between alternatives, and am not rigorously determined to choose one rather than the other. In other words, if classical determinism is a true view (and the fact that it does not square with our present usage is no argument against it), knowledge of it will not increase liberty – if liberty does not exist, the discovery that it does not exist will not create it. This goes for self-determinism no less than for its most full-blown mechanistic-behaviourist variety.

The clearest exposition of classical self-determinism is probably that given in his *Ethics* by Spinoza. Stuart Hampshire represents him,[1] it seems to me correctly, as maintaining that the fully rational man does not choose his ends, for his ends are given. The better he understands the nature of men and of the world, the more harmonious and successful will his actions be, but no serious problem of choice between equally

[1] Stuart Hampshire, 'Spinoza and the Idea of Freedom', *Proceedings of the British Academy* 46 (1960), 195–215.

acceptable alternatives can ever present itself to him, any more than to a mathematician reasoning correctly from true premises to logically unavoidable conclusions. His freedom consists in the fact that he will not be acted upon by causes whose existence he does not know or the nature of whose influence he does not correctly understand. But that is all. Given Spinoza's premises – that the universe is a rational order, and that to understand the rationality of a proposition or an act or an order is, for a rational being, equivalent to accepting or identifying oneself with it (as in the old Stoic notion) – the notion of choice itself turns out to depend upon the deficiencies of knowledge, the degree of ignorance. There is only one correct answer to any problem of conduct, as to any problem of theory. The correct answer having been discovered, the rational man logically cannot but act in accordance with it: the notion of free choice between alternatives no longer has application. He who understands everything, understands the reasons which make it as it is and not otherwise, and being rational cannot wish it to be otherwise than as it is. This may be an unattainable (and perhaps even, when thought through, an incoherent) ideal, but it is this conception that underlies the notion that an increase in knowledge is *eo ipso* always an increase in freedom, i.e. an escape from being at the mercy of what is not understood. Once something is understood or known (and only then), it is, on this view, conceptually impossible to describe oneself as being at the mercy of it. Unless this maximal rationalist assumption is made, it does not seem to me to follow that more knowledge necessarily entails an increase in the total sum of freedom; it may or may not – this, as I hope to show, is largely an empirical question. To discover that I cannot do what I once believed that I could will render me more rational – I shall not beat my head against stone walls – but it will not necessarily make me freer; there may be stone walls wherever I look; I may myself be a portion of one; a stone myself, only dreaming of being free.

There are two further points to be noted with regard to the relationship of freedom and knowledge. (*a*) There is the well-known objection, urged principally by Karl Popper, that the idea of total self-knowledge is in principle incoherent, because if I can predict what I shall do in the future, this knowledge itself is an added factor in the situation that may cause me to alter my behaviour accordingly; and the knowledge that this is so is itself an added factor, which may cause me to alter that, and so on *ad infinitum*. Therefore total self-prediction is logically impossible. This may be so: but it is not an argument against determinism as such (nor does Popper so represent it) – only against self-prediction. If

x can predict the total behaviour of y, and y predict the total behaviour of x (and they do not impart their prophecies to one another), that is all that determinism needs. I cannot be self-consciously spontaneous; therefore I cannot be self-consciously aware of all my states if spontaneity is among them. It does not follow that I can never be spontaneous; nor that, if I am, this state cannot be known to exist while it is occurring, although it cannot be so known to me. For this reason I conclude that, in principle, Popper's argument does not (and is not meant to) refute determinism.

(b) Stuart Hampshire, in the course of some recent remarks,[1] advances the view that self-prediction is (logically) impossible. When I say 'I know that I shall do x' (as against, e.g., 'x will happen to me', or 'You will do x'), I am not contemplating myself, as I might someone else, and giving tongue to a conjecture about myself and my future acts, as I might be doing about someone else or about the behaviour of an animal – for that would be tantamount (if I understand him rightly) to looking upon myself from outside, as it were, and treating my own acts as mere caused events. In saying that I know that I shall do x, I am, on this view, saying that I have decided to do x: for to predict that I shall in certain circumstances in fact do x or decide to do x, with no reference to whether or not I have already decided to do it – to say 'I can tell you now that I shall in fact act in manner x, although I am, as a matter of fact, determined to do the very opposite' – does not make sense. Any man who says 'I know myself too well to believe that, whatever I now decide, I shall do anything other than x when the circumstances actually arise' is in fact, if I interpret Hampshire's views correctly, saying that he does not really, i.e. seriously, propose to set himself against doing x, that he does not propose even to try to act otherwise, that he has in fact decided to let events take their course. For no man who has truly decided to try to avoid x can, in good faith, predict his own failure to act as he has decided. He may fail to avoid x, and he may predict this; but he cannot both decide to try to avoid x and predict that he will not even try to do this; for he can always try; and he knows this: he knows that this is what distinguishes him from non-human creatures in nature. To say that he will fail even to try is tantamount to saying that he has decided not to try. In this sense 'I know' means 'I have decided' and

[1] Iris Murdoch, S. N. Hampshire, P. L. Gardiner and D. F. Pears, 'Freedom and Knowledge', in D. F. Pears (ed.), *Freedom and the Will* (London, 1963), pp. 80–104.

cannot in principle be predictive. That, if I have understood it, is Hampshire's position, and I have a good deal of sympathy with it, for I can see that self-prediction is often an evasive way of disclaiming responsibility for difficult decisions, while deciding in fact to let events take their course, disguising this by attributing responsibility for what occurs to my own allegedly unalterable nature. But I agree with Hampshire's critics in the debate, whom I take to be maintaining that, although the situation he describes may often occur, yet circumstances may exist in which it is possible for me both to say that I am, at this moment, resolved not to do *x*, and at the same time to predict that I shall do *x*, because I am not hopeful that, when the time comes, I shall in fact even so much as try to resist doing *x*. I can, in effect, say 'I know myself well. When the crisis comes, do not rely on me to help you. I may well run away; although I am at this moment genuinely resolved not to be cowardly and to do all I can to stay at your side. My prediction that my resolution will not in fact hold up is based on knowledge of my own character, and not on my present state of mind; my prophecy is not a symptom of bad faith (for I am not, at this moment, vacillating) but, on the contrary, of good faith, of a wish to face the facts. I assure you in all sincerity that my present intention is to be brave and resist. Yet you would run a great risk if you relied too much on my present decision; it would not be fair to conceal my past failures of nerve from you.' I can say this about others, despite the most sincere resolutions on their part, for I can foretell how in fact they will behave; they can equally predict this about me. Despite Hampshire's plausible and tempting argument, I believe that such objective self-knowledge is possible and occurs; and his argument does not therefore appear to me to lessen the force of the determinist thesis. It seems to me that I can, at times, though perhaps not always, place myself, as it were, at an outside vantage point, and contemplate myself as if I were another human being, and calculate the chances of my sticking to my present resolution with almost the same degree of detachment and reliability as I should have if I were judging the case of someone else with all the impartiality that I could muster. If this is so, then 'I know how I shall act' is not necessarily a statement of decision: it can be purely descriptive. Self-prediction of this kind, provided that it does not claim to be too exact or infallible, and meets Popper's objection, cited above, by remaining tentative, allowing for possible alterations of conduct as a result of the self-prediction itself – seems possible and compatible with determinism.

In other words, I see no reason to suppose that a deterministic doctrine, whether about one's own behaviour or that of others, is in principle incoherent, or incompatible with making choices, provided that these choices are regarded as being themselves no less determined than other phenomena. Such knowledge, or well-founded belief, seems to me to increase the degree of rationality, efficiency, power; the only freedom to which it necessarily contributes is freedom from illusions. But this is not the basic sense of the term about which controversy has been boiling for twenty-two centuries.

I have no wish to enter into the waters of the free will problem more deeply than I already have. But I should like to repeat what I have indeed said elsewhere, and for which I have been severely taken to task by determinists: that if a great advance were made in psycho-physiology; if, let us suppose, a scientific expert were to hand me a sealed envelope, and ask me to note all my experiences – both introspective and others – for a limited period – say half-an-hour – and write them down as accurately as I could; and if I then did this to the best of my ability, and after this opened the envelope and read the account, which turned out to tally to a striking degree with my log-book of my experience during the last half-hour, I should certainly be shaken; and so I think would others. We should then have to admit, with or without pleasure, that aspects of human behaviour which had been believed to be within the area of the agent's free choice turned out to be subject to discovered causal laws. Our recognition of this might itself alter our behaviour, perhaps for the happier and more harmonious; but this welcome result itself would be a causal product of our new awareness. I cannot see why such discoveries should be considered impossible, or even particularly improbable; they would bring about a major transformation of psychology and sociology; after all, great revolutions have occurred in other sciences in our own day. The principal difference, however, between previous advances and this imaginary breakthrough (and it is with this surmise that most of my critics have disagreed) is that besides effecting a vast alteration in our empirical knowledge, it would alter our conceptual framework far more radically than the discoveries of the physicists of the seventeenth or twentieth century, or of the biologists of the nineteenth, have changed it. Such a break with the past, in psychology alone, would do great violence to our present concepts and usages. The entire vocabulary of human relations would suffer radical change. Such expressions as 'I should not have done x', 'How could you have chosen x?' and so on, indeed the entire language of the criticism and assessment of one's own and others' conduct, would undergo a sharp transformation, and the expressions we needed both for descriptive and for practical-corrective, deterrent, hortatory etc. purposes (what others would be open to a consistent determinist?) would necessarily be vastly different from the language which we now use. It seems to me that we should be unwise to underestimate the effect of robbing praise, blame, a good many counterfactual propositions, and the entire network of concepts concerned with freedom, choice, responsibility, of much of their present function and meaning. But it is equally important to insist that the fact that such a transformation could occur – or would, at any rate, be required – does not, of course, have any tendency to show that determinism is either true or false; it is merely a consequence which those who accept it as true tend not to recognise sufficiently. I only wish to add that the further issue whether the truth of determinism is or is not an empirical question, is itself unclear. If so revolutionary an advance in psycho-physiological knowledge were achieved, the need of new concepts to formulate it, and of the consequent modification (to say the least) of concepts in other fields, would itself demonstrate the relative vagueness of the frontiers between the empirical and the conceptual. If these empirical discoveries were made, they might mark a greater revolution in human thought than any that has gone before. It is idle to speculate on the transformation of language – or of ideas (these are but alternative ways of saying the same thing) – that would be brought about by the triumph of exact knowledge in this field. But would such an advance in knowledge necessarily constitute an overall increase in freedom? Freedom from error, from illusion, fantasy, misdirection of emotions – certainly all these. But is this the central meaning of the word as we commonly use it in philosophy or common speech?

II

I do not, of course, wish to deny that when we say that a man is free – or freer than he was before – we may be using the word to denote moral freedom, or independence, or self-determination. This concept, as has often been pointed out, is far from clear: the central terms – willing, intention, action, and the related notions – conscience, remorse, guilt, inner versus outer compulsion, and so on – stand in need of analysis, which itself entails a moral psychology that remains unprovided; and in the meanwhile the notion of moral independence – of what is, or should be, independent of what, and how this independence is achieved – remains obscure. Moreover, it seems doubtful whether we should describe a man as being free if his conduct displayed unswerving regularities, issuing (however this is established) from his own thoughts, feelings, acts of will, so that we should be inclined to say that he could not behave otherwise than as he did. Predictability may or may not entail determinism; but if we were in a position to be so well acquainted with a man's character, reactions, outlook that, given a specific situation, we felt sure that we could predict how he would act, better perhaps than he could himself, should we be tempted to describe him as being a typical example of a man morally – or otherwise – free? Should we not think that a phrase used by Patrick Gardiner, a 'prisoner of his personality',[1] described him better? So aptly, indeed, that he might, in certain cases, come to accept it – with regret or satisfaction – himself? A man so hidebound by his own habits and outlook is not the paradigm of human freedom.

The central assumption of common thought and speech seems to me to be that freedom is the principal characteristic that distinguishes man from all that is non-human; that there are degrees of freedom, degrees constituted by the absence of obstacles to the exercise of choice; the choice being regarded as not itself determined by antecedent conditions, at least not as being wholly so determined. It may be that common sense is mistaken in this matter, as in others; but the onus of refutation is on those who disagree. Common sense may not be too well aware of the full variety of such obstacles: they may be physical or psychical, 'inner' or 'outer', or complexes compounded of both elements, difficult and perhaps conceptually impossible to unravel, due to social factors and/or individual ones. Common opinion may oversimplify the issue; but it seems to me to be right about its essence: freedom is to do with the absence of obstacles to action. These obstacles may consist of physical power, whether of nature or of men, that prevents our intentions from being realised: geographical conditions or prison walls, armed men or the threat (deliberately used as a weapon or unintended) of lack of food or shelter or other necessities of life; or again, they may be psychological: fears and 'complexes', ignorance, error, prejudice, illusions, fantasies, compulsions, neuroses and psychoses – irrational factors of many kinds. Moral freedom – rational self-control – knowledge of what is at stake, and of what is one's motive in acting as one does; independence of the unrecognised influence of other persons or of one's own personal past or that of one's group or culture; destruction of hopes, fears, desires, loves, hatreds, ideals, which will be seen to be groundless once they are

[1] op. cit. (p. 186 above, note 1), p. 92.

inspected and rationally examined – these indeed bring liberation from obstacles, some of the most formidable and insidious in the path of human beings; their full effect, despite the acute but scattered insights of moralists from Plato to Marx and Schopenhauer, is beginning to be understood adequately only in the present century, with the rise of psychoanalysis and the perception of its philosophical implications. It would be absurd to deny the validity of this sense of the concept of freedom, or of its intimate logical dependence on rationality and knowledge. Like all freedom it consists of, or depends on, the removal of obstacles, in this case of psychological impediments to the full use of human powers to whatever ends men choose; but these constitute only one category of such obstacles, however important and hitherto inadequately analysed. To emphasise these to the exclusion of other classes of obstacles, and other better recognised forms of freedom, leads to distortion. Yet it is this, it seems to me, that has been done by those who, from the Stoics to Spinoza, Bradley and Stuart Hampshire, have confined freedom to self-determination.

To be free is to be able to make an unforced choice; and choice entails competing possibilities – at the very least two 'open', unimpeded alternatives. And this, in its turn, may well depend on external circumstances which leave only some paths unblocked. When we speak of the extent of freedom enjoyed by a man or a society, we have in mind, it seems to me, the width or extent of the paths before them, the number of open doors, as it were, and the extent to which they are open. The metaphor is imperfect, for 'number' and 'extent' will not really do. Some doors are much more important than others – the goods to which they lead are far more central in an individual's or society's life; some doors lead to other open doors, some to closed ones; there is actual and there is potential freedom – depending on how easily some closed doors can be opened given existing or potential resources, physical or mental. How is one to measure one situation against another? How is one to decide whether a man who is obstructed neither by other persons nor by circumstances from, let us say, the acquisition of adequate security of material necessities and comforts, but is debarred from free speech and association, is less or more free than one who find its impossible, because of, let us say, the economic policies of his government, to obtain more than the necessities of life, but who possesses greater opportunities of education or of free communication or association with others? Problems of this type will always arise – they are familiar enough in utilitarian literature, and indeed in all forms of non-totalitarian practical politics.

Even if no hard and fast rule can be provided, it still remains the case that the measure of the liberty of a man or a group is, to a large degree, determined by the range of choosable possibilities.

If a man's area of choice, whether 'physical' or 'mental', is narrow, then however contented with it he may be, and however true it may be that the more rational a man is, the clearer the one and only rational path will be to him and the less likely will he be to vacillate between alternatives (a proposition which seems to me to be fallacious), neither of these situations will necessarily make him more free than a man whose range of choice is wider. To remove obstacles by removing desire to enter upon, or even awareness of, the path on which the obstacles lie, may contribute to serenity, contentment, perhaps even wisdom, but not to liberty. Independence of mind – sanity and integration of personality, health and inner harmony – are highly desirable conditions, and they entail the removal of a sufficient number of obstacles to qualify for being regarded, for that reason alone, as a species of freedom – but only one species among others. Someone may say that it is at least unique in this: that this kind of freedom is a necessary condition for all other kinds of freedom – for if I am ignorant, obsessed, irrational, I am thereby blinded to the facts, and a man so blinded is, in effect, as unfree as a man whose possibilities are objectively blocked. But this does not seem to me to be true. If I am ignorant of my rights, or too neurotic (or too poor) to benefit by them, that makes them useless to me; but it does not make them non-existent; a door is closed to a path that leads to other, open, doors. To destroy or lack a condition for freedom (knowledge, money) is not to destroy that freedom itself; for its essence does not lie in its accessibility, although its value may do so. The more avenues men can enter, the broader those avenues, the more avenues that each opens into, the freer they are; the better men know what avenues lie before them, and how open they are, the freer they will know themselves to be. To be free without knowing it may be a bitter irony, but if a man subsequently discovers that doors were open although he did not know it, he will reflect bitterly not about his lack of freedom but about his ignorance. The extent of freedom depends on opportunities of action, not on knowledge of them, although such knowledge may well be an indispensable condition for the use of freedom, and although impediments in the path to it are themselves a deprivation of freedom – of freedom to know. Ignorance blocks paths, and knowledge opens them. But this truism does not entail that freedom implies awareness of freedom, still less that they are identical.

It is worth noting that it is the actual doors that are open that determine the extent of someone's freedom, and not his own preferences.[1] A man is not free merely when there are no obstacles, psychological or otherwise, in the way of his wishes – when he can do as he likes – for in that case a man might be rendered free by altering not his opportunities of action, but his desires and dispositions. If a master can condition his slaves to love their chains he does not thereby prima facie increase their liberty, although he may increase their contentment or at least decrease their misery. Some unscrupulous managers of men have, in the course of history, used religious teachings to make men less discontented with brutal and iniquitous treatment. If such measures work, and there is reason to think that they do so only too often, and if the victims have learnt not to mind their pains and indignities (like Epictetus, for example), then some despotic systems should presumably be described as creators of liberty; for by eliminating distracting temptations, and 'enslaving' wishes and passions, they create (on these assumptions) more liberty than institutions that expand the area of individual or democratic choice and thereby produce the worrying need to select, to determine oneself in one direction rather than another – the terrible burden of the *embarras du choix* (which has itself been taken to be a symptom of irrationality by some thinkers in the rationalist tradition). This ancient fallacy is by now too familiar to need refutation. I only cite it in order to emphasise the crucial distinction between the definition of liberty as nothing but the absence of obstacles to doing as I like (which could presumably be compatible with a very narrow life, narrowed by the influence upon me of personal or impersonal forces, education or law, friend or foe, religious teacher or parent, or even consciously contracted by myself), and liberty as a range of objectively open possibilities, whether these are desired or not, even though it is difficult or impossible to give rules for measuring or comparing degrees of it, or for assessing different situations with regard to it.

There is, of course, a sense, with which all moral philosophers are well acquainted, in which the slave Epictetus is more free than his master or the emperor who forced him to die in exile; or that in which stone walls do not a prison make. Nevertheless, such statements derive

---

[1] I should like to take this opportunity of correcting a misstatement on this subject which occurs in my lecture *Two Concepts of Liberty* (Oxford, 1958 [now reprinted in revised form in *Four Essays on Liberty* (London, 1969)]), and of thanking Richard Wollheim for pointing this out.

their rhetorical force from the fact that there is a more familiar sense in which a slave is the least free of men, and stone walls and iron bars are serious impediments to freedom; nor are moral and physical or political or legal freedoms mere homonyms. Unless some kernel of common meaning – whether a single common characteristic or a 'family resemblance' – is kept in mind, there is the danger that one or other of these senses will be represented as fundamental, and the others will be tortured into conformity with it, or dismissed as trivial or superficial. The most notorious examples of this process are the sophistries whereby various types of compulsion and thought control are represented as means to, or even as constitutive of, 'true' freedom, or, conversely, liberal political or legal systems are regarded as sufficient means of ensuring not only the freedom of, but opportunities for the use of such freedom by, persons who are too irrational or immature, owing to lack of education or other means of mental development, to understand or benefit by such rules or laws. It is therefore the central meaning of the term, if there is one, that it is important to establish.

There is yet another consideration regarding knowledge and liberty to which I should like to return.[1] It is true that knowledge always, of necessity, opens some doors, but does it never close others? If I am a poet, may it not be that some forms of knowledge will curtail my powers and thereby my liberty too? Let us suppose that I require as a stimulus to my imagination illusions and myths of a certain kind which are provided by the religion in which I have been brought up or to which I have been converted. Let us assume that some honourable rationalist refutes these beliefs, shatters my illusions, dissipates the myths; may it not be that my clear gain in knowledge and rationality is paid for by the diminution or destruction of my powers as a poet? It is easy enough to say that what I have lost is a power that fed on illusions or irrational states and attitudes which the advance of knowledge has destroyed; that some powers are undesirable (like the power of self-deception) and that, in any case, powers are powers and not liberties. It may be said that an increase in knowledge cannot (this would, I think, be claimed as an analytic truth) diminish my freedom; for to know the roots of my activity is to be rescued from servitude to the unknown – from stumbling in a darkness populated with figments which breed fears and irrational conduct. Moreover, it will be said that as a result of the destruction of my idols I have clearly gained in freedom of

[1] See p. 176.

self-determination; for I can now give a rational justification of my beliefs, and the motives of my actions are clearer to me. But if I am less free to write the kind of poetry that I used to write, is there not now a new obstacle before me? Have not some doors been closed by the opening of others? Whether ignorance is or is not bliss in these circumstances is another question. The question I wish to ask – and one to which I do not know the answer – is whether such absence of knowledge may not be a necessary condition for certain states of mind or emotion in which alone certain impediments to some forms of creative labour are absent. This is an empirical question, but on the answer to it the answer to a larger question depends: whether knowledge never impedes, always increases, the sum total of human freedom. Again, if I am a singer, self-consciousness – the child of knowledge – may inhibit the spontaneity that may be a necessary condition of my performance, as the growth of culture was thought by Rousseau and others to inhibit the joys of barbarian innocence. It does not matter greatly whether this particular belief is true; the simple uncivilised savage may have known fewer joys than Rousseau supposed; barbarism may not be a state of innocence at all. It is enough to allow that there are certain forms of knowledge that have the psychological effect of preventing kinds of self-expression which, on any showing, must be considered as forms of free activity. Reflection may ruin my painting if this depends on not thinking; my knowledge that a disease, for which no cure has been discovered, is destroying me or my friend, may well sap my particular creative capacity, and inhibit me in this or that way; and to be inhibited – whatever its long-term advantages – is not to be rendered more free. It may be replied to this that if I am suffering from a disease and do not know it, I am less free than one who knows, and can at least try to take steps to check it, even if the disease has so far proved to be incurable; that not to diagnose it will certainly lead to dissipation of effort in mistaken directions, and will curtail my freedom by putting me at the mercy of natural forces the character of which, because I do not recognise it, I cannot rationally discount or cope with. This is indeed so. Such knowledge cannot decrease my freedom as a rational being, but it may finish me as an artist. One door opens, and as a result of this another shuts.

Let me take another example. Resistance against vast odds may work only if the odds are not fully known; otherwise it may seem irrational to fight against what, even if it is not known, can be believed with a high degree of probability to be irresistible. For it may be my very ignorance of the odds that creates a situation in which alone I resist successfully. If David had known more about Goliath, if the majority of the inhabitants of Britain had known more about Germany in 1940, if historical probabilities could be reduced to something approaching a reliable guide to action, some achievements might never have taken place. I discover that I suffer from a fatal disease. This discovery makes it possible for me to try to find a cure – which was not possible so long as I was ignorant of the causes of my condition. But supposing that I satisfy myself that the weight of probability is against the discovery of an antidote, that once the poison has entered into the system death must follow; that the pollution of the atmosphere as the result of the discharge of a nuclear weapon cannot be undone. Then what is it that I am now more free to do? I may seek to reconcile myself to what has occurred, not kick against the pricks, arrange my affairs, make my will, refrain from a display of sorrow or indignation inappropriate when facing the inevitable – this is what 'Stoicism' or 'taking things philosophically' has historically come to mean. But even if I believe that reality is a rational whole (whatever this may mean), and that any other view of it, for instance, as being equally capable of realising various incompatible possibilities, is an error caused by ignorance, and if I therefore regard everything in it as being necessitated by reason – what I myself should necessarily will it to be as a wholly rational being – the discovery of its structure will not increase my freedom of choice. It will merely set me beyond hope and fear – for these are symptoms of ignorance or fantasy – and beyond choices too, since choosing entails the reality of at least two alternatives, say action and inaction. We are told that the Stoic Posidonius said to the pain that was tormenting him 'Do your worst, pain; nothing that you can do will cause me to hate you.' But Posidonius was a rationalistic determinist: whatever truly is, is as it should be: to wish it to be otherwise is a sign of irrationality; rationality implies that choice – and the freedom defined in terms of its possibility – is an illusion, not widened but killed by true knowledge.

Knowledge increases autonomy both in the sense of Kant, and in that of Spinoza and his followers. I should like to ask once more: is all liberty just that? The advance of knowledge stops men from wasting their resources upon delusive projects. It has stopped us from burning witches or flogging lunatics or predicting the future by listening to oracles or looking at the entrails of animals or the flight of birds. It may yet render many institutions and decisions of the present – legal, political, moral, social – obsolete, by showing them to be as cruel and stupid and incompatible with the pursuit of justice or reason or happiness or truth, as we now think the burning of widows or eating the flesh of an enemy to acquire his skills. If our powers of prediction, and so our knowledge of the future, become much greater, then, even if they are never complete, this may radically alter our view of what constitutes a person, an act, a choice; and *eo ipso* our language and our picture of the world. This may make our conduct more rational, perhaps more tolerant, charitable, civilised, it may improve it in many ways, but will it increase the area of free choice? For individuals or groups? It will certainly kill some realms of the imagination founded upon non-rational beliefs, and for this it may compensate us by making some of our ends more easily or harmoniously attainable. But who shall say if the balance will necessarily be on the side of wider freedom? Unless one establishes logical equivalences between the notions of freedom, self-determination and self-knowledge in some *a priori* fashion – as Spinoza and Hegel and their modern followers seek to do – why need this be true? Stuart Hampshire and E. F. Carritt, in dealing with this topic, maintain that, faced with any situation, one can always choose at least between trying to do something and letting things take their course. Always? If it makes sense to say that there is an external world, then to know it, in the descriptive sense of 'know', is not to alter it. As for the other sense of 'know' – the pragmatic, in which 'I know what I shall do' is akin to 'I know what to do', and registers not a piece of information but a decision to alter things in a certain way – would it not wither if psycho-physiology advanced far enough? For, in that event, may not my resolution to act or not to act resemble more and more the recommendation of Canute's courtiers?

Knowledge, we are told, extends the boundaries of freedom, and this is an *a priori* proposition. Is it inconceivable that the growth of knowledge will tend more and more successfully to establish the determinist thesis as an empirical truth, and explain our thoughts and feelings, wishes and decisions, our actions and choices, in terms of invariant, regular, natural successions, to seek to alter which will seem almost as irrational as entertaining a logical fallacy? This was, after all, the programme and the belief of many respected philosophers, as different in their outlooks as Spinoza, Holbach, Schopenhauer, Comte, the behaviourists. Would such a consummation extend the area of freedom? In what sense? Would it not rather render this notion, for want of a contrasting one, altogether otiose, and would not this constitute a novel situation? The 'dissolution' of the concept of freedom would be accompanied by the demise of that sense of 'know' in which we speak not of knowing that, but of knowing what to do, to which Hampshire and Hart have drawn attention; for if all is determined, there is nothing to choose between, and so nothing to decide. Perhaps those who have said of freedom that it is the recognition of necessity were contemplating this very situation. If so, their notion of freedom is radically different from those who define it in terms of conscious choice and decision.

I wish to make no judgement of value: only to suggest that to say that knowledge is a good is one thing; to say that it is necessarily, in all situations, compatible with, still more that it is on terms of mutual entailment with (or even, as some seem to suppose, is literally identical with) freedom, in most of the senses in which this word is used, is something very different. Perhaps the second assertion is rooted in the optimistic view – which seems to be at the heart of much metaphysical rationalism – that all good things must be compatible, and that therefore freedom, order, knowledge, happiness, a closed future (and an open one?) must be at least compatible, and perhaps even entail one another in a systematic fashion. But this proposition is not self-evidently true, if only on empirical grounds. Indeed, it is perhaps one of the least plausible beliefs ever entertained by profound and influential thinkers.

Index

Compiled by Douglas Matthews

epistemology: and empiricist tradition, xv; and purpose of philosophy, 10; and verification, 14–15; and phenomenalism, 37, 52; and supplying answers, 144; and political theory, 167; *see also* knowledge

equality: liberal, xix; as human goal, 6; doctrine of, 81–4; and rights, 81–2; and treatment, 82–4, 87; and rules, 84–90, 100; ideal of, 90–6, 102; and other values, 96; and fairness, 97–101; in political theory, 148, 151

ethics, xii, xviii, 58, 69, 89, 147–8, 170

Euclid, 135

Ewing, Alfred Cyril, 18n

existentialism, 45, 49–50, 154, 156, 158, 172, 176

experience, 12–15; *see also* sense data

fairness, 97–101

family, 9

Faraday, Michael, 106

Fascists, 171

Fermat's theorem, 2, 37–8, 145

Festugière, André Jean, 173

Fichte, Johann Gottlieb, 156

freedom: concept and definition of, xvii, 8, 166, 173, 189–90, 193–4, 197–8; and knowledge, xvii, 183–5, 188, 194–6; as human goal, 6; and equality, 93–5; in political theory, 148, 155–7; and self-realisation, 173–4; and self-determination, 174–5, 179–83, 185–6, 188–9, 191, 195, 197; obstacles to, 190–3, 196; *see also* civil liberties

French Revolution (1789), 82, 95, 125, 130–1, 135

Freud, Sigmund, 129, 132, 156

Galileo Galilei, 106, 162

Gardiner, Patrick Lancaster, 143n, 186n, 190

geology, 105

Gracchi, the, 82

Green, Thomas Hill, 171

Hampshire, Stuart Newton, xiii, 143n, 184, 186–7, 191, 197–8

Hardie, William Francis Ross, 35

Hare, Richard Mervyn, 181–2

Hart, Herbert Lionel Adolphus, 94, 143n, 198

Hegel, Georg Wilhelm Friedrich: and objectivity of knowledge, xvi; and absolute, 61; refutes ontological argument, 66; and Ionian fallacy, 76; as historiosopher, 118, 126, 135, 140, 159; on reason and understanding, 140; and value judgements, 149; and self-fulfilment, 156; and laws of social evolution, 177; and freedom, 197

Helvétius, Claude Adrien, 7, 156, 160

and human experience, 129; and historical study, 133–40; and political philosophy, 149, 156, 168, 172; and obedience, 155; as liberating force, 173–6, 179; of self, 177–9; and predictability, 182, 185

Laplace, Pierre Simon, marquis de, 106
Lassalle, Ferdinand, 159
Lavoisier, Antoine Laurent, 135
Leibniz, Gottfried Wilhelm von, 67, 69, 126, 181
Lenin, Vladimir Il'ich, 135, 138, 159
liberalism: and pluralism, xviii, xx; and the state, 9; and equality, 81–2, 93–4, 100–2; and political theory, 156, 168, 172; Lassalle disparages, 159; relevance, 170; and freedom, 194
liberty see freedom
literalness, 80
Locke, John: ontology, 32; and phenomenalism, 36, 38, 41, 44, 49; and confusion of words and things, 40; and empirical propositions, 59; moral uncertainty, 101n; political theory, 156, 159, 163; and acts of will, 181; *The Second Treatise of Government*, 101n
logic: on observed and unobserved objects, xv, 5; and formal deduction, 9,

144–5; and explanation, 10; and verification, 13; on possible and actual, 15, 55; and propositions, 20, 56–8, 61; and meaning, 31; and structure of reality, 66; as ontology, 68; extensional, 73; of language, 75; translation, 76–80; in science, 116–17, 126; in historical explanation, 117–18, 126–9; and rules, 145; uses, 148; and political doctrine, 167–8
logical constructions, 24, 36, 41, 62
logical positivism, xii, xiv–xv, 20, 63, 156
Louis XVI, King of France, 130
Luther, Martin, 135, 155

Machiavelli, Niccolò, 156, 158, 169
Macnabb, Donald George Cecil, 36n
Maistre, Joseph de, 159
Mannheim, Karl, 171
Marx, Karl: insights, 132; as historian, 137, 140; and paths to goals, 149, 156; rejects Encyclopedists, 163; and human fundamentals, 164; rejects Bentham, 164; and sociology of knowledge, 171; and social laws, 177; and freedom, 191
Marxism: and history, 119, 147; and understanding, 129; and value judgements, 149;

state, the, 9–10, 168; *see also*
  political philosophy
Stern, Fritz, 13n
Stoics: and human ends, 153;
  and human relations, 158;
  on reason and nature, 168,
  185; logic, 169; and truth as
  liberating, 173; on rational
  self-control, 174; and social
  independence, 177; on
  knowledge as liberating,
  179; and causation, 180;
  and moral responsibility,
  180, 182; and freedom, 191;
  and acceptance, 196
Stout, George Frederick, 27,
  33–4, 39, 44
subjectivism, xvii, 148, 153
subsistent entities, 65–7
symbols: words as, 59–60, 74

Tacitus, 135
Taine, Hippolyte, 105, 107,
  119, 122–4, 128, 139
Thales, 33
theists, 81
theology, 4n, 14, 163
Thomists *see* Aquinas, St
  Thomas
Thucydides, 135
Tolstoy, Count Lev
  Nikolaevich, 130, 164
Tönnies, Ferdinand Julius,
  158
totalitarianism, 152, 191
Toynbee, Arnold Joseph, 118
translation, logical, xviii,
  34–51, 56–80
truthfulness, xx

understanding, 29, 128–9,
  140; *see also* knowledge
universe, ultimate:
  constituents and structure
  of, 76–7, 80
utilitarianism, 81, 88, 97, 101,
  150, 191

value judgements, 147–9
values, conflicting, xvii–xix,
  86–9, 96, 150–1, 166, 167,
  176–7; *see also* pluralism
verification: and sense-
  perception, xiv; oppositions
  to, xv, 12–13, 27; principles
  and examples, 12–25, 29;
  and phenomenalism, 13, 16,
  20, 24, 26–7, 38, 49, 51–2;
  by observation, 17, 20–1,
  26, 28; 'strong' and 'weak',
  18–20, 23, 27, 29, 32, 58;
  and falsification, 20, 28; and
  significance, 25, 30; and
  material objects, 26–8;
  dependence on
  intelligibility, 29–30; and
  true propositions, 58; of
  historical facts, 134; and
  belief, 168
Verstehen, 128
Vico, Giambattista, xvi, 105,
  109, 132, 135, 137, 140
Viennese school, 57
Voltaire, François Marie
  Arouet de, 130

Waismann, Friedrich, 46n
Warnock, Geoffrey James,
  143n

INDEX